Understanding Human Ecology

We are facing hugely complex challenges – from climate change to world poverty, our problems are part of an interrelated web of social and natural systems. Human Ecology provides an approach to address these complex challenges, a way to understand them holistically and to start to manage them more effectively.

This textbook, which has been road-tested and refined through over a decade of teaching and workshops, offers a coherent conceptual framework for Human Ecology – a clear approach for understanding the many systems we are part of and how we frame and understand the problems we face. By giving rigorous definitions it guides readers out of the current 'conceptual swamp' that hinders communication and collaboration – with a particular focus on terms such as 'sustainability' and 'cultural adaptation' that need generally agreed definitions before they can support clear communication. It also clarifies the role of Human Ecology, and similar disciplines, by bringing ethical and justice considerations into the assessment of different interventions to promote sustainability.

Blending natural, social and cognitive sciences with dynamical systems theory, the authors offer systems approaches that are accessible to all, from the undergraduate student in environmental studies to policy makers and practitioners across government, business, and community.

Robert Dyball convenes the 40-year-old Human Ecology Program at the Fenner School of Environment and Society at the Australian National University (ANU), Australia. He is President of the Society for Human Ecology (SHE) and the Past Chair of the Human Ecology Section of the Ecological Society of America (ESA), USA.

Barry Newell is Adjunct Associate Professor in the Research School of Engineering and Visiting Fellow in the Fenner School of Environment and Society at the Australian National University (ANU), Australia. He is a physicist with a focus on the dynamics of complex social-ecological systems.

D1402632

Human ecology is a critical transdisciplinary approach to creating a better, more sustainable world. We cannot achieve this goal without integrating the study and management of human societies and the rest of nature as tightly interconnected dynamic systems. This valuable book points the way.

Robert Costanza, Professor and Chair in Public Policy,
Crawford School of Public Policy, The Australian National University,
Australia and Editor in Chief, Solutions

A central challenge for enhancing human wellbeing is to establish a sustainable society in harmony with nature across all regions of the world. Integrating rigorous research, education, and policy-making to meet this challenge is urgently needed. *Understanding Human Ecology* provides an insightful guide to how this might be achieved.

Kazuhiko Takeuchi, Senior Vice-Rector, United Nations University, Japan

It is time to move beyond the simplistic approaches of cause-effect logic and the triple bottom line that typify many attempts to meet the sustainability challenge. This timely textbook brings the powerful approach of systems thinking to the most pressing, seemingly intractable problems that face humanity in the 21st century.

Will Steffen, Senior Fellow, Stockholm Resilience Centre, Sweden

Understanding Human Ecology by Dyball and Newell provides a novel and transdisciplinary framework for understanding sustainability. This "must-read" book explains why people have historically made such a mess of the environment and provides a convincing case of why we must and can switch from a paradigm of limitless growth to one of ethical living, content with sufficiency.

Terry Chapin, University of Alaska Fairbanks, USA,
and Past President Ecological Society of America

We live in an era of rapid environmental change. If this change is to benefit people in both developed and developing countries, then it needs to be guided by collaborative interdisciplinary research into sustainable development. The approach to human ecology developed in this book should help us to meet the challenge of steering humanity towards a just and sustainable future.

Yonglong Lu, Professor and Co-Director, Research Center for Eco-
Environmental Sciences, Chinese Academy of Sciences, China

This important book helps to elucidate the interplay between planetary change and human health, with profound implications for our understanding of the dynamics of global epidemics of obesity and non-communicable diseases.

Anthony Capon, Director, United Nations University
International Institute for Global Health

Understanding Human Ecology

A systems approach to sustainability

Robert Dyball and
Barry Newell

LONDON AND NEW YORK

First published 2015
by Routledge
2 Park Square, Milton Park, Abingdon, Oxon OX14 4RN

and by Routledge
711 Third Avenue, New York, NY 10017

Routledge is an imprint of the Taylor & Francis Group, an informa business

British Library Cataloguing-in-Publication Data
A catalogue record for this book is available from the British Library

Library of Congress Cataloging-in-Publication Data
  Understanding human ecology: a systems approach to sustainability/Robert Dyball, Barry Newell.
  pages cm
  Includes bibliographical references and index.
  1. Nature – Effect of human beings on. 2. Human ecology.
  3. Ecosystem management. 4. Sustainability. I. Newell, Barry. II. Title.
  GF75.D93 2014
  304.2 – dc23
  2014021434

ISBN: 978-1-84971-382-5 (hbk)
ISBN: 978-1-84971-383-2 (pbk)
ISBN: 978-0-203-10955-7 (ebk)

Typeset in Sabon
by Florence Production Limited, Stoodleigh, Devon, UK

Dedicated to
Stephen Boyden, pioneer in human ecology

and to the memory of
Don Nicholls
and
Edward James (Ken) Newell

Contents

Figures

Tables

Boxes

Foreword
A challenge for human evolution

Human ecology is now the most important discipline in both the academic and political worlds, since humanity is on a straight course toward a likely collapse of civilization (Ehrlich and Ehrlich 2013). The human population is far beyond a size sustainable in the long term, and growing. Increasing per capita consumption among relatively wealthy groups, aggravated by the use of environmentally malign technologies and flawed socio-political–economic arrangements, is causing rapid deterioration of our life-support systems. This is manifested by the dramatic increases in climate disruption, ocean acidification and eutrophication, global toxification, the impoverishment of biodiversity, escalating resource conflicts, persistent levels of hunger and micronutrient malnourishment, growing threats of vast epidemics, and expanding gaps between rich and poor that we are now experiencing. The challenges of diverting humanity from its present course, at both theoretical and practical levels, are daunting.

Human ecology can be thought of as dealing with the intersection of two complex adaptive systems (Levin 1999), a human social–economic–technological system that is embedded in a physical–chemical–living biosphere. Each of these generates emergent properties that are unpredictable, and the combined system is rocked by the increasing scale of the once-trivial human system, dramatic changes in it produced by rapid cultural evolution, and the devastating effects of a 'we can grow forever' ideology. Cultural change, in turn, is made ever more complex by the pressing need to enhance understanding of these interacting systems and their evolution and to begin moving society away from lethal growthmania and toward sustainability (Ehrlich and Ehrlich 2012). Some climate scientists, for example, think we have at most 20 years to make the necessary changes in course to mitigate global warming, which is an increasingly critical threat to biodiversity and human health (especially nutrition) and is strongly related to other resource constraints.

Human ecology is central to meeting this great set of challenges. The discipline needs to mature quickly and attract many more scholars with diverse skills in the social and natural sciences and humanities, as well as generating students who literally want to change the world. This book should provide a most welcome push in those directions.

Paul R. Ehrlich

References

Ehrlich, P. R. and Ehrlich, A. H. (2012). 'Solving the human predicament'. *International Journal of Environmental Studies* 69: 557–565.

Ehrlich, P. R. and Ehrlich, A. H. (2013). 'Can a collapse of civilization be avoided?' *Proceeding of the Royal Society* B280(1754): http://rspb.royalsocietypublishing.org/content/280/1754/20122845

Levin, S. (1999). *Fragile Dominion*. Reading, MA, Perseus Books.

Preface

The task of charting a course to a humane, worthwhile, and sustainable future for all is complex and multifaceted. Its dimensions range from the biophysics of Earth to the ethics of human behaviour. Human ecology has enormous potential to help in this endeavour. Its practitioners have long recognized that the challenges we face necessarily require collaborative efforts that draw on knowledge and understanding from a wide range of perspectives. Human ecology can provide a forum where insights from these different perspectives can be juxtaposed and given licence to interact freely. For many, the possibility that novel insights, partnerships, and opportunities can arise from this free thinking is one of the major attractions of the subject. Nevertheless, this intellectual freedom can result in an amorphous approach that leads nowhere in particular, and even obscures the nature of human ecology itself. It is sometimes portrayed as an 'anything goes' approach that says nothing of value. Thus, one of the major strengths of human ecology can be construed as one of its main weaknesses.

We have long been aware of a tension within human ecology – a tension between those who favour an open-ended approach and those who seek a more 'scientific' way of proceeding. Such a tension can be divisive, or it can be creative. In this book we have attempted to weigh in on the side of creativity. As we see it, one of the most salient tasks facing human ecologists is to develop a coherent theoretical framework that can support their efforts to be holistic, without opening them to the charge of attempting to create a Science of Everything. Our aim has been to take a step in this direction. The adaptation of society to the realities of a finite planet requires change, and so we believe that a shared understanding of the basic dynamics of social–ecological systems – of how and why things change over time – can lead to a more coherent human ecology. As a first step towards such an understanding we have gathered together selected concepts from the natural, social, and cognitive sciences, and have attempted to integrate them using ideas and principles from dynamical systems thinking. While our discussion is necessarily tentative, we hope that it provides human ecologists with a glimpse of the possibility of taking a more rigorous approach without falling captive to the rigid thinking that can typify traditional disciplines.

Although we are concerned primarily with the application of human ecology to the persistent problems of today's world, we are not unduly pessimistic. Our central assumption is that human beings are highly creative, and will eventually attempt to 'do the right thing' by their fellow humans and the environment. The principal danger is that the required changes will not be achieved soon enough to avoid catastrophe. What is needed is a powerful vision for the future, a vision based on an overarching understanding and respect for the planet as a living system, and the assumption that environmental and social goals are inseparable. A prerequisite to achieving this vision is a transformation in thought and practice, away from a focus on ever-increasing consumption of resources toward a more biosensitive worldview. If human ecologists can contribute to this transformation they will truly have realized their potential. We hope that this book will, in some small way, help them to achieve that aim.

This book would not have been possible without generous support and contributions from a very wide range of people. This includes all who have participated in the Human Ecology program at the Australian National University (ANU) over more than 40 years, since its establishment by Stephen Boyden. The immediate past-convenor of the programme, David Dumaresq, warrants special acknowledgement. We owe a great debt to the vast number of students – doctorate, masters, and undergraduate – who have studied human ecology at the ANU. Their critical engagement with the subject has lent a great deal to its development over the years, with many original contributions arising from student theses. In addition to the formal academic programme in human ecology, there is the long-running Human Ecology Forum, an open community of transdisciplinary scholars. This forum has hosted innumerable in-depth discussions on all aspects of human ecology, and both of us have benefited greatly from our participation over the years. Human Ecology at the ANU sits within The Fenner School of Environment and Society, home to scholars of sustainability from across the humanities, and the social and environmental sciences – a genuinely cross-disciplinary school that is all-too-rare in contemporary academia. We are both affiliated with The Fenner School and owe much to the many and varied discussions, seminars, and presentations that are part of the daily life of the school. We thank the Director of the Fenner School, Stephen Dovers, for his continued support. One of us (BN) is also affiliated with the ANU Research School of Engineering, and acknowledges the support of its Director, Thushara Abhayapala.

Beyond the ANU there is a wide network of human ecology scholars whose ideas have influenced our writing. The Society for Human Ecology (SHE) is home to many of these scholars, as is the Human Ecology Section of the Ecological Society of America (ESA). It would be impossible to thank all of these people by name but Rich Borden, Stephen Boyden, Helen Brown, Val Brown, Chris Browne, Tony Capon, Bruin Christensen, Paul Compston, Bob Costanza, Federico Davila, Paul Ehrlich, Alfredo Fantini, Catherine Gross, Nordin Hasan, Eskild Hohlmann, Ayako Kawai, Luke Kemp, Brendan Mackey, Eleanor Malbon, Craig Miller, Brendan Moloney, David Newell, John Porter, Katrina Proust, Michael Reddy, Jacqui Russell, John Schooneveldt, Tom Sloan, Will Steffen, Rachael Wakefield-Rann, Bob Wasson, Chiho Watanabe, and Alan Ziegler are just a few of those who have provoked various chains of thought that have ended up in this book. Many of these colleagues have given us constructive criticism of early drafts of the manuscript. Tracy Harwood edited parts of the manuscript and compiled the index, and Clive Hilliker created the maps. We thank Helen Bell and the team at Routledge for their patience.

On a personal note, Robert would like to thank his family and friends. Don and Jane Nicholls in particular – it is deeply regretted that Don died before this book was published. Jim, Sarah, and Bryndon formed the backbone of the support group at Wilburs. The Neighbours, for demonstrating that vibrant community is still possible. Special thanks are due to Ngaire for her love and patience. Finally, thanks to Jack, Claudia, and Hazel – you helped make a personal connection to the task of writing about humane, worthwhile, and sustainable futures.

Barry thanks his family for their forbearance. You have made it deceptively easy for me to be an elusive father and grandfather. I am particularly grateful to Katrina for her love and unwavering support. It is a rare privilege to have such a close professional colleague and friend with whom to share the journey.

Robert Dyball
Barry Newell
Canberra

Prologue

Six impossible things before breakfast

Alice laughed. 'There's no use trying,' she said: 'one can't believe impossible things.'
'I daresay you haven't had much practice,' said the Queen. 'When I was your age,
I always did it for half-an-hour a day. Why, sometimes I've believed as many as six
impossible things before breakfast.'

(*Through the Looking Glass*, Lewis Carroll, 1871)

7.20 am

The alarm buzzed. Already half awake, Alex reached over, pushed the mute button, and pulled the covers up over her head. She'd set her bedside alarm 10 minutes fast in the hope that this would help get her up more promptly. As a device to trick herself it was not really working. Knowing it was fast, she had long since adapted her behaviour to simply add an extra 10 minutes in bed from the time it went off. Throughout the night the clock's glowing display had been dutifully counting off the seconds, steadily consuming electricity. Elsewhere in her small apartment five other time-keeping devices had also been keeping track. There were displays on her microwave, television, sound system, washing machine, and air conditioner. None of these were telling the same time as any other – the air conditioner she had never even set as she could not see the point of it. That morning it was the washing machine display that was the most accurate. It was just 57 seconds slow. None of this troubled Alex. She always used her mobile phone to check the time. However, as the features were built into the units by their manufacturers, she could not turn them off and so simply ignored them. But, along with the standby power used by many of her devices, these electronic clocks contributed to a phantom energy drain that was close to 18 per cent of her electricity consumption.

7.30 am

Alex began to doze again, but then remembered she had set the alarm because her friend was coming over for breakfast. She dragged herself from bed and shuffled across the corridor to the bathroom. She spent almost a minute adjusting the hot and cold taps of the shower to achieve a comfortable temperature. During this time, 25 litres of potable water, collected and transported from river systems over 100 kilometres from her apartment, ran down the drain to be treated as effluent. The waste of water irritated her, but there was little she could do. The apartment was poorly designed, with the water heater placed too far from the shower. The consequent delay in delivery from the heater meant it was almost inevitable to overcorrect the taps' setting. In the 10 minutes that she took to shower Alex successfully removed about a gram of dirt, body oil, and her own dead skin, using a quarter of a tonne of water. The water was heated by electricity generated by a power plant that, in the process, released some 7 kilograms of carbon dioxide into the atmosphere.

7.45 am

Shower over, Alex reached for her moisturizer. She used this glycerine-based product to replace the natural body oils that she had just washed down the drain. Without this, her skin would be left feeling dry. Palm oil was a basic ingredient in her moisturizer, as it was in the soap and shampoo that she had washed herself with in the first place. The palm oil in all the products she used had been grown in huge plantations across Southeast Asia. Many of these plantations had high environmental and social impacts, including habitat destruction that was endangering the orangutan. The plight of the orangutan was the subject of a television documentary that had upset Alex last night, leaving her angry at the selfishness and greed of the people responsible. However, she was also aware of the contribution her own choice of soap, shampoo, and moisturizers was making. Guilty though this made her feel she knew of no affordable and readily available alternative. She tried to mollify herself with the thought that the amounts she used were only very small.

7.50 am

Alex returned to her room to dress. From a choice of over 30 different T-shirts, Alex selected one with a mildly humorous slogan that she thought fitted the casualness of the day and was fairly sure she was not wearing last time she caught up with her friend. Not having thought about it, Alex would be hard-pressed to say why she needed so many. However, it would be unlikely that she thought her collection excessive – it was certainly no larger than that of most of her friends. The cotton for each of Alex's shirts was grown in large-scale cropping systems under intensive irrigation, with high fertilizer and pesticide inputs. Around 3,000 litres of water were required to grow the 250 grams of cotton lint that went into the manufacture of each one. After harvesting and local processing, the extracted lint was shipped overseas to be woven into cloth. The cloth was then bleached, dyed, and finished using a mixture of toxic chemicals, much of which ended up in local waterways. It was then made up into T-shirts by lowly paid workers in sweatshop factories. The finished garments were then exported to regional wholesale centres that in turn distributed them to local retailers, including the one where Alex had bought hers. Alex's preference was for cotton as she considered it to be a 'natural' product.

7.55 am

Although she knew that her friend was unlikely to forget their breakfast arrangement, Alex sent her a reminder – a text message from her mobile phone. Texting is an essential communication mechanism for Alex and her friends. More than just staying in touch, it forms a social 'glue' without which Alex simply could not participate in the group. Alex's mobile phone contained over 400 separate components manufactured by subcontractors across the globe and shipped to one huge factory for final assembly by hand. Her handset had been assembled in a city of some 14 million people, which had grown from nothing in just a few decades, powered almost entirely by the telecommunications industry. Over 30 kilograms of ore-bearing rock had been clawed out of the earth to provide the base materials for Alex's phone – iron, aluminium, arsenic, gold, cobalt, lithium, chromium, silver – yet the phone itself weighed only 75 grams. Its lightness was due in part to the use of miniaturized tantalum capacitors. The tantalum in her phone was derived from a mineral nicknamed 'coltan', which had been mined in the Congo. Coltan fetched a high price in world markets, and illegal mining and sales were credited with supporting civil war in the region. As a consequence, the Congo was one of the most violent and dangerous war zones in the world. The coltan that went into the capacitors for Alex's phone had been dug by hand by child soldiers in the service of a local warlord.

8 am

Alex headed into the kitchen to prepare breakfast. The coffee that she used was made from beans shipped from Mexico. Coffee's international supply chain of importers, roasters, and retailers makes it the second-largest traded commodity in the world. However, the farmer who grew the coffee Alex was consuming was paid only a minute fraction of the price she paid at the shops. Some years back the farmer had switched from subsistence food production to coffee cash-cropping as part of an international aid 'modernization' programme. However, commodity prices had since tumbled and the farmer was now deeply in debt. In an effort to get ahead the farmer had increased production, but this required fertilizers he could scarcely afford. The demands of higher production were also starting to erode the productive capacity of his once-fertile soils. Furthermore, as thousands of other farmers were in a similar situation and also trying to increase yields, the collective outcome was simply to glut the coffee market and drive commodity prices lower still. Alex was aware of 'fair trade' and 'organic' coffee options, and was in principle prepared to buy them if the cost difference to conventional supplies was not too great. However, because demand for these more social and ecologically sound brands was low, the supermarket where Alex shops was not prepared to carry them. There was a specialty coffee shop in the next suburb that did sell these products, but Alex reasoned it was too inconvenient to make the trip that far just for coffee.

Alex remembered that today she was going to make omelettes for her friend. She reached into her refrigerator for some eggs. The carton displayed a logo certifying that the eggs were 'free range'. Alex insisted on buying only free-range eggs. It was one of the few ways she thought she could align her consumption choices with her concerns for the ethical consequences of her actions.

Reference

Carroll, L. (1871). *Through the Looking Glass*. New York, Bantam Classics.

Part I

The challenge

Robert Dyball

Humanity today is facing hugely complex challenges. The catalogue of problems can be overwhelming – over-population and over-consumption are driving climate change, loss of biodiversity, despair, illness, soil degradation, poverty, alienation, deforestation, pollution, inequality, and stress. At times it can seem that our every action has some impact, from the local to the global, that is environmentally unsustainable, or socially unjust, or both. Little wonder that many people close their eyes to the evidence that change is urgently needed, and simply try to get on with life as best they can.

However, giving in to this sense of disempowerment is a recipe for disaster. It is also premature. Across history, humans have shown that when they work collaboratively towards common goals they can achieve great things. The challenge for human ecology, as discussed in this book, is to help develop an idea of what a worthwhile, humane, and sustainable modern society might be like, and to see how we might get to that situation from where we are now. If our current collective demands on the environment exceed its capacity, then we will have to develop new social systems where demand is safely below environmental thresholds. This goal of more moderate consumption faces the additional challenge of redressing the fact that for many people in the world today, levels of consumption are so low they are unable to meet basic standards of living – a situation that is ethically intolerable. Ultimately, we need to consider the role of dominant knowledge and belief systems in legitimising our collective behaviour. If, as seems obvious, change is required, then we have to understand how social-learning processes adapt our culture so that we can value new social-environment systems – specifically ones that are more in tune with environmental reality and social justice.

1 Human ecology

An evolving discipline

For this knowledge of right living, we have sought a new name ... As theology is the science of religious life, and biology the science of [physical] life ... so let Oekology be henceforth the science of [our] normal lives ... the worthiest of all the applied sciences which teaches the principles on which to found a healthy and happy life.

(Ellen Swallow Richards, 1892)

1.1 Introduction

Why 'six impossible things before breakfast'? Alex's story illustrates some of the central challenges facing human ecologists. She regards her morning routine as perfectly normal. She and her peers undertake activities such as these on a daily basis. Indeed, Alex may well feel that she has no choice in these matters. She can certainly choose one item of clothing over another, but she hardly has a genuine choice as to whether to wear clothes in public or not. Her friends would certainly pass comment if she wore the same T-shirt every day or refused to wash. But this mix of choice and social obligation results in Alex's everyday 'normal behaviour' consuming at levels far above what the vast majority of Earth's population can access or afford. It is not possible for Alex to justify her having access to a level of goods and services that others are denied on the arbitrary grounds of circumstances of birth. Nor is it possible for Earth's environments to provide the resources needed for everyone on the planet to consume at similar levels. In this sense Alex has done 'six impossible things before breakfast'. Her morning's activities would be impossible to sustain if 7 billion people could act as she does. Furthermore, it is ethically impossible for her to defend actions that allow her to satisfy her expectations, if these actions impose a heavy cost on others and the planet.

Alex is not a 'bad' or 'selfish' person, indifferent to the social and environmental problems of the world. Indeed, she is predisposed to caring for the environment and her fellow human beings. Unlike many of Earth's inhabitants she is not so constrained by poverty, and the daily struggle to stay alive, that she has little or no choice about her actions. Nor is she profoundly ignorant. She is literate, reasonably worldly wise, and has instant access to globally connected information systems. Yet, despite being well-intentioned, knowledgeable, and free to choose, her actions lead to a range of socially and environmentally harmful outcomes.

Human ecology aims to understand how such problems can be addressed. It has a practical interest in how systems of production, distribution, and consumption might be redesigned, so that the reasonable daily needs of people such as Alex might be met, without causing harmful impacts. It is in Alex's own interest to face up to these practical concerns. The social and environmental systems that provide her with the things she needs might decline and eventually cease to function if they are too badly damaged by human activity. In the long run societies such as Alex's are at risk if the means by which they provision themselves cause such a collapse.

In addition to a pragmatic concern for self-interest, human ecology has an ethical concern for how that self-interest is satisfied. Human ecologists want to know how, in satisfying our own needs, we can make sure that we do not prevent others from adequately satisfying their needs. This is not merely to ensure that, when one community has taken the resources it believes it needs, some residual remains with which another community might satisfy what it believes are its needs. Human ecology extends to the idea that there is something fundamentally wrong if what one community regards as a reasonable expectation *can be met only* if other communities must settle for much lower levels of consumption. This imbalance is unethical, particularly where it imposes low levels of consumption that prevent individuals achieving even a basic level of health and wellbeing. The injustice of this situation cannot be addressed by attempting to raise levels of consumption in poorer communities, if continued profligate consumption by affluent communities means there are simply not enough resources to go around.

A central premise of this book is that sustainability issues are inseparable from issues of justice and fairness. How Alex, and people like her, might reconcile a reasonable level of desire and satisfaction, while avoiding excessive harm to others and to the environment, is one of the central questions of human ecology.

1.2 Human ecology: an evolving discipline

Over 100 years ago, Ellen Richards first proposed 'Human Ecology' as a form of enquiry seeking 'knowledge of right living' (Richards, quoted in Clarke 1973: 120. Figure 1.1). As Borden says, the subject matter of human ecology is fundamentally concerned with the age-old questions of the human condition, 'what makes life possible?' and 'what makes life worthwhile?' (Borden 2014: xvii). Since then, in one way or another, human ecologists have sought to better understand the answers to these questions and their implications. As human ecology has evolved, many different perspectives have come and gone, different concepts and methodologies have dominated, and different ways of thinking have been employed. Knowledge of human ecology has been generated both from within formal academic institutions and from outside academia among practitioners, communities, artists, and traditional peoples. Indeed, as a developing school of thought, the history of human ecology can be characterized as an ever-widening network of knowledge and ideas, as the inadequacy of any one perspective on its subject matter has become apparent (Tengström 1985, Boyden 1986, Dyball 2010, Borden 2014). Many human ecologists today would take issue with Ellen Richards' notion that their subject is a science at all – arguing that science, as a way of thinking, can provide only limited insights into the human condition (Steiner 1993). Many would label human ecology as *transdisciplinary*, spanning or integrating many disciplines, or even *adisciplinary* and not a discipline at all (Christensen 2014). In this book we explore the idea that human ecology can be a *disciplined* form of inquiry and practice, even if it is not regarded as a discipline (Young 1989, Dyball 2011).

Figure 1.1 Ellen Swallow Richards (second from right, front row). First woman graduate from the Massachusetts Institute of Technology (MIT), first woman member of MIT faculty, and first to use the term 'Human Ecology'. Shown here with MIT Chemistry staff, 1900.

Source: photo courtesy of MIT Museum.

If human ecology is to move towards the rigour and coherence of a discipline, while avoiding the rigidity and narrowness of thinking that disciplines can suffer, it needs an underlying conceptual framework. A conceptual framework for human ecology can be considered adequate only if it can accommodate and support the characteristic concerns of its practitioners. For human ecology, these concerns can be summarized under four themes – ethics, social–ecological systems, learning from experience, and dominant human-belief systems. These themes point to aspects of the subject matter studied by human ecologists. These include, for example, the interactions between social and biophysical elements; the intrinsically ethical concern for the health and wellbeing of humans (but arguably extending to other sentient beings) and the biosphere; processes of evolution and adaptation through time, with humans capable of experience-driven behaviour change; the overriding influence of dominant cultural paradigms (worldviews, beliefs, and values) on different human communities; and a community's expectations and judgements about 'sensible' behaviour. The challenge for human ecology is to comprehensively understand these aspects as inseparable parts of a unified whole.

1.3 The challenge of human ecology

We begin here by briefly characterizing the kinds of problems that human ecology deals with. Any minimally adequate conceptual framework for human ecology will have to aid understanding of these kinds of problems. The characteristic features of human ecological problems make them exceedingly difficult to tackle. They typically include some or all of the following features:[1]

- *Unclear definitions.* Stakeholders typically don't agree on what 'The Problem' actually is, even if they use similar words to describe it. If the nature of the problems is presupposed – for example, that it is an 'economic problem' – then the nature of 'the solution' is also presupposed. Economic problems are tackled using economic measures to achieve economic solutions. This may not be how others see things. And such a focus is likely to be too narrow to avoid unintended outcomes.
- *Scale issues.* There is no 'correct' level of abstraction across time and space. Interventions that solve problems at local scales may not solve them at national or global scales. For example, an effort to improve urban air quality by building a taller smokestack at a regional power station may simply result in sulphur poisoning of forests in another state or nation downwind. It can be very hard to see how actions taken in one place connect to outcomes far away in time and space.
- *Solution management.* Solutions can be better or worse than one another, but not right and wrong in an absolute sense. A conservationist might wish to see landscape-scale conservation measures implemented to protect the habitat of a large carnivore, such as a bear. However, a solution that includes local land-owners' rights to manage their properties within a landscape-scale plan of management might be a better outcome than either no measure at all or one that angers the landowners by locking them out. Social–ecological problems are not so much 'solved' as rendered manageable.
- *'Solutions' create new problems.* Intervening to 'fix' complex human–environment problems inevitably puts in train a range of outcomes. Some of these are desired and intended, but others are not. In time, these undesired and unintended outcomes emerge as new problems to be tackled. Often the urgency of the problem appears to warrant the intervention, but caution should be taken in thinking solutions are 'obvious'. In particular, solutions that are intended to 'make the problem go away' often make the problem worse over time. Building freeways to reduce commute times can work in the short term, but can lead to even longer commute times because it encourages more private vehicle use. Increasing the height of a flood-control levee is an obvious solution to rising flood levels. But the increased home building in flood-prone districts that follows from this intervention exposes settlers to even greater risk of flood damage.
- *No objective measure of success.* Which variable to monitor as an indicator of 'success' is often not obvious, but must be critically considered. A government department of roads might measure its success by reference to the total kilometres of road constructed within a set budget. A department of health might measure the success of its interventions by a reduction in the number of patients with respiratory tract ailments. The increased road use and consequent increases in

vehicle particulate emissions generated by the success of the former are directly at odds with the population health goals of the latter.

- *Intervention stresses.* Every intervention changes the situation and very often these changes cannot be easily reversed. Social–ecological systems can suffer 'regime shifts' following management interventions. People learn and adapt as a result of experience. A poorly presented proposal to install technology such as wind farms in a region can cause anger, distrust, and hostility in the community – causing rifts that take a very long time to repair. The proposer can certainly rework the proposal, but the second time around they will be dealing with a deeply sceptical community whose members will be predisposed to object. Adding sea water to rice paddies to farm shrimp yields greater profits to the farmer. However, the farmer cannot opt to go back to growing rice as the soil now carries a salt load in which rice cannot be grown. This becomes an even greater problem if the price of shrimp collapses.

- *Solutions must be collaborative.* Sustainability challenges are never 'owned' by one person or interest group. They always require a range of skills, perspectives, and understandings to be brought together in management collaborations. This is one reason why human ecology is necessarily transdisciplinary. Since 'disciplines' are ways of thinking that sit mostly within academia, human ecologists need to extend their conceptual reach to include knowledge held by all relevant stakeholders. Bringing these diverse and partial knowledge sources together is tricky, and how this might be done is a preoccupation of this book. However, it is only when we do successfully blend these various contributions that novel alternative pathways to just and sustainable futures can be found. An additional benefit is that a more lasting commitment to a particular innovation is generated when stakeholders have been included in the process of generating solutions to shared problems.

- *Moral, ethical, political, or professional dimensions.* Social–ecological problems are not only issues of environmental resource allocation. They are inextricably woven through issues of justice and fairness. It is not hard to imagine scenarios where a reduced human population lives in balance with the environment. Yet versions of balance that are achieved through death, destruction, and enforced misery cannot be ethically countenanced. Furthermore, people's moral stances are guided by their value and belief systems, including their sense of right and wrong, and thus influence what interventions they believe to be acceptable. These moral stances are grounded in cultural, religious, and peer-group allegiances, as well as in pragmatic political affiliations and professional codes of practice. Once taken up, such stances are not readily changed, and certainly not by scientific evidence. Yet their role in explaining a community's attitudes and actions is fundamental and cannot be overlooked.

- *Aesthetic motivations.* People do not tackle social–ecological problems in a purely 'rational' manner. When people are inspired to act it is for a suite of reasons that have judgemental, emotional, spiritual, aspirational, and aesthetic dimensions, in addition to any evidential knowledge base. Indeed, recalcitrance, ignorance, and irrationality all play their part. But that is part and parcel of human nature and it is, after all, human nature that human ecology has to deal with.

One of human ecology's major tasks is to contribute towards the re-imagination and rearrangement of social–ecological systems in order to bring into being the kind of humane, sustainable, and worthwhile futures that the broader community will willingly embrace.

1.4 Conclusion: a systems approach to sustainability

The four thematic areas of human ecology – ethical priority; social–ecological interactions; learning and behaviour change; and meeting, or changing, the expectations built into dominant belief systems – will be pursued throughout this book. The inquiry will, of necessity, be transdisciplinary (or comprehensive), due to its dependence on a wide range of knowledge and perceptions. In order to keep the discussion coherent we will develop a fifth theme as the book progresses. This is the 'systems approach' promised by the book's subtitle. A systems approach will help us, as human ecologists, to understand the interplay between the various aspects of the situations under investigation and how the parts of a social–ecological system drive change in each other. Where change is found to be unsustainable, a systems approach will help a community to identify leverage points for effective intervention and system redesign to develop more acceptable patterns of behaviour. Finally, the systems approach will point the way towards a theoretical structure that can help human ecology evolve as a comprehensive, disciplined form of inquiry and practice. The case study in Chapter 2 demonstrates the need for this comprehensive approach.

Note

1   This list is adapted from Rittel, H. J. and Webber, M. (1973). 'Dilemmas in a general theory of planning'. *Policy Sciences* 4(2): 155–169. A more up to date extension of these ideas can be found in Brown, V. A., Harris, J. A. and Russell, J. Y. (2010). *Tackling Wicked Problems Through the Transdisciplinary Imagination*. London; Washington, DC, Earthscan.

References

Borden, R. (2014). *Ecology and Experience: Reflections from a human ecological perspective.* Berkeley, CA, North Atlantic Books.

Boyden, S. (1986). 'An integrative approach to the study of human ecology'. *Human Ecology: A gathering of perspectives.* R. Borden. Maryland, MD, The Society for Human Ecology, 3–25.

Brown, V. A., Harris, J. A., and Russell J. Y. (2010). *Tackling Wicked Problems Through the Transdisciplinary Imagination.* London, Washington, DC, Earthscan.

Christensen, C. (2014). 'Human ecology as philosophy'. *Human Ecology Review* 20(1): 31–49.

Clarke, R. (1973). *Ellen Swallow: The Woman Who Founded Ecology.* Chicago, IL, Follett Publishing Company.

Dyball, R. (2010). 'Human Ecology as open transdisciplinary inquiry'. *Tackling Wicked Problems Through the Transdisciplinary Imagination.* V. A. Brown, J. A. Harris, and J. Y. Russell. London, Earthscan, 273–284.

Rittel, H. J. and Webber, M. (1973). 'Dilemmas in a general theory of planning'. *Policy Sciences* 4(2): 155–169.

Steiner, D. (1993). 'Human ecology as transdisciplinary science, and science as part of human ecology'. *Human Ecology: Fragments of anti-fragmentary views of the world*. D. Steiner and M. Nauser. New York, Routledge, 47–73.

Tengström, E. (1985). *Human Ecology – A New Discipline? A Short Tentative Description of the Institutional and Intellectual History of Human Ecology*. Gothenburg, Gothenburg University, Institute for Human Ecology.

Young, G. (1989). 'A conceptual framework for an interdisciplinary human ecology'. *Acta Oecologiea Hominis: International Monographs in Human Ecology* 1(1): 1–137.

2 Water conflicts in the Snowy Mountains

He hails from Snowy River, up by Kosciusko's side,
Where the hills are twice as steep and twice as rough,
Where a horse's hoofs strike firelight from the flint stones every stride,
The man that holds his own is good enough.
And the Snowy River riders on the mountains make their home,
Where the river runs those giant hills between;
I have seen full many horsemen since I first commenced to roam,
But nowhere yet such horsemen have I seen.
(*The Man from Snowy River* – A. B. 'Banjo' Paterson)

2.1 Introduction

This chapter presents a case example of how an environment changes as different groups of people try to obtain resources from it. When the resource is insufficient to satisfy the demands of every group, one or other will miss out. If a group is denied access to resources they believe they are entitled to, and if they feel that they were unfairly treated in the decision-making process, conflict results. Unresolved, conflict can lead to a number of groups competing for the same resource. This can potentially result in the collapse of that resource, with negative social and environmental outcomes for all. Consequently, issues of justice and fairness are a major consideration if conflict is to be avoided and resources managed sustainably. In this case example, the water resources of the Australian Snowy Mountains are finite. The challenge is how the different groups wishing to use that water might collectively learn to fairly and equitably respect the limits imposed by this basic environmental reality. This is a good example at a landscape scale of the kinds of situations that human ecology deals with more generally. As a whole, the chapter demonstrates the need for a comprehensive framework through which we can better understand interactions in complex social–ecological systems, such as this one. The development of such a framework is necessary if we are to avoid piecemeal interventions that are intended to improve a situation but which are ineffective, unfair, or unsustainable.

2.2 The Australian Snowy Mountains

The Snowy Mountains are located in the south-east of the Australian continent, as the highest point in a mountain-range complex that runs 3,500 kilometres along the eastern coast. Although it has no precise boundary, the 'High Country' covers an

Figure 2.1 The rounded, soil-covered mountains of the Australian High Country, seen through European eyes as 'meadows'.

Source: photo credit Peter Meusburger.

area of about 2,500 square kilometres, with the highest peaks centred on Mount Kosciuszko at an elevation of 2,228 metres. By world standards this is not high, reflecting the extreme age of the continent and the consequence of millions of years of erosion. The resulting landscape is characterized by rounded, soil-covered hills, where prolonged weathering has left gentle slopes, except where rivers have incised deep valleys (Figure 2.1). The soils are fragile, acidic, poor in nutrients, and generally shallow over most of the region. At about 300 metres elevation the upper slopes give way to flat tablelands that mark the lower boundary of what would normally be considered 'part of' the Snowy Mountains (Costin 1954).

Temperatures peak in January (summer) with average highs around 20 degrees Celcius (°C). Average lows in July (winter) are around –4°C, but can reach minimums below –12°C. All averages are subject to considerable annual and decadal variations, including the periodic droughts that are endemic to Australia's weather systems. Three extreme droughts have been recorded in the past 100 years, with the most recent lasting from 1997 to 2009. In the worst year of this drought, 2006, precipitation was around 25 per cent of the annual average. Evidence from records across the twentieth century indicates patterns of longer term climatic change tending towards generally warmer and drier conditions. This is predicted to result in shorter snow seasons, with less total snow falling at higher elevations than in the recent past.

Water run-off from the High Country feeds an extensive network of bogs and fens before draining through a number of small montane streams into one of three major river systems that rise in this area (Box 2.1 and Figure 2.2). During winter, precipitation falls as snow when the temperature is low enough. Accumulated snow eventually melts in spring, which occurs around September. This results in extremely high discharge rates. The energy in this snow melt water is crucial to the health of these montane waterways, as it scours out boulders, invasive plants, and silt and other debris that would otherwise accumulate and eventually choke them. During summer, average precipitation is low and stream flow is much reduced, with some waterways ceasing to flow altogether.

In the Snowy Mountains above about 1,800 metres elevation is an area of about 370 square kilometres where prolonged snow cover results in treeless alpine eco-systems. Here, feldmark and various forms of heath-like plant communities dominate. These alpine plant communities are adapted to the low-nutrient environment of thin fragile soils and the short growing season. There are also large areas of bogs and fens that are associated with permanently saturated peat. In their undisturbed state these bogs retain vast amounts of water. Below the alpine zone is a characteristic

---

Box 2.1 Rivers of the High Country

Three major rivers are fed by water from the Snowy Mountains. Rates of flow in all three rivers have been significantly modified by the construction of the Snowy Mountains Hydro-Electric Scheme (Snowy Hydro), as will be discussed. Their unmodified flows (pre-European settlement) off the High Country catchment area are described below.

The Snowy River rises at about 1,700 metres elevation. It flows in a roundabout fashion, heading north and then east, before eventually finding its way south to the sea. It has a total length of about 500 kilometres. The average flow into the Snowy River is in the order of 1,150 gigalitres per annum. Spring snow melt discharges could exceed 2,000 megalitres per day. Summer flows are about 200 megalitres per day.

The Murrumbidgee River rises at about 1,600 metres. It initially flows south-easterly before swinging around in a great loop to head to the west, joining the Murray River after some 1,500 kilometres. The flow into the Murrumbidgee was about 620 gigalitres per annum, with a spring to summer ratio similar to that of the Snowy River.

The Murray River rises near Mount Kosciuszko, at approximately 1,430 metres elevation, and takes a fairly direct route west to the Southern Ocean some 2,530 kilometres away. Despite its length, around 40 per cent of its flow comes from the 2 per cent of its catchment that is in the High Country – this flow amounts to some 650 gigalitres per annum.

Although the combined average discharge into these three rivers is around 2,500 gigalitres per annum, this figure is a long-term average. Flows can range from maximums close to 5,000 gigalitres per annum, to minimums that are less than 600 gigalitres per annum. This extreme range of variation is typical of Australian rainfall patterns.

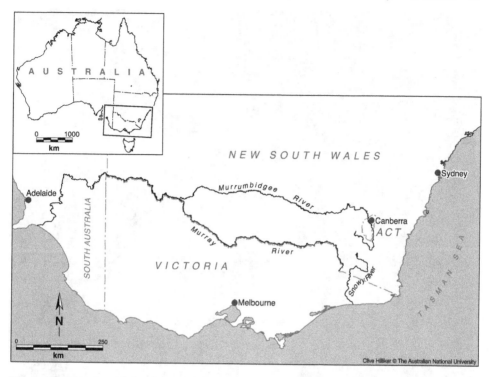

Figure 2.2 Location of the three major river systems rising in the catchment of the High Country.

subalpine landscape that experiences varying amounts of winter snow. The subalpine is typified by the presence of the snow gum (*Eucalyptus pauciflora*) but can be dominated by shrub, heath, or grasslands, depending upon local landform, exposure, soils, and drainage. At lower levels the High Country gives way to montane woods and sclerophyll forests that predominate down to the surrounding tablelands (Williams *et al.* 2003).

These landscapes are fire prone and many of the species have evolved resilience to fire. Natural wildfire is often started by summer lightning strikes, and a range of factors affect fire intensity. Key influences are temperature, wind speed, and fuel load. Fuel load is mostly the amount of fine flammable material, such as grasses, smaller shrubs, and accumulated forest litter, and is affected by how dry this material is. This is in turn influenced by how many extreme heat days in a row there have been prior to ignition (Good 1986).

The fauna of the alpine areas of the Snowy Mountains have adaptations that allow them to survive despite temperature extremes, low nutrient availability, and the limits on food energy that result from the short growing season. Reproduction strategies are typically geared to take advantage of the short periods when food is abundant. An extreme example of alpine specialization is provided by the pygmy possum (*Burramys parvus*, Figure 2.3), the only marsupial that goes into energy-saving hibernation during winter. The specialist adaptation of alpine fauna ties their future survival to the continuation of their unique habitat conditions – something that climate change threatens as snow seasons become shorter, the snow line becomes higher, and

Figure 2.3 Mountain Pygmy Possum. Critically endangered by climate change, habitat
　　disturbance, and predation by feral animals.

Source: photo credit Charlotte Corkran and Rebecca Plum.

snow pack becomes thinner. Other, more generalist, species are able to migrate
seasonally, which allows them to overwinter in warmer, more sheltered regions where
food is more abundant. This freedom of movement extends to feral animals, such as
foxes and cats, which nowadays exert a major survival pressure on the alpine
specialists.

　　In summary, the Snowy Mountains high-country ecosystem includes a relatively
small alpine area characterized by severe weather, low nutrient stocks, and short
growing seasons. Its geophysical and biological characteristics are extremely tightly
linked and are naturally low in productivity. Lower in the landscape natural productivity is higher as less extreme challenges are presented. Humans have been
attracted to the region for millennia, with very different environmental consequences.
The original occupants, with by far the longest period of custody, are the Aboriginal
peoples of the area.

2.3 Aboriginal people: at home in the High Country

Aboriginal people have lived in Australia for at least 55,000 years. Firm archaeological
evidence for Aboriginal presence in the High Country dates from 21,000 years ago.

With this ancient association, Aboriginal belief systems and social arrangements evolved so that they could live in their country in ways compatible with both its and their own wellbeing.

A number of different Aboriginal communities lived in and around the region, drawing on the resources of the subalpine and lower woodlands. Rights of access to manage and appropriate these resources were governed through traditional laws and codes of practice (Crabb 2003). Management regimes involved deliberate setting on fire for a range of reasons, including habitat creation for key species, ease of hunting and movement, and the belief that the country needed fire to keep it vibrant. Such fires were set with great consideration to the appropriate circumstances and resulted in low-intensity burns. The true alpine areas do not hold essential resources of use to humans, although some transient resources exist. Notably, the seasonal influx of bogong moth (*Agrotis infusa*) was an important food source. However, the area has great non-material value to Aboriginal people, including its spiritual significance.

In the subalpine areas the pattern was one of seasonal coming and going from camps in established lower altitude home territories to access resources during the warmer seasons. Population density in the region would have varied, but a figure of around 500 individuals has been estimated, spread over a number of tribal groups and divided into smaller kinship units (Flood 1980). Although population density at any one place varied during the year, a figure of about 1 person per 5 square kilometres can be estimated.

Although Aboriginal groups traded goods across the continent, for their immediate health and wellbeing they relied on the productive capacity of the environments they occupied. In environments such as those of the Snowy Mountains, where seasonal variation in resource abundance occurs, people physically moved in phase with ecological cycles. This means that at any one time they were located in a region where sufficient food and other essential resources were available to support them. Some steps were taken to enhance the environment's productivity, including the use of fire as already mentioned. However, their main strategy for accessing resources was not manipulation of the environment but understanding its behaviour. Through observation and an unbroken chain of intergenerational cultural learning, Aboriginal people knew their environments intimately. This knowledge enabled them to relocate to places where the environment could readily absorb the impacts of their presence with few lasting effects on its productive capacity.

The need for mobility limited personal possessions, since everything they owned had to be carried from place to place. Items of cultural significance or status were small and easily transported. Hence, in strictly material terms, there was little difference between people in levels of ownership and possessions. The various items they did manufacture were fashioned from stone or from organic sources such as wood, bone, fur, and fibres. Their summer shelters were simple, as these were annually abandoned for more permanent homes in the lower river valleys. Among the few permanent structures they built were stone fish traps, which can still be found in the area, as can evidence of stone working for tool making. Trade with other groups outside the region did not represent a significant loss of any resource – nor did goods imported represent any significant accumulation. Overall, their effect on the material balance of the landscape was local, temporary, and well within the ecosystem's resilience threshold. In many ways, Aboriginal 'impacts' actually enhanced the environment's capacity to provide a home for them.

2.4 New arrivals: stockmen and graziers

The traditional way of life of Aboriginal people, with its associated environmental management practices, was catastrophically affected by the arrival of European settlers in Australia in 1788. From the time of contact, relationships between the new arrivals and the original occupants were marred by forced dispossession, devastating disease epidemics and, at times, deliberate acts of genocide. Aboriginal resistance to the occupation of their land eventually proved ineffective. Although some individuals remained in the Snowy Mountains area to try to maintain their traditional way of life, for the vast majority this was impossible. The culture of the new arrivals, with their beliefs about private and exclusive ownership of the environment and its resources, was completely at odds with traditional practice. Aboriginal people were forced off their land or removed themselves to kinship groups outside the region. How many died is unknown. Those who remained typically found themselves in low-status employment. Although Aboriginal connection to their country remains to this day, their ability to actively manage the environment at this time was broken. Their predominant culture was suddenly replaced by one that believed the environment was there to be dominated and controlled.

The first Europeans to arrive in the Snowy Mountains were graziers and their stockmen in search of suitable land for sheep and cattle. From the 1820s, large grazing properties were established in the lowland plains at the foot of the mountains. It was not long until animals from these properties were being brought up into the High Country for summer grazing (Figure 2.4). Driving stock up into the mountains from the plains was an arduous business and not lightly undertaken. However, the reward was that the open heaths and fens of the alpine areas held both feed and secure water for their animals. With their European backgrounds, these landscapes were seen as 'meadows'. Even though in ecological terms a fertile deep-soiled European meadow was quite unlike the infertile, thin, and fragile soils of the Snowy Mountains, the stockmen put them to similar uses. By the early 1850s there were large numbers of grazing animals in the High Country for as much of the year as the weather allowed (Hueneke 1994).

The cultural background of the graziers and stockmen strongly endorsed the exploitation of the environment. Within their belief system, harnessing environmental resources is the process by which value is generated. The provision of food and fibre to satisfy the needs of consumers was held to be a virtuous activity. Indeed, the wellbeing of those consumers depended upon such provisions. More generally, graziers and stockmen were contributing to the economic development of the nation, which was seen as one of the primary measures of progress. Within these sets of assumptions and priorities their behaviour was completely rational and had the approval and support of the broader community (Merritt 2007). Indeed, for many Australians at the time, the free-spirited stockman at home in 'the bush' epitomized the quintessential national character – as the 1890 Paterson poem at the front of this chapter attests.

A major consequence of this difference in attitude to environmental management was that the size of the population the High Country was called on to support was much greater than it had been under Aboriginal management. Furthermore, within the class-based European culture, large income disparities existed. This meant that not only were more people being supported but the amount of resources each person demanded varied depending on their status. A high-income individual might expect

Figure 2.4 Stockmen mustering cattle in the High Country, *c.* 1936.
Source: photo courtesy of the National Library of Australia – an23488110.

resources many times greater than that of a low-income individual. These resources were sourced from environments far from their point of consumption, including being shipped from overseas. However, in material terms, people at the lower end of the social scale had more material goods than the Aboriginal people before them. Not only did European colonisation start to increase the population, it brought a culture whose per capita resource use was significantly greater than before.

This novel state of affairs started to generate a one-way flow of resources out of the High Country. This material flow was not only in the form of the exported commodities, such as beef and wool, but also in major coincidental flows, such as soil loss. The systems of production occurring in the Snowy Mountains were now embedded in larger systems of production, distribution, and consumption. Changes to the local environment and social arrangements would increasingly reflect these external forces.

The number of animals brought up to the High Country in any year reflected the quality of the season in the lowlands. When drought occurred, which happens regularly in Australia, large numbers of animals would be brought in. Graziers who had access to the mountains could keep more animals and deliver them to market in better condition for greater financial reward than those who did not. Because the alpine areas provided a safety net in times of drought, these graziers could maintain more animals on their home farms than they otherwise would. In 1869 the *Sydney Morning Herald* reported:

> [D]uring a favourable season like the present, when the district is covered, from one end to the other, by rich waving grass, there is feed enough for the entire half million [sheep]; but . . . when there is a drought – as there was last year or may be in any year – the district [the lower tablelands] must prove unable to support such numerous flocks; they will die in thousands or must be driven 'to the mountains'.

> (Hancock 1972: 135)

The profitability of maintaining large stocks fed back to increase stock numbers, which in turn increased the pressure on the environments that were supporting them.

The management practices introduced by the stockmen had profound environmental effects. This was partly the consequence of introducing large numbers of big grazing animals into a landscape that had no co-evolutionary relationship with such animals. Particularly vulnerable were the fens and bogs, as animals naturally gathered there to drink. In many places this led to breaking down the sides of the bogs and with it a loss of water. Once exposed to air, the peat substrate soon dried out. This process is essentially irreversible, and resulted in vast areas of bog vanishing from the High Country, dramatically altering the water-holding capacity of the region. Also, with repeated grazing, an animal's dietary preference places selective pressure on the foods they find most palatable. Over time, this changes the composition and structure of the plant community. Plants that the animals do not favour, such as woody shrubs, tend to proliferate. This change in distribution and type of vegetation produced by the animals' food choices was one reason that led stockmen to deliberately set fire to the landscape.

Wildfire is a natural phenomenon in many Australian environments. The deliberate setting of fire to manage the landscape was practised by Aboriginal people for millennia. However, the pattern of burning that the stockmen introduced was unlike previous regimes. When conditions allowed, they would set fire to the landscape as they moved their animals out for the winter. This functioned to clear woody vegetation and also stimulated new plant growth in the following spring. The young shoots were a ready food source for their animals when they returned. However, the practice also tended to reinforce the scrubby growth it was intended to control. Although grasses were the first kinds of plants to recolonize the burnt areas they were soon succeeded by further woody plants and shrubs. About the only strategy to prevent such regrowth was further burning – essentially using fire to control the consequences of using fire (Leaver 2004). That this practice was making the situation worse was noted in a report by naturalist Richard Helms to the New South Wales Government as early as 1893:

> This [deliberate setting of fires] has only a temporary beneficial effect in regard to the improvement of the pasture by the springing up of young grass in places so cleared, for after a year or so the scrub and underwood spring up more densely than ever.

> (quoted in Banks 1989: 269)

Removing the soil's protective plant cover through grazing and burning had the unintended consequence of causing erosion. Left exposed, the region's fragile soils were easily mobilized by flowing water, especially melting snow. As a result, vast amounts of soil were lost from across the High Country, carried downhill to end up in the streams and rivers of the lowlands. Because it was seen as impacting on the value of water assets, this erosion of soil into waterways brought the stockmen into conflict with other groups. Chief and most powerful of these were the inland irrigators.

2.5 Inland irrigators

Australia is a large continent. At 7.7 million square kilometres, it has a land surface area fractionally larger than the contiguous United States and half the size again of Europe. However, it also has low and unreliable volumes of rainfall. An indicator of this is that its land area is 5 per cent of the world's total, yet it has only 1 per cent of the world's total rainwater run-off. To the early European settlers, discovering that this vast wealth of land was coupled with such tiny flows of water seemed a cruel hoax.

Land with reasonably reliable rainfall primarily occurs in a narrow coastal strip along the south-east of the continent. These areas were soon occupied by Europeans. By the mid nineteenth century settlers were moving into the wide inland plains. Here rainfall variability was a major issue. In 'good' years, when rainfall was above average, large stocks of sheep and cattle could be carried. In drought years animals died in their thousands, and the settlers suffered extreme hardship. In agricultural terms, the challenge was how to get these environments to yield the meats – and later grains – that the European-style diets of their customers required. The stakes were high. If water could be found they could 'make the deserts bloom'. Capturing this sentiment at the time, Wills wrote:

> [If] more water can be conserved and applied to the land, then the future will be secure. If not, to talk of the future may well be to speculate about that time when food will have become the scarcest resource ... If such a situation eventuates, our struggle to develop this continent will indeed have gone for nothing.
>
> (Wills 1955: vii)

Not only would water secure the food demands of Australia's rapidly growing population, but also through exports Australian landscapes could help provision the British Empire. From this time, the impacts on Australian environments resulted from meeting the resource demands of remote consumers, an increasing percentage of whom were overseas. Material flows were now not just off the environments of origin, they were off the entire continent.

Unlike their Snowy Mountains counterparts, the settlers of the inland plains did not have the option of driving their stock to where the water was. Rather, their solution lay in trying to bring water to their stock. Small-scale private schemes to impound and divert water appeared along waterways in the region by the end of the 1800s. However, as the success with which one individual could divert and store water almost invariably came at the expense of his downstream neighbour, these schemes often led to conflict. When major droughts occurred, such as the 'Federation Drought' of 1895 to 1902, irrigation was of little use, as even major rivers stopped flowing. The solution to the extreme economic, social, and personal hardship caused by drought was sought in much larger and properly administered irrigation schemes.

Figure 2.5 Digging irrigation channels in the 1920s.
Source: Courtesy of the National Library of Australia – an10571345–41.

Such schemes required the finances and institutional power of government and intense political pressure was applied to realize them.

Scientific concerns at the time were that irrigation in semi-arid areas could lead to salinity problems. Experience from similar projects elsewhere, notably India, showed that the additional water could bring salts held in the soil to the surface. However, the political imperative to act overruled scientific advice. Commencing in the early twentieth century, major government-funded irrigation projects were developed on just such salinity-prone landscapes adjoining the Murrumbidgee River. Irrigation projects on the Murray River were slower to get underway, as they required complex political negotiations between the three states – New South Wales, Victoria, and South Australia – that shared that river's water. However, these obstacles were eventually overcome and by the 1930s a range of irrigation works were under construction on the Murray. Water along both rivers was regulated by a series of dams and distributed to farmers along a vast network of supply channels (Figure 2.5). With these works, engineers successfully removed the natural variability of rainfall as an obstacle to conducting European-style agriculture in Australia. Regular water supply allowed for pasture irrigation, which was much more productive and secure than its dryland equivalent. In time, irrigation also supported the production of grains and horticultural produce. However, while the application of water achieved much higher outputs per hectare, it also had, as scientists had warned, the unintended consequence of bringing salt to the surface. Over-irrigation rendered large tracts of land barren – a problem that irrigators struggle to manage to this day.

Government financial investment in the system was significant and large numbers of politically influential rural communities were dependent on its output. Consequently, anything that put it at risk generated concern. Attention soon turned to the soil eroding from the High Country. As this material entered the waterways it accumulated on the floor of the reservoirs behind the dam walls. Siltation reduced the volumes of water that reservoirs could store, and hence reduced water security for the irrigators. By the early 1930s government reports were strongly linking grazing and burning with downstream siltation. This unintended consequence of the stockmen's environment management strategy meant that conflict with the irrigators was almost inevitable. The political power balance was probably already in the irrigators' favour, but a major new player was about to enter the stage that would tip it even further. This was the proposed Snowy Hydro scheme.

2.6 Changing flows: the Snowy Hydro scheme

The engineering works on the Murray and Murrumbidgee rivers reduced the variability in their flow patterns and underpinned a highly productive and profitable irrigation-based agriculture. This in turn drew more settlers to the region and saw more farms converting to irrigation. However, the dams could not increase the total amount of water available for distribution. Hence, although water resources were now more reliable, with large numbers of irrigators calling upon them they were soon fully allocated. From that point, additional volumes supplied to the irrigation areas was only possible if inflows to the irrigation impoundments could be increased. This brought the water of the Snowy River into consideration.

The Snowy River flowed for much of its upper reaches through rocky gorge country not suitable for farming. From a farmer's point of view, this water was 'wasted' (Seddon 1994). Harnessing this 'wasted' water for human use had been considered before. A wide variety of more or less feasible options to divert it inland were sketched from the 1880s onwards. These early plans foundered over political differences over how the water, and the cost of accessing it, would be shared between what were originally independent colonies. When the colonies formed a Federation in 1901 they became states, with each retaining sovereign jurisdiction over environmental resources, including water. Eventually it took the intervention of the federal government to break this state-based impasse. In 1945 Australia emerged from the war years under a 'left' leaning federal government, predisposed to centralized programmes, large-scale infrastructure building, and welfare schemes. During the course of the war, the federal government had consolidated income taxation powers previously administered by the states as a war revenue-raising measure. For the first time it could bring considerable financial backing to the schemes that it pursued, and large-scale nation-building public works appealed to it strongly.

The proposal that gained the federal government's interest was a water diversion project that would also generate hydro-electric power. The capacity to earn money by generating electricity would be used to refund the money advanced to build the scheme and to cover its operating costs. The Snowy River would be dammed on the eastern side of the Snowy Mountains and its waters diverted for storage in a number of reservoirs across the High Country. When this water was needed for irrigation it would be released to the west. As this requires the water to fall from a considerable height, hydropower stations could be constructed at the outlet point to capture the energy of the water and convert it to electricity. The diverted waters would be delivered in equal parts to the Murray and Murrumbidgee rivers, and thus their respective irrigation communities, doubling the natural volumes of flow in both. Not only would this require tunnelling over 150 kilometres through the mountains, but the impoundments would need an enormous storage capacity, equivalent to two years' average precipitation. This capacity would allow the scheme to average out the wide variation in volumes of annual inflow and convert it to reliable, constant rates of outflow. The engineering task was on a scale never tried before, which arguably enhanced its attraction to a nation eager to establish its 'first world' status.

Politically, the scheme had to survive some delicate negotiations between the federal and state governments, particularly as water remained a state government asset. However, there was broad agreement that secure and reliable energy was key to the nation's economic growth and the social wellbeing of its growing population. Power outages were a common occurrence at this time. There was a general concern that Australia's per capita energy consumption was far too low, being significantly less than the developed nations it typically compared itself to – the United States and Britain. A more diverse energy mix would also weaken the Coal Miners' Union, which had engaged in industrial action in the post-war years and was seen by some as too powerful. Above all, there was common agreement that if more irrigation water could flow to farmlands out west, then Australia could flourish as the 'breadbasket of the Empire', and help secure its position as an 'outpost of Europe' in what was then seen as a hostile Asian region (Wills 1955).

This broad alliance between the various levels of government, the irrigation communities and the energy requirements of urban and industrial development stood in opposition to the stockmen. However unfairly, the stockmen found themselves portrayed as standing in the way of 'national progress', a politically untenable position (Merritt 2007). From the late 1940s stock numbers in the High Country were progressively limited and, over a longer time frame, withdrawn. Largely due to catchment protection, but over time also because of conservation and recreation interests, the entire area was converted into national park, with grazing of all kinds excluded by the 1970s. From the stockmen's perspective they had lost the fight to maintain a traditional way of life they had practised for generations. The enduring sense of injustice and accompanying anger and resentment continues in many High Country communities to this day.

As an engineering feat the Snowy Hydro scheme justly deserves its reputation. In extraordinarily challenging conditions, and with technology that by today's standards seems extremely primitive, the engineers and labourers did what was requested of them, on time and on budget. They constructed 16 dams, tunnelled through 150 kilometres of rock and built seven major power stations and a range of associated infrastructure, include aqueducts and roads. Almost the entire precipitation falling over 7,800 square kilometres is captured and stored in reservoirs capable of holding more than two years' average inflows – some 7,000 gigalitres. The water of the Snowy River was turned inland and divided in a way that placated the political imperatives of the time by being shared almost equally between the users on the Murrumbidgee and Murray rivers. As the Snowy had a flow equal to the Murray and Murrumbidgee combined, its waters served to roughly double what was available before. As this water is released from the scheme it generates about 5,000 gigawatt hours of pollution-free electricity (McHugh 1989). To indicate the efficiency with which the engineers completed their task, post-construction flows in the Snowy River below the scheme were reduced effectively to zero. Not a drop was missed (Figure 2.6).

Figure 2.6 Constructing the trans-mountain tunnels of the Snowy Mountains Hydro-Electric scheme.

Source: photo courtesy of the National Library of Australia – vn3415857.

The primary purpose of the scheme is both to significantly increase the amount of water flowing from the High Country to the west and to ensure that it does so reliably. In order to provide the guaranteed minimum flows that it was designed to deliver, water storages are carefully managed from year to year. Inflows from the relatively rare above-average precipitation years are stored to augment flows in the more common below-average years. In other words, the scheme holds back water from above-average rainfall years and uses it to 'top up' below-average rainfall years so that a reliable annual outflow is provided. In any year the scheme stores enough water to fulfil that year's required annual release, as well as volumes estimated to meet future needs. The amount of water required to achieve this minimum flow is based on a series of rolling estimates that assume that the worst drought sequence Australia will experience in the future is no greater than the most severe drought it has experienced in the past (Department of Industry 2000). Responding to political pressure from downstream users, including irrigators, to release larger volumes risks the scheme running dry during a future drought. Irrigators, who understandably would like higher annual releases, can have either the smaller, effectively guaranteed figure, or a larger annual figure and risk going without more often. They cannot have both.

Conflicts can arise from failure to appreciate the difference between how much water is stored to meet required annual releases and amounts stored over and above those volumes. The managers of the scheme carefully account and accumulate any volumes of water above what is needed to provide the required annual releases. This 'above target' water is very valuable to them, both for the price they can get from it for generating electricity and because it allows them to provide a range of other lucrative services to the energy industry. It is one of the primary ways that Snowy Hydro makes the money to cover its operations and enable the provision of water at no charge to the user. The key is that it is entirely at their discretion when or whether they release above-target water. Required annual-release water has limited financial value for Snowy Hydro. This is because, in Australia, the price paid to an electricity generator changes as demand in the market changes. The difference between the price paid late at night when demand is low and in the morning when everyone is using power can vary considerably. The really big peak in prices occurs when something unpredictable happens, such as a heat wave or a big power generator going offline. Since required annual-release water has to be provided according to legally binding schedules, Snowy Hydro has limited capacity to respond to these market prices. With above-target water they have absolute discretion and can choose to release it when prices on the electricity market are at their highest. Although the amount of electricity generated per litre of water passing through the turbines is identical, it is worth much more to them. For example, although above-target water accounts for just 15 per cent of the water released in an average year, it accounts for 60 per cent of the revenue from power generation.

In the past, irrigators got above-target water as a bonus, since it would flow into their downstream impoundments. However, above-target water can also be used to underwrite various auxiliary services that Snowy Hydro is capable of providing. Many of these require that the water not be released at all. For example, they can underwrite the generation capacity of other power companies by guaranteeing to generate for them if their station has to go offline. This allows the power station that is taking out the contract to enter high-value 'no fail' contracts with industrial bulk consumers. In order to provide this service, Snowy Hydro is paid to *not* release water, as it has to ensure that it has sufficient volumes available to respond to any calls made on the contracts it has entered into. More recently, Snowy Hydro has bought its own fossil fuel power stations and can now extend this service guarantee to its own assets. This has the somewhat perverse consequence that a renewable energy supply is held offline in order to keep an unrenewable one online.

Ultimately, the amount of inflow from rain and snowfall places a limit on how much hydropower Snowy Hydro can generate. The scheme already captures it all and, with the possible and very limited exception of cloud seeding, cannot get any more. Once all the accumulated water is released the turbines stop turning and no further power can be generated. As energy demand in Australia continues to grow the proportional contribution of Snowy Hydro shrinks. Consequently, the value of electricity production to Snowy Hydro's overall profit is diminishing and the value of provision of other kinds of services, such as those described above, is increasing.

This will see fewer and fewer years in which Snowy Hydro releases anything more than the guaranteed minimum required annual releases. In accumulating above-target water for economically rational purposes, some see Snowy Hydro as betraying its primary purpose. Irrigators especially were incensed to be told during the height of the millennium drought that there was no more water, when Snowy Hydro still held above-target water in its reservoirs.

However, as Snowy Hydro is increasingly run more as a business and less as a public service, these sorts of conflicts are likely to become more common. Once, a phone call from the agricultural minister's office would probably have seen additional flows of above-target water, but this is no longer the case. Within the new paradigm, only market signals would prompt such releases. For a range of reasons, these signals are weaker and rarer and so Snowy Hydro's operating patterns are likely to change accordingly. Flows above required annual-release levels are likely to be rarer, with timing less well suited to meeting irrigation needs. On top of this, reduced inflows due to climate change will almost certainly make matters worse. However, a more immediate threat is from groups demanding the restoration of environmental flows to the Snowy River. If significant volumes were to be returned to the Snowy River, the entire scheme would be potentially compromised.

2.7 New expectations – new pressures

At the time of construction of the Snowy Hydro scheme the health of the alpine landscape was not a central concern to either the irrigators or electricity generators. Their primary interest was in the quantity of water that could be harvested from it. However, remediating the catchment from the effects of grazing livestock created a new interest group. Soil conservation authorities worked with scientists whose interest was the environmental significance of the landscape. Joining them were small but increasingly influential groups of bushwalking enthusiasts, often travelling from urban centres to enjoy 'nature'. Over time, a park system was created, originally for utilitarian purposes but increasingly given intrinsic value by urban-based, conservation-concerned visitors whose political influence was to grow.

For another group of visitors the park came to be valued as a 'winter playground'. These users were attracted to the snow-covered slopes and opportunities for skiing. The potential the area offered for commercial ski activities was first noticed by Northern Europeans who had been employed in the ski industry in Europe, before coming to Australia in the mid 1900s to help build the Snowy Hydro scheme. From small beginnings using the clearings abandoned by the evicted stockmen, skiing has grown to be a major activity within the park. In addition to the ski lifts and groomed ski runs are major resorts with accommodation, shops, and catering, and infrastructure such as roads, car parks, and sewage treatment plants. These winter resorts now also promote significant summer visitation with an emphasis on comfort and convenience – as against 'roughing it' by camping and bushwalking. They make a major contribution to the estimated annual 2.8 million visitor nights to the region (a 'visitor night' being the number of people multiplied by the number of nights they stay). The economic contribution of visitors is significant. In addition to fees charged to commercial operators are park entry fees. These are a major source of revenue for the New South Wales National Parks and Wildlife Service and cross-subsidize the maintenance of less popular parks elsewhere in the state. However, the expectations of visitors to the ski resorts do not always align with those of the 'wilderness' seekers or with habitat conservation. These are all sources of potential conflict that the parks service has to manage.

Conflict with conservation concerns is not restricted to landscape management in the park. River conservation groups have been agitating for flows to be returned to the Snowy River. This is both for reasons of recovering the environmental health of the river and for the wellbeing of the old riverside communities. From their perspective, the once-mighty 'Snowy' has been stolen from them. Meeting their demands requires the return of adequate volumes of water. Scientific advice is that it will require at least 20 per cent of previous flow patterns to restore some semblance of health to the river. Others are calling for significantly more. The more successful the river restoration groups are, the less water there will be for hydro-electric generation and irrigation. From the perspective of the irrigators, restoring large volumes to the Snowy River would do them an injustice. Rightly or wrongly, they argue, the Snowy was turned inland and is now part of the headwaters of the Murray and Murrumbidgee rivers. They have invested in irrigation-dependent farming that would not be commercially viable without water from the Snowy River. There are also ramifications for the distant communities that rely on food produced from the irrigated agriculture. For some product types, around 60 per cent of these consumers are overseas. Although they are almost certainly unaware of it, their food security depends in part on how Australia resolves the conflict between competing demands on its finite environmental resources.

2.8 Conclusion

The example of water conflict in the Snowy Mountains of Australia exhibits many of the issues common to social–ecological problems. These are the kinds of problems human ecology seeks to understand and, if possible, help change. Different groups decide to act the way they do because, for whatever reason, these actions seem like a good idea from the worldview that dominates at the time. Most human-caused problems we face are not the product of random behaviour, but of deliberate choice. Construction of the Snowy Hydro scheme reflected the mindset that dominated at the time. Within this mindset, the challenge was to make the environment useful by fixing its perceived limitations. Water shortages in semi-arid landscapes were seen as an environmental problem for engineers to solve. When the missing element of water was supplied, these improved environments would become 'like' their highly productive European and North American counterparts, and could be farmed accordingly. Resources, such as water, were viewed as something that could be managed to maximize output under the authority of strong, confident institutions. No consideration was given to the broader social–ecological systems of which the resource is a part. Ultimately, managing environmental resources was seen as key to increasing the nation's population and its wealth, and was regarded as intimately linked with national progress.

Times change, and new values become influential as the unintended social and environmental impacts of earlier activities become apparent. Some elements of the belief system that motivated the construction of the Snowy Hydro scheme start to appear outmoded. Whether the scheme can reinvent itself to keep pace with these changing beliefs is difficult to answer. With the mindset and concerns that dominate today it is unlikely that the scheme would be built. In Australia, large, future-oriented nation-building programmes funded by the federal government do not have the public and political support they once did – although such schemes remain popular elsewhere in the world. Certainly the social and environmental costs would be given very different consideration to the weighting they got in the 1950s. Serious doubts would probably be cast on the equity with which the costs and benefits of the scheme were shared among stakeholders. However, we might also consider whether this contemporary aversion to large, ambitious programmes is itself a problem. The collective effort required to move towards sustainability will need programmes of intervention on at least the scale of the Snowy Hydro scheme, and is unlikely to be achieved without inconveniencing anyone.

Nevertheless, many Australians are rightly concerned about the impact the Snowy Hydro scheme has had upon environments and communities. The challenge for these concerned individuals is to design interventions that fairly, equitably, and sustainably improve the situation. This includes recognition on their part that they themselves are ultimately the consumers of the products of environments such as these. Complex questions then follow. If they wish these social–ecological systems to be treated differently, what does that mean for their own expectations? Do existing consumers have to consume fewer resources and does this mean going without some of the products they currently enjoy? How and why would they be willing to do this – or is it imagined that the decision to reduce will be imposed upon them? If consumers are to willingly reduce the impacts of their consumption, does this require that they know and care about what those impacts are? It seems impossible that we could all know – and then care – what all the impacts were of everything we did. If the decision to reduce is imposed, then by whom, with what authority, and what resentment and response is this likely to create? In asking such questions, we must acknowledge that the greater proportion of Earth's population currently consume very little. Far from expecting these individuals to share in reducing consumption there would seem to be a moral imperative to try to increase their share. One thing is certain – if a landscape is taken out of production but existing levels of consumption are to continue then the social–ecological impacts being experienced there will be relocated elsewhere. Whether that can be done in a socially just and environmentally sustainable manner is an empirical question that depends very much on how and where the impact is relocated. However, on a finite planet, addressing impacts felt in one place by moving them elsewhere is a strategy that cannot continue for long.

Among all the conflicts, alliances, collaborations, and misunderstandings that influence how human groups interact with the environment, one important factor must be held in mind. Human use of ecosystem services rests on supporting the environment's ability to maintain basic ecosystem functionality. For many services this means respecting the rates at which the stock from which the service is drawn replenishes. If human expectations of the environment exceed its capacity to deliver it will be the humans who are disappointed.

The situation described in this chapter is typical of many social–ecological problems in the world. If we are to avoid reactive, piecemeal policy responses to conflicts like the ones described here we need to be able to understand them comprehensively. Otherwise, we risk interventions that, however well intentioned, attempt to tackle aspects of the problem in isolation from the whole. Such interventions typically fail, often making matters worse environmentally or socially, or both. Steps towards the development of a theoretical framework for understanding such social-ecological problems are presented in Part II.

References

Banks, J. (1989). 'A history of forest fire in the Australian Alps'. *The Scientific Significance of the Australian Alps: The proceedings of the first Fenner conference on the environment.* R. Good. Canberra, The Australian National Parks Liaison Committee in association with the Australian Academy of Science, 265–280.

Costin, A. (1954). *A Study of the Ecosystems of the Monaro Region of New South Wales: With specific reference to soil erosion.* Sydney, Soil Conservation Service of New South Wales.

Crabb, P. (2003). *Managing the Alps: A history of cooperative management of the Australian Alps national parks.* Canberra, A joint publication of the Australian Alps Liaison Committee and the Centre for Resource and Environmental Studies, Australian National University.

Department of Industry, S. a. R. (2000). *Corporatisation of the Snowy Mountains Hydro-electric Authority.* Canberra, Commonwealth of Australia.

Flood, J. (1980). *The Moth Hunters : Aboriginal prehistory of the Australian Alps.* Canberra, Australian Institute of Aboriginal Studies.

Good, R. (1986). 'A basis for fire management in Alpine National Parks'. *Australia's Alpine Areas: Management for conservation.* K. Frawley. Canberra, National Parks Association, 86–104.

Hancock, W. (1972). *Discovering Monaro: A study of man's impact on his environment.* Cambridge, Cambridge University Press.

Hueneke, K. (1994). *People of the Australian High Country.* Palmerston, ACT, Tabletop Press.

Leaver, B. (2004). 'Fire values'. *An Assessment of the Values of Kosciuszko National Park: Interim Report.* CD Rom, Kosciuszko Independent Scientific Committee.

McHugh, S. (1989). *The Snowy: The people behind the power.* Sydney, Harper Collins.

Merritt, J. (2007). *Losing Ground: Grazing in the Snowy Mountains 1944–1969.* Bungendore, Turalla Press.

Seddon, G. (1994). *Searching for the Snowy.* St. Leonards, Allen & Unwin.

Williams, R., Mansergh, I., Wahren, C.-H., Rosengren, N. and Papst, W. (2003). 'Alpine Landscapes'. *Ecology: An Australian perspective.* P. Attiwill and B. Wilson. Melbourne, Oxford University Press, 352–369.

Wills, N. R., Ed. (1955). *Australia's Power Resources.* Melbourne, F. W. Cheshire.

Part II

Building shared understanding

Barry Newell

At the beginning of the geological epoch called the Holocene, some 10,000 years ago, there was a basic asymmetry in the interactions between humans and nature. While natural ecosystems had a strong effect on humans, humans did not have an equally strong effect on ecosystems. Now, however, human populations and technological power have grown to the point where the asymmetry is reducing rapidly. Human activity is having a more and more significant impact on ecosystem structure and function. This is happening at all scales, from local to global. Crutzen (2002) has suggested that the period when human culture has become a significant planetary force, should be called the Anthropocene. In the Anthropocene it is no longer effective to study social systems and ecosystems in isolation from one another.

Nevertheless, social–ecological systems are complex. Investigations of their behaviour, and likely response to policy and management initiatives, require strong, long-term collaborations between people with a wide range of knowledge and worldviews. The creation and maintenance of such collaborations depends on an iterative process that produces, and uses, the shared understanding necessary for effective communication between individuals with different backgrounds, training, and experience. Fundamental to this process is the construction of a generic theoretical framework that embodies mutually agreed explanations of the behaviour of complex systems. In Chapters 3 through 7 we explore key concepts, drawn from cognitive science and system dynamics that are potential elements of the required theoretical framework. Our hope is that the ideas discussed here can support the development of a truly collaborative human ecology.

Reference

Crutzen, P.J. (2002) 'Geology of mankind', *Nature* 415: 23.

3   Thinking together

Indeed, in our view, the persistence of so many of the problems facing humankind in the modern world is to a large extent due to the excessive compartmentalization, fragmentation, and specialism which are so characteristic of education, research and government today. There is an urgent need for more intellectual effort aimed at improving knowledge and understanding of the patterns of interplay between different cultural and natural processes in human situations, and of the principles relevant to this interplay. We use the word 'comprehensive' to describe work which has this objective.

(Boyden *et al.* 1981)

3.1 Introduction

There is a story that arose, in various forms, in a number of ancient cultures. A group of blind men come upon an elephant in the jungle. Several members of the group reach out and feel a part of the elephant. Because they cannot see the whole animal, each imagines it differently. One slides his hand along a tusk and says, "It's a spear!" Another feels its trunk and says, "It's a snake!" The third puts his arms around a leg and says, "It's a tree!" The fourth grabs its tail and says, "It's a rope!" They begin to argue loudly. Meanwhile, the elephant wanders away to find a quieter place to browse.

It is a basic principle of systems thinking that no one person can 'see the whole elephant'. People with different backgrounds and life experiences will usually see the world differently. They are likely to have different opinions about causation – about the way that the world works. They will tend to have different aims, hopes, and fears, and be concerned about different aspects of a given situation. As a result, there may be little overlap between their lists of important issues, and they may disagree about which policy initiatives are likely to fail and which to succeed. Such situations, which are common in complex social–ecological systems, can seem intractable.

What is often overlooked, however, is that the contrast between different perspectives can be a source of valuable new insights. If the protagonists are prepared to work together, they can mesh their different views of cause-and-effect to generate new understandings of the forces that drive system behaviour. The shared understandings that emerge from such collaborative efforts are likely to be more useful and more powerful than those constructed by individuals working in isolation. Such understandings can provide the broad, systemic foundations necessary for the generation of sustainable policies and management practices. We will follow Boyden and his colleagues and use the term 'comprehensive' to refer to integrative, systemic approaches of this kind. We consider that 'comprehensive' means much the same as the term 'transdisciplinary', but its use reduces the focus on academic disciplines and expresses more naturally an approach that values the expertise of people drawn from many walks of life.

In calling for a comprehensive approach to the study of human situations, as shown in the opening quotation, Boyden and his colleagues send a strong message to the human-ecology community. Their perception, that the *persistence* of some of the major problems facing the world community is due to the fragmented approach taken to education, research, and government, is as true today as it was in 1981. In particular, there are still fundamental conceptual and communication barriers that slow the development of comprehensive approaches (Newell *et al.* 2005; Newell 2012). Thus, while considerable progress has been made, there is still an urgent need for a deeper understanding of the interplay between the components of social-ecological systems.

In this chapter we take an initial step towards such an understanding. Our approach draws on key insights from modern studies of the nature of human understanding and communication. We are particularly interested in ideas that can help multi-sector, multidiscipline teams to see conflicting worldviews as a valuable resource in efforts to build sustainable societies. We agree with early systems thinker C. West Churchman (1968) that "the systems approach begins when you first see the world through the eyes of another". But, how can you see through the eyes of another person? There are no short cuts. You need to work with that person – to talk together, to wrestle together with system complexity. Such endeavours require strong cross-discipline, cross-sector collaborations, and long-term dialogues where participants' deepest assumptions are suspended, like washing on a clothes line, for all to examine (Bohm 1996). In order to understand how such collaborations might work, and why it is essential to take up the challenge of bringing them into being, it is necessary to take a brief excursion into modern cognitive science.

Cognitive scientists want to know how people perceive and conceptualise the world, and how their perceptions and conceptualisations govern their behavioural policies and actions. They draw their methods and concepts from areas as diverse as anthropology, computer science, linguistics, neurophysiology, philosophy, psychology, and sociology. Early workers in the field were preoccupied with studies of thought as a disembodied logical process that involved serial symbol-processing (Gardner 1985). From this perspective, brains are seen as digital computers and thought is considered to be similar to computation. Over the last 20 to 30 years, however, there has been a shift in emphasis on the part of some cognitive scientists. These second-generation researchers perceive the mind as embodied (that is, human understanding is based on real-world experience), and have made extensive use of empirical studies of language-use as a way to study mental processes. Their efforts have produced powerful new insights into the nature of human conceptual systems. A study of some of the key discoveries of this science can help us to define the meaning of basic terms such as 'concept', 'mental model', 'conceptual framework', 'powerful idea', and 'shared understanding' as they are used in this book. It can also clarify the nature of the dialogue methods that are needed for effective comprehensive research.

3.2 Mental models and prediction

One of the earliest discoveries made by cognitive scientists is that humans build mental models of themselves and their environment. They use these models in attempts to predict the future and base their decisions and actions on these predictions (Gardner 1985: 383). As described by Senge (1990: 175):

> Mental models can be simple generalisations such as "people are untrustworthy," or they can be complex theories, such as my assumptions about why members of my family interact as they do. But what is most important to grasp is that mental models are *active*—they shape how we act. If we believe people are untrustworthy, we act differently from the way we would if we believe they were trustworthy. If I believe that my son lacks self-confidence and my daughter is highly aggressive, I will continually intervene in their exchanges to prevent her from damaging his ego.

Why are mental models so powerful in affecting what we *do*? In part, because they affect what we *see*. Two people with different mental models can observe the same event and describe it differently, because they've looked at different details. When you and I walk into a crowded party, we both take in the same basic sensory data, but we pick out different faces. As psychologists say, we observe selectively. This is no less true for supposedly "objective" observers such as scientists than for people in general.

A mental model can make up a large part of its owner's understanding of some event or behaviour. Prominent among your collection of mental models are those that contribute to your understanding of how causation operates in the world around you. These models of cause-and-effect are crucially important parts of your conceptual system. They are based on your experiences of manipulating real-world objects (including other people), and therefore can play a predictive role in your thinking. Because they can be operated mentally, in advance of actual events, they allow you to imagine the potential outcomes of alternative courses of action. You can then select the action that you judge most likely to produce your favoured outcome.

An ability to anticipate future events, even to a limited extent, confers an immense adaptive advantage. For this reason, human beings have evolved to be modellers. Today the term 'modeller' is usually reserved for professionals who build formal, mathematical, computer-based models, but there is more to modelling than mathematics. Formal models lie at one end of a wide spectrum. Mental models lie at the other end of the spectrum. If you try to examine your own mental models you will find that they are elusive. Some are held consciously, but many others are tacit. While you are usually unaware of their existence, the tacit models still strongly influence your perceptions, thoughts, and actions. You appear to see the world as it is, and your reasoning and actions appear to be sensible. But your behaviour is largely controlled by your mental models, which can never be completely adequate. Like your observations, they are unavoidably limited and idiosyncratic (Box 3.1). Furthermore, your mental models can be hard to improve. Once constructed they tend to 'lock-in'. That is, you use your existing models to decide what you should pay attention to and what you can ignore. This leads you to ignore things that contradict your models. This tendency makes it difficult for you to learn new things from experience.

Box 3.1 All imaginary sports cars are red

Many years ago one of us (BN) was standing on a street corner with a friend, waiting for the traffic lights to change. Suddenly a sports car swung around the corner, travelling fast to beat the lights, and ran across the concrete strip in the middle of the road. There was an awful crunch as the sump at the bottom of the car's engine was ripped off by a short metal pipe that was protruding from the concrete. The car coasted to a stop, leaving its sump spinning around on the road and spilling hot oil everywhere. The driver got out to inspect the damage. But the lights had changed and, as the driver was obviously unhurt, we hurried away across the road. About 20 minutes later we were describing the incident to some colleagues over a cup of coffee:

> "We were standing on the street corner when a red sports car came around . . ."
> "The car was blue."
> "No, it was red!"

As our conversation proceeded it became apparent that, even though we had both witnessed the scene from exactly the same vantage point, our stories differed to a surprising extent. We were definite about the different colours. One of us thought the driver was a man, the other insisted that it was a woman. One of us had a vivid image of the sump spinning around on the road, the other was not sure what had been damaged. To this day we are no closer to the truth, but we have never forgotten the occasion. How could we have such strikingly different memories of an event that *seemed* so simple and that had occurred less than an hour before?

The answer is that we had simply noticed different aspects of the event. While both of us assumed, without conscious thought, that we had accurately observed everything that had happened, we had done no such thing. Events had unfolded rapidly and we had not lingered at the scene. Neither of us had time to develop a full picture. We each noticed the things that we considered important and ignored the things that we considered unimportant. These classifications reflected our interests and experiences, and were made more or less instantaneously and without conscious thought. When we came to tell the story it became clear immediately that we had used different assumptions about what was important and what was unimportant. The conflict between our stories was not due to memory failure, but to an idiosyncratic blend of observation and imagination. We each based our account on the observations we had made, and filled in the unnoticed details imaginatively using our mental models of sports cars, drivers of sports cars, and the structure of engines. An imagined sports car can be red, even if the real one was blue.

Indeed, the main aim of the scientific method is to counter this natural shortcoming of human observation, in order to build models (both mental and formal) that are as reliable as possible.

When faced with a decision you gather information about the state of the world around you, and then use your cause–effect models to decide what action to take in order to preserve or change that state. Thus, when you examine the state of your bank account and see that the balance is zero you can safely predict that, in the absence of additional deposits, any further expenditure will drive the balance negative. In this simple case the relationship between cause and effect is clear, and your predictions will be reliable. But as the connections between cause and effect become more complex, your cause–effect models will become less adequate and your ability to anticipate the consequences of your actions will diminish. The requirement for reliable models has been expressed well by Donaldson (1978: 111):

> Now on even the simplest notion of what is involved in adaptation, it can come as no surprise that dissatisfaction arises when prediction fails. As soon as a species abandons reliance on instinctual patterns of behaviour and begins to rely instead on building inner representations and making predictions then it becomes critical for survival to get the predictions right. Thus the realization of incongruity between our notion of the world and what it turns out to be like should naturally lead us to want to understand it better. And many different theories about the growth of intelligent thought stress that this kind of cognitive conflict is unacceptable to us, that it is something we try to get rid of. After the early stages, the conflict may be between different parts of our world model. If we come to face the fact that we hold two inconsistent beliefs we find this uncomfortable. And so we should. For it is axiomatic that the different parts of a model must fit together.

Surprise is inevitable when your models of causation are inadequate. In such circumstances you might accidentally generate a welcome surprise, but it is much more likely that most of the surprises will be unwelcome. After all, in the face of complexity and uncertainty there is a strictly limited number of ways to make good decisions, but an almost unlimited number of ways to make poor decisions.

In this book we take the phrase 'to understand X' to mean 'to have an adequate mental model of how X works'. An adequate mental model is one that leads to useful predictions – predictions that are reliable more often than not. Decision makers, at all levels, need adequate mental models (a good understanding) of how causation operates in their system-of-interest. You are no exception. In those circumstances where your mental models are adequate, where you understand what is going on, your predictions will be reliable and your selected actions stand a good chance of producing the desired effects. In situations where your mental models are inadequate, where you don't understand what is going on, you are bound to be surprised.

3.3 Conceptual metaphor, understanding, and reasoning

Your mental models of cause-and-effect underlie all of your attempts to anticipate the future. Modern cognitive scientists have demonstrated that such models are metaphorically structured. That is, they work by providing a way for you to understand and experience one kind of thing in terms of another (Lakoff and Johnson 2003: 5).

Cognitive scientists distinguish between concepts that are 'literal' and those that are 'metaphorical'. A literal concept is an abstraction that summarises the common properties of a number of superficially different concrete things or actions. These common properties allow the individual items to be classified as examples of the concept. For example, the concept COFFEE MUG is literal. It has been formed by separating (a) the essential characteristics of a large number of coffee mugs, from (b) their individual characteristics. The coffee mugs in most collections have a wide range of shapes, motifs, and colours. These superficial differences between individual *real* coffee mugs are irrelevant when it comes to forming the concept COFFEE MUG. In other words, COFFEE MUG is an abstract concept that captures the *essential attributes* of all coffee mugs. From this abstract point-of-view coffee mugs are more-or-less-cylindrical containers with open tops, constructed from rigid materials that provide some insulation from the heat of the coffee, and with handles that give a sure grip and additional insulation. These are the attributes that determine the usefulness of coffee mugs.

Literal concepts capture the *invariant* aspects of things and actions; characteristics that you can rely on to be present in all instances of the concept. They are valuable because, in any given situation, they speed and sharpen your perceptions. They do this by allowing you to ignore much of the detail that the world presents to your senses. Many basic concepts are literal. They are used unconsciously and, because they are literal, almost everyone understands them in exactly the same way. But there are many more concepts that are metaphorical. And these concepts are not necessarily understood in exactly the same way by everyone. The existence of metaphorical concepts, and their central role in human understanding, rational thought, and communication, is a relatively new discovery. In this book the word 'metaphor' will always mean 'metaphorical concept'.

The ubiquity and importance of metaphors was discovered by cognitive scientists interested in linguistics (Lakoff and Johnson 2003). Cognitive linguists use empirical studies of language as a way to investigate mental processes. Ordinary statements, made in the course of everyday conversations, provide them with clues to the workings of the mind. This work has led to the development of a robust theory of metaphor. The ideas involved in this theory are unfamiliar to many people, and can be difficult to grasp at a first encounter. A good place to begin is to ask, how does language-use reveal the existence of conceptual metaphor?

Consider the following sentence:

Fish stocks are falling in the North Sea.

We expect you to interpret this statement to mean that fish populations in the North Sea are decreasing over time and, as a consequence, the average catch is lower now than it was in the past. We do not expect you to infer that there are fish falling out of the sky over the North Sea. Why do people say that fish stocks are *falling* when they are not literally falling? Taken literally the statement makes no sense. The fact that you derived a sensible meaning from this nonsensical statement, even though it cannot be literally true, demonstrates that your understanding involves imagination and metaphor. In this case, you constructed a meaning for the sentence using the MORE IS UP, LESS IS DOWN metaphor. The same metaphor enabled you to construct a sensible meaning from the phrase 'the average catch is *lower* now'.

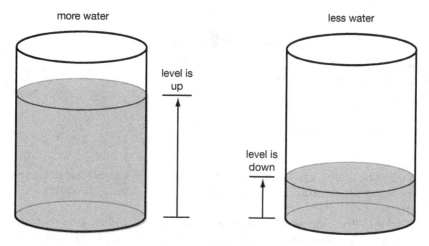

more water   less water

level is
up

level is
down

Figure 3.1 The physical basis for the MORE IS UP, LESS IS DOWN metaphor.

Cognitive scientists classify the MORE IS UP, LESS IS DOWN metaphor as a 'primary metaphor' (Lakoff and Johnson 2003: 45). It is based on a simple physical correlation (Figure 3.1). As any child knows, the *level* of the water in a glass increases as the *amount* of water in the glass increases. Conversely, the level decreases as the amount of water decreases. This commonly experienced correlation, between amount and level, is captured by the metaphor and used by people to think and communicate about an immense range of more abstract perceptions and experiences. I have *built up* my trust in him. The stakes are *high*. His income is *low*.

It is essential to realise that metaphorical concepts are more than a mere matter of words. They provide a way for people to use their common perceptions and experience of physical movements (their sensorimotor experiences) as a basis for understanding and reasoning about the way that the world works. The evidence from cognitive science makes it clear that human conceptual systems contain a large number of metaphorical concepts organised into a more-or-less coherent structure. Such a structure comprises a set of complex metaphors built on a foundation of primary metaphors and image schemata. An 'image schema' is a very simple cognitive structure that captures and summarises a commonly experienced pattern of sensorimotor experiences. For example, the PATH SCHEMA captures key aspects of our experiences of movement through space (Johnson 1987: 28).

In the PATH SCHEMA a moving entity (or 'trajector') travels along a path (or 'trajectory') from a starting location towards a destination or goal. In Figure 3.2 the trajector is represented by the filled circle labelled T, the starting location is represented by the open circle labelled S, and the destination is represented by the open circle labelled D. The arrow F represents the force that induces T to move. The path already traversed by the trajector is represented by the continuous curve, and the dashed curve represents that segment of the path yet to be travelled. The point labelled L represents one of the locations that the trajector has already passed.

The basic structure of the PATH SCHEMA can be elaborated metaphorically in a wide variety of ways – to think about physical or intellectual journeys, the action of giving something to someone else, the change (movement) of some entity from one

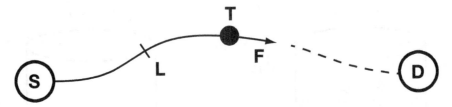

Figure 3.2 The PATH SCHEMA.

state to another, and so on. In all these cases some thing moves (changes), under the action of some driving force, from one place (or initial state) to another place (or final state).

Each schema has associated with it a basic logic that allows us to make valid inferences about any metaphorical elaboration of the schema. For example, the logic of the PATH SCHEMA allows us to infer that T must pass through all points on the trajectory as it moves from S to D. We also can infer that, if T has passed point L by time *t*, then it must have been at L at a time earlier than *t*. You can apply this logic metaphorically to any kind of movement. Thus, when you decide to undertake a course of study you must begin at the admissions office (S). Your ambitions (F) drive you to study each of the course components, in the order specified in the curriculum, to achieve the required grades at various assessment times (L) during the course. Finally, once you have satisfied all of the requirements of the course, you are awarded the degree (you have reached your goal D).

For example, The PATH SCHEMA provides the basic logic for a FORMAL STUDY IS A JOURNEY metaphor that can be invoked when you reason about, talk about, and attempt to understand your educational endeavours.[1] The FORMAL STUDY IS A JOURNEY metaphor is a 'complex metaphor'. It depends on a correspondence between two sets of concepts:

Source Concepts – which, in the case of journey metaphors, are a set of concepts concerning the act of travelling. These concepts are embodied. They are based on peoples' everyday bodily experiences, as abstracted in the PATH SCHEMA. Because they relate to fundamental sensorimotor experiences, essentially everyone will have much the same understanding of the words used to label them. The connections comprising the FORMAL STUDY IS A JOURNEY metaphor start from concepts built up around the PATH SCHEMA, so this set of concepts is an example of what cognitive scientists call a 'conceptual source domain'.

Target Concepts – which are, in this case, a set of concepts concerning the process of formal study. These concepts are more abstract than concepts about travelling, and so they can be more difficult to understand. There will be a tendency for people with different experiences of studying and learning to have different understandings of the processes involved. This will be true even within a given cultural setting. Think of the difficulties that some students have in communicating with their parents about their university activities. The FORMAL STUDY IS A JOURNEY metaphor provides a way for people to use their common experience of journeys as the basis of a shared language that helps to overcome

Table 3.1 The FORMAL STUDY IS A JOURNEY metaphor

Conceptual source domain: journeys		*Conceptual target domain: formal study*
The journey	⇒	The educational endeavour
Travelling	⇒	Studying
The traveller	⇒	The student
Travelling companions	⇒	Fellow students
A part of the motive force	⇒	An interest in ideas
Another part of the motive force	⇒	A desire for qualifications
The starting location	⇒	The admissions office
The destination	⇒	A degree conferred
The road map	⇒	The course syllabus
Check points along the way	⇒	Assessments
Rest stops	⇒	Vacations
A barrier to progress	⇒	A very active social life
An aid to progress	⇒	Self discipline
An aid to progress	⇒	A good lecturer

communication difficulties. The connections comprising the metaphor terminate on concepts to do with studying, so this set of concepts is an example of what cognitive scientists call a 'conceptual target domain'.

Some of the correspondences that constitute the FORMAL STUDY IS A JOURNEY metaphor are displayed in Table 3.1. Source-domain concepts are listed in the first column of the table. The small arrows shown in the second column represent the links between source-domain concepts and target-domain concepts. Target-domain concepts are listed in the third column.

The language that you use to talk about your educational experiences sends a clear signal that the PATH SCHEMA is involved. I am *following* a particular *course* of study. I am getting *bogged-down* in this subject. It's an *uphill* struggle. I have concluded that this topic is *taking me down a side-track*. This subject is *easy going*. I have *fast-tracked* my progress by taking a summer course. I have almost *reached* my educational *goals*. I've *arrived*!

The PATH SCHEMA is held in common by all who have experienced journeys of any kind – from a baby's first hesitant steps to intercontinental travel by supersonic jet. The schema captures a basic pattern that is common to all journeys. This means that different individuals will tend to have similar mental models of how journeys work. Because individuals conceptualise journeys in the same way, using the PATH SCHEMA, they can use this schema as the source domain for metaphors that help them to communicate about life, love, and other elusive concepts. Consider the complex metaphor LOVE IS A JOURNEY. According to Lakoff and Johnson the existence of this metaphor is signalled by our widespread use of the language of journeys when we talk about love (Lakoff and Johnson 1999: 60). It has been *smooth sailing* so far. We are *at the cross-roads* in our relationship. We have *hit a dead-end*. I think that we have *burnt our bridges* – there is *no going back* now. These are not just colourful

Box 3.2 Multiple metaphors for the abstract concept 'Idea'

Lakoff and Johnson (1980: 46) provide the following list of the multiple metaphors that are commonly used to structure the concept 'idea'. In each case we name the metaphor and quote a few of the sentences that they give to demonstrate its existence:

IDEAS ARE FOOD

There are too many facts here for me to *digest* them all. I just can't *swallow* that claim. That's *food for thought*. This is the *meaty* part of the paper.

IDEAS ARE PEOPLE

The theory of relativity *gave birth to* an enormous number of ideas in physics. He is the *father* of modern biology. His ideas will *live on* forever.

IDEAS ARE PLANTS

That idea *died on the vine*. That's a *budding* theory. Mathematics has many *branches*. She has a *fertile* imagination. Here's an idea that I'd like to *plant* in your mind.

IDEAS ARE PRODUCTS

We've *generated* a lot of ideas this week. He *produces* new ideas at an astounding rate.

IDEAS ARE COMMODITIES

It's important how you *package* your ideas. That idea just won't *sell*. There is always a *market* for good ideas. Your ideas don't have a chance in the *intellectual marketplace*.

IDEAS ARE RESOURCES

He *ran out of* ideas. Don't *waste* your thoughts on small projects. Let's *pool* our ideas. We've *used up* all our ideas.

IDEAS ARE MONEY

He's *rich* in ideas. That book is a *treasure trove* of ideas. He has a *wealth* of ideas.

IDEAS ARE CUTTING INSTRUMENTS

That's an *incisive* idea. That was a *cutting* remark. He has a *razor* wit. She *cut* his argument *to ribbons*.

IDEAS ARE FASHIONS

That idea went *out of style* years ago. That idea is *old hat*! That's an *outdated* idea. *Old-fashioned* notions have no place in today's society.

THEORIES ARE BUILDINGS

Is that the *foundation* for your theory? The theory needs more *support*. Here are some more facts to *shore up* the theory. So far we have put together only the *framework* of the theory.

phrases – they carry a tight logic that allows us to reason and communicate about love. For example, the logic of journeys provides the inference that vehicle breakdown will prevent the travellers from reaching their destination. The LOVE IS A JOURNEY metaphor allows a couple to apply PATH SCHEMA logic to infer that relationship breakdown will prevent them from reaching their (previously) shared life goals.

There are hundreds of metaphors in regular use within a given cultural group. They provide a rich mapping from experience to inference. There is often more than one metaphorical way to represent a key concept. For example, there are many different metaphors that are used to understand and communicate about the abstract concept 'idea'. One of these, the ACQUIRING IDEAS IS EATING metaphor, builds on the observation that *eating healthy foods* helps you to develop and maintain *a healthy body*. You can use this logic, via the metaphorical mapping, to infer that *acquiring good ideas* can help you to develop and maintain *a well-functioning mind*. Other metaphors that are used to understand 'idea' are displayed in Box 3.2.

In this book we define a metaphor (metaphorical concept) to be a unidirectional mapping, between a conceptual source domain and a conceptual target domain, where the mapping (a) is selective, (b) makes sense in the target domain, and (c) provides a way to use the inferential logic of the source domain as the basis for inferences in the target domain.[2] This idea is illustrated in Figure 3.3. Note that the mapping is selective. That is, not all of the source domain concepts are mapped into the target domain, and not all of the target domain concepts are mapped onto it. Metaphorical mappings are selective because they must make sense in the target domain.

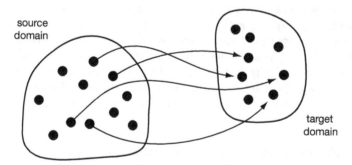

Figure 3.3 The basic structure of a metaphorical mapping. In this diagram the enclosed areas represent a conceptual source domain and a conceptual target domain. The filled circles inside the enclosed areas represent the concepts that are included in each domain. The arrows indicate the cross-domain correspondences that constitute the metaphorical mapping.

Such mappings are called *analogies* in the basic sciences and engineering. We use sentences of the form B IS A when we want to name a metaphor. Here A represents a source domain and B represents a target domain. It is important to realise that the sentence B IS A means that B *metaphorically* is A, not that B *literally* is A. When we want to show the details of the correspondence between A and B we will use a visual representation of the form

an item in A $\Rightarrow$ an item in B,

where the arrow ⇒ can be taken to mean "this item in the source domain A *corresponds to* this item in the target domain B" or "this item in A *maps to* this item in B".

3.4 Categories – classical and fuzzy

Categorisation is a fundamental cognitive process. It is what you do to simplify the flood of information entering through your senses. For example, it enables you to build concepts that allow you to see a forest as a collection of trees and not be distracted by the myriad differences in the arrangement of leaves and branches that distinguish one tree from the next. According to Lakoff (1987: 5):

> Categorization is not a matter to be taken lightly. There is nothing more basic than categorization to our thought, perception, action, and speech. Every time we see something as a *kind* of thing, for example, a tree, we are categorizing. Whenever we reason about *kinds* of things—chairs, nations, illness, emotions, any kind of thing at all—we are employing categories. Whenever we intentionally perform any *kind* of action, say something as mundane as writing with a pencil, hammering with a hammer, or ironing clothes, we are using categories. The particular action we perform on that occasion is a *kind* of motor activity (e.g., writing, hammering, ironing), that is, it is in a particular category of motor actions. They are never done in exactly the same way, yet despite the differences in particular movements, they are all movements of a kind, and we know how to make movements of that kind. And any time we either produce or understand any utterance of any reasonable length, we are employing dozens if not hundreds of categories: categories of speech sounds, of words, phrases and clauses, as well as conceptual categories. Without the ability to categorize, we could not function at all, either in the physical world or in our social and intellectual lives. An understanding of how we categorize is central to any understanding of how we think and how we function, and therefore central to an understanding of what makes us human.

Most people assume that objects are always assigned to a category on the basis of what they have in common. This is also the basic assumption of classical category theory, which holds that a category is defined by properties that are common to *all* members. A corollary of this definition is that no one member of a classical category can be a better example of the category (concept) than any other member. But, while many of our everyday categories do work this way, a great many more do not. There is strong empirical evidence for the existence of categories with 'graded membership'. That is, fuzzy categories that have some members that are good examples of the category and other members that are poor examples of the category.[3]

The difference between classical categories and categories with graded membership is illustrated in Figure 3.4. The diagram shown in the left-hand panel represents a classical category. The diagram is based on the CATEGORIES ARE CONTAINERS metaphor that underlies the classical theory of categories. In this metaphor categories are understood as bounded areas with an inside and an outside (Lakoff and Núñez 2000: 43). Accordingly, the category is represented in this diagram as an oval area with a sharply defined boundary. Objects are represented by filled circles that can

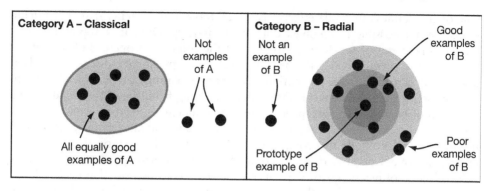

Figure 3.4 Classical and radial categories.

fall inside or outside the bounded areas. All of the points within the boundary represent objects that are equally good members of the category. Objects represented by points that fall outside the boundary are not members of the category. The COFFEE MUG concept is an example of a classical category.

The diagram shown in the right-hand panel of Figure 3.4 represents a category with graded membership. In this diagram the area representing the category is shaded in a radial direction, dark at the centre and light at the rim. An object whose representative point falls close to the centre of the bounded area is considered to be a better example of the category than an object whose representative point falls out towards the edge of the bounded area. Objects at the centre of the category are the best examples, or 'prototype members', of the category. Because fuzzy categories can be thought of as having a centre and a periphery they are also called 'radial categories'.

Human ecologists need to be aware of the existence of radial categories. Why? Because the classical view, that all members of a category are equally good examples of that category, impedes attempts to build a shared understanding. A metaphorical concept can be based on mappings from more than one concrete example. For example, the metaphor A SYSTEM IS A FEEDBACK STRUCTURE can draw its source domain concepts and inferential structures from a wide variety of real-world feedback mechanisms – physical, chemical, biological, economic or social. Each concrete mechanism gives rise to a corresponding version of the metaphorical concept 'system'. While some of these versions of 'system' will be in harmony with each other, others will be discordant. As long as there is an underlying belief that all of the concrete mechanisms must be equally good examples of a single classical category, any incompatibility will give the impression that the abstract concept 'system' cannot be defined clearly. Jordan (1968: 46) has observed this tendency in scientific discussions:

> It is a fact that many who speak about systems are uneasy with 'system'. They assert that they will not try to define it, that it is vague, ambiguous, fuzzy, and even meaningless. And yet, since both the speakers and the audience do have a concrete system in mind, the subsequent discourse using this undefinable term generally proves to be valuable and rewarding. 'System' is, of course, now defined as the concrete system under discussion. This permits the ensuing discussion to be fruitful, but it also has some undesirable side effects.

One of the "undesirable side effects" is the all-too-common belief that sharp definitions are not possible in complex domains of inquiry. Once it is appreciated that there can be better or worse ways to abstract the common properties of the entities being studied, then the door is open for much more productive discussions. These discussions can start from the notion that there is a range of possible definitions (metaphors) for a given concept, rather than adopting from the outset the dead-end approach of blaming the concept itself for being undefinable.

High-level concepts usually do have multiple metaphorical underpinnings (Box 3.2). It is essential to recognise this complexity and allow for it in attempts to build shared theoretical frameworks. A rich collection of metaphors provides a correspondingly rich collection of meanings for a given term. Once it is recognised that such richness exists, then it becomes clear that an exploration of the range of possible meanings of a given term (such as 'system') is a part of the work required to establish a shared theoretical framework for human ecology. Each meaning can be sharply defined, by describing the corresponding metaphor, and the most useful one selected for any given discussion. In some cases prototype examples will be found that provide a basis for simple metaphors that are useful in a wide range of contexts – in Section 3.6 we will explain why these metaphors are powerful ideas that are fundamental in attempts to build a comprehensive theoretical framework.

3.5 The CONDUIT metaphor and communication

The development of a comprehensive approach requires effective communication between people from different walks of life. Ultimately this requirement can be met only if there exist practical procedures for bridging the gaps between individuals' worldviews. The development and application of such procedures is a challenging task. Your conceptual system is not arbitrary; it reflects the way that your body works and your experience of activity in your local environment. This means that there will always be some commonality between your conceptual system and those of others who share your world. But, there will also be differences – particularly at the more technical, more abstract levels. Indeed, as noted above, cognitive scientists have discovered that it is common for people to use a number of different metaphors to understand and reason about a single abstract concept (Box 3.2).

Differences of perception and understanding are invaluable in attempts to build better theoretical frameworks. No one person can see the whole of a social–ecological system. The development of an adequate understanding of the behaviour of such systems requires the collaborative meshing of many perspectives. This is the reason why human ecology needs to be comprehensive. But, when people use different metaphors to understand and talk about a given situation, it is likely that their conversation will be marred by ambiguity and confusion. This is not any one person's fault. According to linguist Michael Reddy, misunderstandings are to be expected in normal human conversation (Reddy 1993). This insight runs counter to popular belief. Most people assume that, in normal conversations, the exchange of meaning is largely automatic and trouble free. In his classic paper Reddy demonstrated that, at least for speakers of the English language, this assumption rests on the unconscious use of the CONDUIT metaphor (Table 3.2).

The CONDUIT metaphor is deeply entrenched in the minds of English speakers. Language is commonly seen as a conduit (a pipe or channel) that can be used to

Table 3.2 The CONDUIT metaphor

Conceptual source domain: Conduits (pipes, channels)		Conceptual target domain: Languages
A conduit (pipe, channel)	⇒	A language
Physical objects	⇒	Ideas
Containers	⇒	Words and word-groupings (sentences)
Put an object into a container	⇒	Put an idea into a word or word-grouping
Send a container down a conduit	⇒	Communicate with another person
Take an object out of a container	⇒	Take an idea out of a linguistic expression

convey ideas directly from one mind to another. Thus, if you want to communicate with a friend, you put your ideas into words and then give the words to your friend. Your friend then takes your ideas, unchanged, out of the words. This view of communication is revealed by the use of such expressions as:[4]

> You know very well that I *gave* you that idea. Jane *gives away* all her best ideas. Marsha *got* those concepts *from* Rudolf. Next time you write, *send* better ideas. It is very difficult to *put* this concept *into* words. Harry always *fills* his paragraphs *with* meaning. Don't *force* your meanings *into* the wrong words.

As Reddy points out, expressions like these are evidence that the CONDUIT metaphor is based on the assumption that thoughts are objects that can exist outside the thinker's head. Because they can be externalised, these objects can be bundled up *in* words and passed around easily from person to person. It is this assumption that leads people to view communication as something automatic, something that requires little effort. There are, however, good reasons to believe that the opposite is true – that communication is a chancy process that requires a lot of time and energy if it is to be successful. This is an unusual view of communication but, if it is correct, it has major implications for subjects such as human ecology that require a comprehensive approach. In order to explain why this is so we need to introduce some basic ideas from information theory (Reddy 1993: 166).

It is essential to recognise the difference between a concept and its name. As expressed by Skemp (1971: 23):

> The distinction between a concept and its name is an essential one for our present discussion. A concept is an idea; the name of a concept is a sound, or a mark on paper, associated with it. This association can be formed after the concept has been formed ('What is this called?'), or in the process of forming it. If the same name is heard or seen each time an example of a concept is encountered, by the time [the] concept is formed the name has become so closely associated with [the concept] that it is not only by children that it is mistaken for the concept itself.

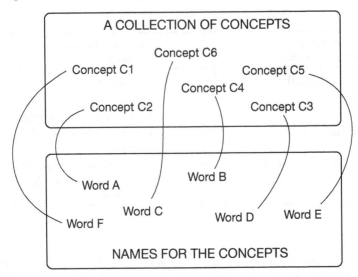

Figure 3.5 A hypothetical concept↔name code relating concepts and their assigned names.

The name of a concept is a word that labels the concept, and allows you to refer to it; the concept itself is the meaning of the word. Contrary to the assumptions underlying the CONDUIT metaphor, words do not carry meaning. Spoken or written words are just physical signals. As Reddy (1993: 184) points out, "Signals *do something*. They cannot *contain* anything."

Consider what happens when you want to tell your friend about an idea that has just occurred to you. In your mind you have a set of metaphorical concepts (the upper box in Figure 3.5). We will call this your 'conceptual repertoire'. You also have a set of words that are the labels (or names) that you associate with each of these concepts (the lower box in Figure 3.5). The set of two-way links between the concepts and the words (the curved lines in Figure 3.5) constitute what we will call your 'concept↔name code'.

Michael Reddy (2013, private communication) points out that the high-level abstract concepts discussed by human ecologists and other scientists are better thought of as hierarchical clusters of concepts. Whenever we talk about a concept in this book, we do so simply for convenience – we will always be referring to such an hierarchical structure.

To express your new idea in words you (unconsciously) take the following steps:

1   select relevant concepts from your conceptual repertoire and assemble them into an ordered (non-random) sequence that captures your idea;
2   use your concept↔name code to assemble a sequence of words (concept names) that matches your ordered list of concepts;
3   generate an ordered set of physical signals (sounds, marks on paper) corresponding to your list of words and transmit the signals to your friend.

The problem is that, while you expect your friend to congratulate you on your brilliant new idea, your friend may simply look puzzled. Accurate communication is possible only when you and your friend have identical conceptual repertoires, and use identical concept↔name codes. If your idea is really new, then this condition may not be met.

Imagine a conversation between a cognitive scientist, a physicist, and a politician. The cognitive scientists says, "The CONDUIT metaphor violates the entropy law."[5] The other two look at him blankly. The physicist, of course, understands (has adequate mental models of) entropy and the second law of thermodynamics. She also uses simple concrete mechanisms and case studies as ways to explain abstract concepts, but she refers to such explanations as 'analogies'. She thinks of metaphors simply as poetic speech. She can't understand how a figure of speech can be in conflict with a physical law. The politician is also baffled. Like the physicist he considers a metaphor to be a figure of speech. In his mind 'metaphor' labels the kind of rhetorical language that he uses in parliament and the television studio. And he has no understanding at all of the term 'entropy'. There are two communication barriers acting here: first, the interlocutors do not use identical concept↔name codes. They use the word 'metaphor' to label quite different concepts. Second, the interlocutors' conceptual repertoires do not overlap sufficiently. For example, the cognitive scientist uses the word 'entropy', which is familiar to the physicist but does not link to any significant conceptual structures in the politician's mind.

The essential insight from information theory is that people cannot fully understand each other's ideas unless they have (a) overlapping conceptual repertoires, and (b) identical concept↔name codes. When these requirements are met the collaborators have what is called an '*a priori* shared context' for communication. In the absence of an a priori shared context it is simply not possible to establish dialogues that are both effective and efficient. That is why human ecologists need a generally agreed theoretical framework. Such a framework is an essential component of the a priori shared context required for productive comprehensive work.

3.6 Powerful ideas

The existence of fuzzy categories, and the widespread, unconscious use of the CONDUIT Metaphor, explains why George Bernard Shaw was led to remark[6] that "[t]he single biggest problem in communication is the illusion that it has taken place". The view that human communication is automatically effective, that words effortlessly carry unambiguous meanings along conduits that connect mind to mind, leads to the tacit conclusion that the deliberate construction of a shared theoretical framework is not necessary. As a result, much of the discourse in the subject has been carried out in what Jaques (1996: 10) calls a "conceptual swamp".

The development of mutual understanding is an iterative process. It involves the basic communication loop that is sketched in Figure 3.6. The iterative process works as follows: You have an idea that you want to share. You initiate the three-step procedure outlined above (Section 3.5). That is, to express your new idea you assemble an ordered sequence of concepts (S1) from your repertoire. You then apply your concept↔name code to produce a string of words (concept names), generate a corresponding physical signal (spoken or written words), and transmit the physical signal to your friend (Arrow 1 in Figure 3.6). Your friend receives the signal, applies her concept↔name code, and generates an ordered sequence of concepts drawn from her repertoire (Arrow 2). This sequence does not make complete sense to her as it stands, so she rearranges it, removing some concepts and adding several new ones

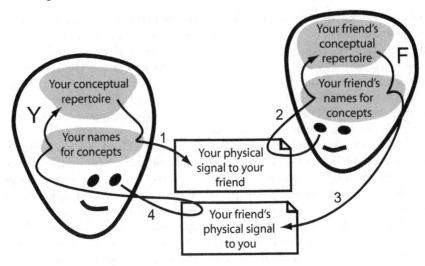

Figure 3.6 The basic communication loop. In this diagram the closed outlines labelled Y
  and F represent your head and that of your friend, respectively. Arrows 1 and 3
  represent the actions of speaking or writing words (generating physical signals).
  Arrows 2 and 4 represent the actions of hearing or seeing words.

from her repertoire, to produce a new sequence (S2) that she believes represents your
idea. She applies her concept↔name code to S2 to generate a physical signal, and
then transmits her signal to you (Arrow 3). You receive her signal, apply your
concept↔name code, and so generate a third ordered sequence of concepts (S3) that
you consider to represent her understanding of your new idea (Arrow 4). You
compare S3 with S1 to see how they agree. If they match well you declare that mutual
understanding has been achieved. If they do not match you think about it for a while,
assemble a new sequence of concepts (S4) that you hope will be easier for your friend
to understand, and initiate a new iteration of the whole loop.

 In everyday situations this process is carried out more or less automatically,
without either you or your friend being particularly aware of it. You are dealing with
reasonably concrete concepts that are understood in terms of the same metaphors
and have commonly used names, so you have the a priori shared context required
for effective communication. This situation is represented by the lowest pair of filled
circles in Figure 3.7. As you move to more and more abstract concepts, however,
your conceptual repertoires overlap less and less and you lose the ability to
communicate easily. There appears to be a dilemma here. You can't communicate
without an a priori shared context, but you can't build an a priori shared context
without communicating. The dilemma is, of course, only apparent. There are effective
methods for building a shared understanding of new concepts. The most effective of
these methods involve some form of what cognitive scientists call 'idea analysis'
(Lakoff and Núñez 2000: xi).

 Idea analysis involves an investigation of the cross-domain mappings that underlie
a given metaphorical concept. Your understanding of such a concept, and so the
meaning that you ascribe to the words that you use to label that concept, depends
on the characteristics of the source domain of the defining metaphor. Different source

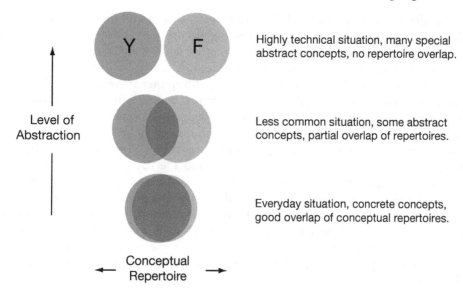

Figure 3.7 Overlap of conceptual repertoires depends on the level of abstraction. The filled circles represent conceptual repertoires. Those on the left (the upper one is labelled Y) represent your repertoire, and those on the right (the upper one is labelled F) represents your friend's repertoire.

domains give rise to different understandings and so lead to different word meanings. It follows that conflict over the meaning of a term signals the use of different conceptual source domains (different metaphors).

The construction of shared understandings, and the shared languages that depend on them, requires the development of shared metaphors. As Newell (2012) has emphasised, this process can be supported by the identification of powerful ideas. He defines a 'powerful idea' to be a metaphorical concept (metaphor) whose source domain is relatively simple and understood in much the same way by people from a wide range of backgrounds. The identification of such ideas is a critical step in the development of an a priori shared context for comprehensive conversations.

It is common for the members of an integrative group to have trouble defining the key terms used in their discussions. They use different words to label concepts that they hold in common, and so do not notice that they are talking about the same things. They use the same word to label different concepts, and so do not realise that they are talking about different things. Nevertheless, there almost always are metaphors that are held in common across these boundaries. It is possible to identify such powerful ideas and use them as the basis for coherent theoretical frameworks (Newell 2012: 780).

Keep in mind that not all powerful ideas are 'good' ideas. For example, the widely accepted notion that unlimited economic growth is both desirable and necessary is certainly simple and generic. But it drives behaviour that greatly reduces a society's chances of becoming sustainable (Daly and Farley 2011: chapter 2). One of the major aims of human ecology, in its normative aspects, is to distinguish 'good' ideas from 'bad' ideas – to identify or develop powerful ideas that can support the emergence of a world society that is both sustainable and just.

The identification of powerful ideas requires creativity and imagination, both of which are stimulated by dialogue between people with different worldviews. It can be difficult to establish such dialogues. Misunderstandings are common early in the process and participants can become discouraged. It can be hard to justify the time and energy required. There will always be plausible, alternative theories about the nature and behaviour of social–ecological systems. Some of the misunderstandings will reflect the existence of these different worldviews. Differences of worldview, particularly where they involve causal explanations, are of crucial importance in a group's attempts to build more comprehensive worldviews. First, they signal the lack of an a priori shared context for discussion and the need for focused dialogue. Second, they signal opportunities to learn from each other. Provided that there is lively discussion of alternative theories, and a balance is achieved between the need to maintain conceptual richness and the desire to identify the most useful ideas, dialogue aimed at establishing the required a priori shared context can be empowering. As shared understandings emerge from the dialogue, the group's ability to conduct productive dialogue improves. When it works well, the process is powerfully self-reinforcing.

3.7 Conclusion

In this chapter we have taken an initial step towards the development of a theoretical framework that can support comprehensive work in human ecology. We based our approach on several key ideas from modern, 'second generation' cognitive science. These ideas were selected to illuminate the nature of human understanding and communication. Such ideas are important in human ecology because no one person can have expert knowledge of the whole of a complex social–ecological system – each of us can have only a limited, idiosyncratic understanding. This constraint mandates that human–ecological studies involve collaboration between individuals from many walks of life. Such collaborations can succeed only if the collaborators can articulate their own explanations of causation and can communicate these explanations clearly to each other.

We began with a discussion of the human ability to build mental models of causal mechanisms and to use those mental models in attempts to anticipate the outcomes of their own decisions and actions. A key insight from cognitive linguistics is that such mental models are structured metaphorically. Here we used the term 'metaphor' to mean 'conceptual metaphor' – a mapping from a conceptual source domain to a conceptual target domain. A defining property of a conceptual metaphor is that it projects the inferential logic of the source domain into the target domain. We explored the nature of conceptual metaphor, beginning with a brief discussion of the evidence from cognitive linguistics that much language use is metaphorical. Once it is recognised that understanding is imaginative, and based on metaphor, then it becomes clear that a 'shared understanding' can exist only if people have 'shared metaphors'. We discussed a number of barriers to the development of shared understanding: the possibility that a single concept can be understood in terms of a variety of metaphors, the existence of fuzzy categories, and the CONDUIT metaphor. Metaphor theory helps to explain the nature of such barriers, and makes it clear that crisp definitions are not only possible but essential for effective communication.

The CONDUIT metaphor is particularly misleading. According to this widely held metaphor, communication works automatically because words carry meaning. When you want to communicate with a friend you put your message into words and transmit the words to your friend. Your friend then takes your message (unchanged) out of the words. This is incorrect. People cannot understand each other's statements unless they have an a priori shared context for communication. That is, they must have conceptual repertoires that overlap, and they must use the same words to represent each concept or cluster of concepts. These conditions are satisfied in everyday situations, where people have similar experience-based concepts, but they are often not satisfied in situations where the concepts used are based on highly technical or idiosyncratic experiences. This is where the identification of powerful ideas can help. A 'powerful idea' is a conceptual metaphor that is relatively simple, yet is of fundamental importance in a wide range of disciplines and circumstances.

In Chapters 4 and 5 we explore some of the powerful ideas that have been crafted in the field of system dynamics. Such ideas can be used to build bridges between different explanations of how the world works. For this reason they can contribute significantly to the construction of comprehensive theory.

Notes

1   The basic metaphor is LONG-TERM PURPOSEFUL ACTIVITIES ARE JOURNEYS.
2   While this view of the nature of metaphor has a limited ability to capture the neurological mechanisms of embodied thought, it is adequate for the present discussion. See Lakoff and Johnson (2003: 252).
3   Lakoff (1987) provides an excellent (but highly technical) review.
4   Taken from Appendix, Part One, of Reddy (1993). Emphasis added.
5   The perception that the CONDUIT metaphor is in conflict with the second law of thermodynamics comes from Reddy (1993: 175).
6   This aphorism is widely attributed to George Bernard Shaw, but we have been unable to find its source.

References

Bohm, D. (1996) *On Dialogue*, London: Routledge.
Boyden, S., Millar, S., Newcombe, K., and O'Neill, B. (1981) *The Ecology of a City and Its People: The Case of Hong Kong*, Canberra: Australian National University Press.
Churchman, C.W. (1968) *The Systems Approach*, New York: Dell.
Daly, H.E. and Farley, J. (2011) *Ecological Economics: Principles and Applications*, 2nd edn, Washington: Island Press.
Donaldson, M. (1978) *Children's Minds*, London: Fontana/Croom Helm.
Gardner, H. (1985) *The Mind's New Science: A History of the Cognitive Revolution*, New York: Basic Books.
Jaques, E. (1996) *Requisite Organization*, Arlington, VA: Cason Hall.
Johnson, M. (1987) *The Body in the Mind: The Bodily Basis of Meaning, Imagination, and Reason*, Chicago, IL: University of Chicago Press.
Jordan, N. (1968) *Themes in Speculative Psychology*, London: Tavistock.
Lakoff, G. (1987) *Women, Fire, and Dangerous Things: What Categories Reveal about the Mind*, Chicago, IL: University of Chicago Press.
Lakoff, G. and Johnson, M. (1980) *Metaphors We Live By*, Chicago, IL: University of Chicago Press.
Lakoff, G. and Johnson, M. (1999) *Philosophy in the Flesh: The Embodied Mind and its Challenge to Western Thought*, New York: Basic Books.

Lakoff, G. and Johnson, M. (2003) *Metaphors We Live By*, Chicago, IL: University of Chicago Press.

Lakoff, G. and Núñez, R.E. (2000) *Where Mathematics Comes From: How the Embodied Mind Brings Mathematics into Being*, New York: Basic Books.

Newell, B. (2012) 'Simple models, powerful ideas: Towards effective integrative practice', *Global Environmental Change* 22 (3): 776–783.

Newell, B., Crumley, C.L., Hassan, N., Lambin, E.F., Pahl-Wostl, C., Underdal, A. and Wasson, R. (2005) 'A conceptual template for integrative human-environment research', *Global Environmental Change* 15 (4): 299–307.

Reddy, M.J. (1993) 'The conduit metaphor: A case of frame conflict in our language about language', in A. Ortony (ed.), *Metaphor and Thought*, 2nd Edition 1993, Cambridge: Cambridge University Press, 164–201.

Senge, P.M. (1990) *The Fifth Discipline: The Art and Practice of the Learning Organization*, Sydney: Random House.

Skemp, R.R. (1971) *The Psychology of Learning Mathematics*, Harmondsworth: Penguin.

4 System dynamics I
Stocks and flows

Understanding and managing stocks and flows – that is, resources that accumulate or deplete and the flows that alter them – is a fundamental process in society, business, and personal life.

(Cronin *et al.* 2009)

4.1 Introduction

System dynamics is a mature discipline, initially developed in the 1950s by Jay Forrester at the Massachusetts Institute of Technology. It is designed to support investigations into the behaviour of complex systems, particularly those involving human decision making. Its practitioners have a strong focus on the development of effective management policies. As John Sterman (2000: 4) defines it: "[s]ystem dynamics is a method to enhance learning in complex systems." An excellent introductory discussion is given by Meadows (2009). Sterman (2000) has thoroughly reviewed the field, its concepts, systems-thinking tools, and modelling methods.

The term 'system' has many definitions in common use – as used here, however, the term will always mean 'feedback system'. We define a feedback system to be a set of parts (components, agents) that *interact* to constrain each other's behaviour. The word 'interact' means to act in such a way as to influence each other – that is, the influence is two-way. A change in the value of any one of the variables in a feedback system will eventually cause a change in the values of all of the other variables. These changes then 'feed back' to influence the value of the variable that was initially changed. Feedback interactions cause social–ecological systems to behave in counterintuitive ways (Forrester 1969: 109). Because an understanding of causation (how and why things change the way they do) is of central importance in any management endeavour, the theory of feedback systems provides some of the foundational concepts that are needed in human ecology.

The term 'dynamics' originally referred to that branch of physics that deals with the way that material bodies move under the influence of applied forces. Galileo Galilei (1564–1642) was the father of the subject. His experimental methods supplanted Aristotle's long reigning metaphysical approach. The mathematical core of the subject was developed over the next 250 years by Newton, Leibniz, Poincaré, Liapounov, and their contemporaries. The conceptual framework that emerged from their work became known as 'dynamical systems theory'. These basic ideas from physics gradually spread to other disciplines as scholars considered how systems of different kinds change from one state to another. Applications in the biological and social sciences were made in the twentieth century, following early work by Lotka, Volterra, and Rashevsky (Richardson 1991). More recently the subject has been enlivened by numerical exploration of many aspects of non-linear dynamics, prompted in particular by the discovery of deterministic chaos and the development of digital computers (Gleick 1987). Because questions of adaptation and sustainability are fundamentally question of change and consistency, dynamical concepts are necessarily invoked in any discussion of the future of human societies.

The dynamical consequences of feedback have been investigated widely by researchers drawing on the pioneering work of, among others, members of the MIT System Dynamics Group, the Santa Fe Institute (Axelrod and Cohen 1999; Mitchell 2009), and the Resilience Alliance (Walker and Salt 2006; Scheffer 2009). While all of this work provides valuable insights into the behaviour of social–ecological systems, the concepts and tools developed by the system dynamics community are particularly well matched to the needs of human ecologists. These concepts are both generic and simple, and therefore can be classified as *powerful ideas* (Section 3.6). They can be expressed in terms of easily understood metaphors, and so provide an effective way to build shared explanations of causation in complex systems.

System dynamics studies are focused on the way that a feedback system changes state in response to both endogenous (internally generated) and exogenous (externally generated) forces, and on applying this knowledge in practice to improve policy-making and management outcomes. The concept of 'accumulation' provides a good starting point for a general discussion of change. In system dynamics terminology an accumulation is called a 'stock' and the processes that change the amount accumulated are called 'flows'. The epigraph quotation above is taken from a paper by Cronin *et al.* (2009), in which they stress the central importance of stock-and-flow thinking in decision making. In their paper Cronin and his colleagues present evidence that a majority of people (even those with strong technical backgrounds) do not reason accurately about the effects that accumulation has on system behaviour. They see this as a significant problem, because "[a]ccumulation is a pervasive process in everyday life, and arises at every temporal, spatial and organisational scale" (Cronin *et al.* 2009: 116). It follows that human ecologists need to understand the nature of accumulation and its effects on the behaviour of social–ecological systems. The stock-and-flow concepts introduced in this chapter pave the way for a discussion of feedback mechanisms in Chapter 5.

4.2 Accumulation and the WATER TANK metaphor

In its most concrete form accumulation involves material collecting in, and draining from, containers. The accumulation of water in lakes, tanks and tubs provides a good conceptual metaphor. The metaphor is *powerful* because it is simple and generic (Section 3.6). Essentially everyone has had experience with the filling and draining of containers, and so the logic of the process is easily understood. The BATHTUB metaphor is traditionally used by the system dynamics community (Sterman 2000: 194). An analysis of this metaphor is given by Newell (2012: 781).

In this book we use the WATER TANK metaphor. At any given time a water tank (Figure 4.1) will hold a certain amount of water – in system dynamics terminology this water is a 'stock'. There will be inflow processes and outflow processes that change the amount of water accumulated – these state-change processes are called 'flows' in

Figure 4.1 A water tank. The tank has an input pipe that leads water in from the roof gutters, a water-delivery pipe with a tap, and an overflow pipe. It might also have holes, where water leaks from the tank, but none can be seen in this photograph.

Source: photo credit: Barry Newell.

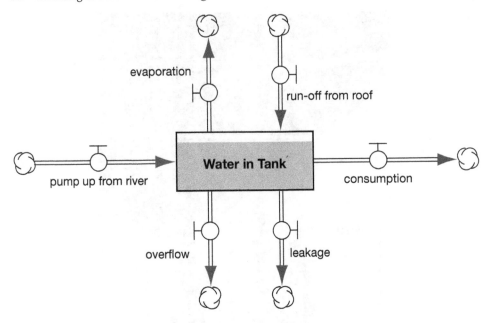

Figure 4.2 A stock-and-flow map representing the stock of water in a tank and six of the flows (state-change processes) that can change the level of that stock. The diagram is drawn using the graphical conventions defined in Box 4.1.

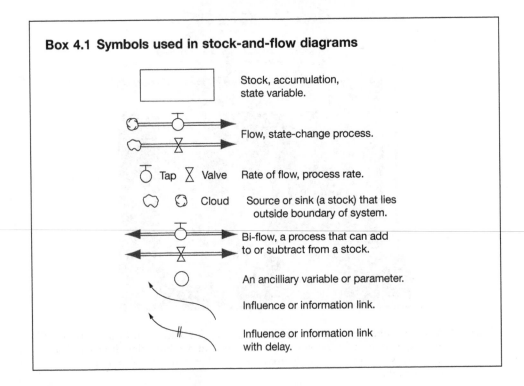

Box 4.1 Symbols used in stock-and-flow diagrams

Stock, accumulation, state variable.

Flow, state-change process.

Tap   Valve   Rate of flow, process rate.

Cloud   Source or sink (a stock) that lies outside boundary of system.

Bi-flow, a process that can add to or subtract from a stock.

An ancilliary variable or parameter.

Influence or information link.

Influence or information link with delay.

system dynamics. A 'stock-and-flow diagram' that identifies some of the flows associated with water tanks is shown in Figure 4.2. The diagram is constructed using the graphical symbols defined in Box 4.1. These symbols are employed also in the graphical user-interfaces of simulation programs such as STELLA® and Vensim™.

The WATER TANK metaphor provides a powerful way to apply these ideas. Because it is *literally* a stock-and-flow structure, a water tank is a very effective source domain for a metaphor that allows stock-and-flow logic to be applied in a wide range of real-world contexts. The conceptual mapping that enables this process is outlined in Table 4.1.

Recall that a conceptual metaphor is not just a matter of poetic language (Section 3.3). It is a mapping that provides a way to project the inferential logic of the source domain into the target domain. This projected logic then becomes the basis for understanding phenomena in the target domain. For example, experience-based water-tank logic tells us that, as long as water is flowing out of a tank faster than it is flowing in, the water level in the tank will fall. The mapping of Table 4.1 allows us to project that inference into the domain of change in general – thus, as long as processes that decrease the level of a stock run at a faster rate than that of processes that increase the level of the stock, the level of the stock will fall. Water-tank logic

Table 4.1 The WATER TANK metaphor

Conceptual source domain: A *water tank*		Conceptual target domain: A *dynamical-system component*
the water in the tank	⇒	an accumulation, a stock, a variable that measures the state of the system component at time t
'water'	⇒	the name of the accumulation, stock, state variable
the amount of water in the tank	⇒	the amount accumulated, the level of the stock, the magnitude or value of the state variable at time t
'volume of water', $V(t)$	⇒	the phrase and symbol used to label the amount of water accumulated (the level of the stock)
water entering the tank from the roof	⇒	an inflow, a flow that increases the level of the stock, a process that increases the value of the state variable
water leaving the tank through the water-delivery pipe	⇒	an outflow, a flow that decreases the level of the stock, a process that decreases the value of the state variable
the setting of the tap on the water-delivery pipe	⇒	the rate of a flow that reduces the level of the stock, the rate of a process that reduces the value of the state variable
water leaving the tank through a hole	⇒	another outflow, another flow that decreases the level of the stock, another process that decreases the value of the state variable
the way the amount of water in the tank changes over time	⇒	the behaviour of the stock, the way that the state of the system component changes over time

tells us also that it takes time to fill or drain a tank. The metaphor therefore implies that it will always take time to change the level of a stock, and so we can infer that the presence of stocks in a dynamical system will cause delays in the system's response to changed conditions – that is, stocks give rise to what we can call 'system inertia'.

Water tanks also act as buffers that decouple outflows from inflows. If a family used rainwater as it flowed off the roof of their home, with no intervening water-storage tanks, then they would have water only when it rained. Their water supply would be impacted by the natural variability of the local rainfall patterns. There would be dry periods when they had no water at all, and periods of heavy rain when they had an oversupply of water. A water tank makes the water-supply system workable by smoothing out the variations – by storing the excess water gathered during rainy periods and making it available for use during dry periods. We can therefore expect, from the WATER TANK metaphor, that stocks will play critical roles as buffers in systems of all types. This expectation is borne out in practice. For example, food energy is stored in our bodies, freeing us from the need to eat continually. Similarly, the metaphor helps us understand why just-in-time (JIT) manufacturing systems are vulnerable to supply failures. A JIT system runs with very little, if any, buffering stocks of the raw materials that are used in the manufacturing process. This is done to reduce the cost of holding raw-material inventories. But it means that any break in the flow of these materials into the factory brings the whole manufacturing process to a halt. This vulnerability can be reduced, at a cost, by increasing the size of the factory's buffering stock (inventory) of raw materials.

In system dynamics terminology an accumulation is called a 'stock' and the processes that affect the amounts accumulated are called 'flows'. There are material stocks, such as the water in a tank, an inventory of goods for sale, the number of frogs in a pond, and the amount of money in a bank account. There are also stocks that are often described as 'non-material' or 'intangible'. Examples include stress and emotions such as fear, anger and happiness, that can be thought of as building up and draining away over time. While all of these stocks may be considered to be non-material, they are actually manifestations of real biochemical states, they do exist in real containers – namely, human brains – and they do build up and drain away. Political will, national pride, commitment to economic growth, and level of under-standing are also examples of stocks that can be thought of as being non-material, but that can easily be thought about as if they are material stocks. Any material or non-material thing that takes time to accumulate or dissipate, under the influence of one or more causal processes, can profitably be thought about in 'stock-and-flow' terms, even if it cannot be actually measured.

In thinking about stocks it is important to distinguish clearly between *the container* that holds the stock, the *name* of the stock (that is, the *kind of thing* that has accumulated in the container), and the *amount* accumulated at a particular time. In our water tank example, the 'tank' is the container, 'water' is the name of the stuff accumulated, and the 'volume of water' is the amount accumulated. The distinction between the name of an accumulation and the amount accumulated can be maintained by careful use of terminology. The *name* of an accumulation does not change over time – in this book such names will always be nouns ('water', 'oil', 'stress', 'trust') or noun phrases ('political power', 'aerobic fitness', 'income equality'). The *amount* accumulated does change over time – such amounts will usually be labelled with either a phrase indicating that we are dealing with a time-dependent quantity ('volume of water', 'level of fitness', 'number of fish') or a symbol such as $V(t)$, $S(t)$, and $F(t)$. In these symbols the 't' in brackets is intended to make it clear that the quantity referred to is dependent on time. In contexts where it is obvious that a time-dependent variable quantity is involved the t may be omitted. Another exception to this rule occurs when words such as 'population' are used to label both a stock (i.e., a collection of people or animals) and the level of that stock (i.e., the number of individuals). The context will usually make the intended meaning clear.

4.3 Stocks control flows, flows change stocks

Stocks and flows interact. Flows change the levels of the stocks (the amount accumulated), but the levels of the stocks control the flow rates. Such stock-flow interactions give rise to the feedback behaviour that is characteristic of dynamical systems.

The level of a stock can change only if there is a net inflow or a net outflow. A net inflow increases the level of a stock, a net outflow reduces its level. Therefore, the way that the level of a stock varies over time depends on the 'net flow rates' – that is, the moment-to-moment *differences* between the inflow and outflow rates. The case of a water tank with one inflow and one outflow is illustrated in Figure 4.3. It is assumed that the flow rates are controlled by pumps. In this diagram the symbols F_{in} and F_{out} represent the *rates* of water inflow and outflow, respectively. While both F_{in} and F_{out} are time-varying quantities, the 't' in brackets will usually be omitted in this book because the labels $F_{in}(t)$ and $F_{out}(t)$ are somewhat unwieldy. The symbol $V(t)$ represents the volume of water accumulated in the tank at a specific time t.

In the situation depicted in Figure 4.3(a) both pumps are stopped – there is no water flowing in and none flowing out ($F_{in} = F_{out} = 0$). As shown in the corresponding graph, under these conditions the amount of water in the tank will remain constant over time. The water level is said to be in 'static equilibrium'. In Figure 4.3(b) there is water flowing. The inflow rate exceeds the outflow rate ($F_{in} > F_{out}$), and so $V(t)$ will rise linearly over time. In Figure 4.3(c) the inflow rate is less than the outflow rate ($F_{in} < F_{out}$), and so $V(t)$ will fall linearly over time.[1] Finally, in Figure 4.3(d), the inflow and outflow rates are equal ($F_{in} = F_{out}$). In this case $V(t)$ will remain constant, *even if the flow rates vary*, as long as the rates remain equal. Now the water level is said to be in 'dynamic equilibrium'.

A flow rate can be changed more or less instantaneously, but the same is not true for a stock. It always takes time for the level of a stock to respond to a change in flow rates. A hypothetical example is shown in Figure 4.4. The story sketched in this diagram is that F_{in} remains constant over the time period considered, while F_{out} jumps between three different levels. The time-axis is subdivided into three time periods, labelled a, b, and c, during each of which F_{out} remains constant. The level $S(t)$ of the stock changes over time in response to the net flow rate ($F_{net} = F_{in} - F_{out}$). The relative flow rates, the net flow rate, and the consequent behaviour of the stock are as follows in the three time periods:

a) $F_{out} < F_{in}$ so F_{net} is positive and $S(t)$ rises steadily;
b) $F_{out} > F_{in}$ so F_{net} is negative and S(t) falls steadily; and
c) $F_{out} < F_{in}$ so F_{net} is positive again and $S(t)$ rises steadily.

When there is a sudden change from a net outflow ($F_{net} < 0$) to a net inflow ($F_{net} > 0$), as shown at the start of Period c in Figure 4.4, $S(t)$ stops falling and begins to rise. The essential point is that sudden changes in the net flow rate produce sudden changes in the *slope* of the graph of $S(t)$ over time. They do not produce sudden jumps in $S(t)$.

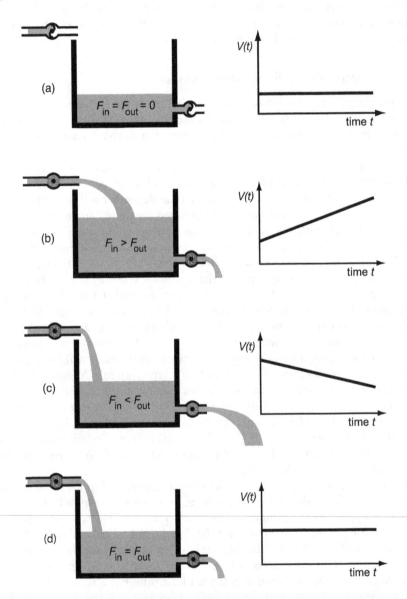

Figure 4.3 Stocks and flows. The diagrams on the left-hand side represent a water tank with one pumped inflow and one pumped outflow. The symbols F_{in} and F_{out} represent the *rates* of inflow and outflow, respectively. Four flow situations are shown. The sketch graphs on the right-hand side represent the way that the volume $V(t)$ of water accumulated in the tank will change over time under the corresponding flow conditions.

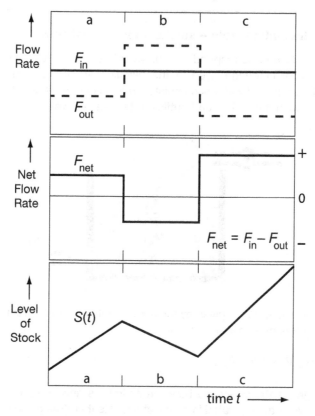

Figure 4.4 The relationship between changes in flow rates and the associated changes in stock levels. The horizontal axis represents time, divided into three periods labelled *a*, *b*, and *c*. *Upper panel*: The vertical axis represents flow rates. The solid horizontal line labelled F_{in} represents a constant inflow rate. The dashed line labelled F_{out} represents a stepped outflow rate. F_{out} is constant for the duration of each of the time periods labelled *a*, *b*, and *c*. *Middle panel*: The heavy line represents the net flow rate $F_{net} = F_{in} - F_{out}$ and the vertical scale shown on the right-hand side indicates that F_{net} runs from negative values (outflow), through zero, to positive values (inflow). *Lower panel*: The vertical axis represents the level of a particular stock. The solid line labelled $S(t)$ represents the way that the level of the stock changes in response to the net flow rates.

At each point in time the state of a dynamical system can be described by listing the levels of its stocks (i.e., the values of its state variables). The way that these levels change over time is driven by the interactions that take place between the stocks. It is important to recognise that stocks cannot affect each other directly – all that they can do is influence the flow rates of each other's state-change processes. A basic rule of system dynamics is that *stocks and flows always alternate along a causal chain* (Forrester 1971: 4).

Box 4.2 Mathematical note – stocks integrate net flows

There is a one-to-one correspondence between stock-and-flow terminology and the mathematical language used in the calculus. In the diagram below, $V(t)$ represents the volume of water accumulated in a tank at time t, and $F_{in}(t)$ and $F_{out}(t)$ are the time-dependent inflow and outflow rates, respectively.

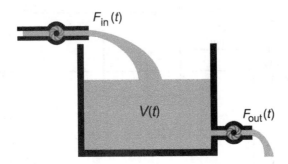

The time-derivative of $V(t)$ is given by the net flow rate $F_{net}(t)$ which is the difference between the rates of inflow and outflow:

$$\frac{dV(t)}{dt} = F_{net}(t) = F_{in}(t) - F_{out}(t).$$

A stock integrates the *difference* between its inflows and its outflows over time. The stock of water accumulated in a tank at time t is therefore given by the integral equation:

$$V(t) = V_0 + \int_{\tau=0}^{t} \left(F_{in}(\tau) - F_{out}(\tau) \right) d\tau,$$

where V_0 is the volume of water in the tank at time $\tau = 0$.

4.4 Causal diagrams

Causal diagrams are powerful systems-thinking tools. They provide a simplified view of the interplay between the variables of a system-of-interest, and so support discussion of feedback structures and presentation of dynamic hypothesis. In this book we define a 'dynamic hypothesis' to be a causal structure that is proposed to explain the behaviour of a system in terms of endogenously generated feedback effects.

An understanding of how causal diagrams work, and their strengths and weaknesses, can be gained by examining the relationship between a stock-and-flow map and a corresponding causal diagram. Consider, for example, the simple stock-and-flow structure shown in Figure 4.5. This diagram represents part of a hypothetical food-supply system operated by a farming family. There are three stocks, *Area Farmed*, *Food Reserves*, and *Consumers*, that have levels $A(t)$, $R(t)$ and $N(t)$, respectively. While a more-complete representation would show flows that affect all three

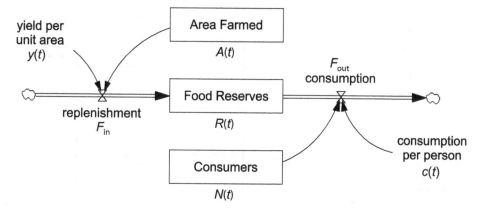

Figure 4.5 Part of an agricultural production system. The three stocks, *Area Farmed*, *Food Reserves*, and *Consumers*, have levels $A(t)$, $R(t)$, and $N(t)$, respectively. Two of the flows that influence *Food Reserves* are shown. The rate of replenishment F_{in} is equal to the product of *yield per unit area* $y(t)$ and the area farmed $A(t)$. The rate of consumption F_{out} is equal to the product of *consumption per person* $c(t)$ and the number of consumers $N(t)$.

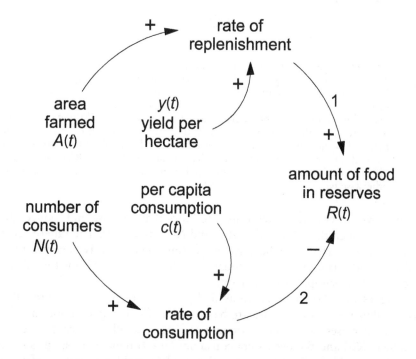

Figure 4.6 A causal diagram corresponding to the stock-and-flow structure of Figure 4.5. In this diagram the blocks of text represent the levels of the stocks, the flow rates and the values of the parameters $y(t)$ and $c(t)$. The arrows represent the influence links and the + and − signs are the link polarities. Links 1 and 2 are labelled for ease of reference.

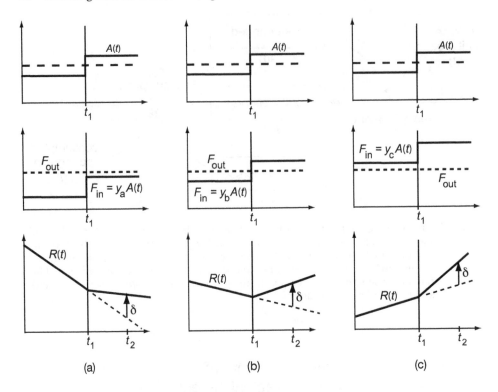

Figure 4.7 Three possible behaviours of the stock-and-flow structure shown in Figure 4.5. The graphs are arranged in columns, labelled *a*, *b*, and *c*. In all graphs the horizontal axis represents time. The vertical axes represent either stock levels (upper and lower rows) or flow rates (middle row). The quantities plotted are defined in Figure 4.5. The increase in $A(t)$ is the *same* in all three cases (see upper row). In the lower row the light dashed line shows how $R(t)$ would have behaved in the absence of the increase in $A(t)$. The small vertical arrows labelled δ are all the same length and show that, while the effect on $R(t)$ appears to be different in the three cases, in all cases $R(t)$ is the *same* amount greater than it otherwise would have been at time t_2.

stocks, here we are concerned with just the flows that increase and reduce the level of $R(t)$. It is through these flows that $A(t)$ and $N(t)$ affect $R(t)$. The rate of replenishment F_{in} is equal to $y(t)A(t)$, where $y(t)$ is the time-dependent average yield per unit area. The rate of consumption F_{out} is equal to $c(t)N(t)$, where $c(t)$ is the time-dependent average rate of consumption per person.

Three cases are shown in columns a, b, and c of Figure 4.7. Note that the behaviours illustrated in the figure are based on the following assumptions; the area farmed $A(t)$ increases by the *same* amount at time t_1 in all three cases; the number of consumers $N(t)$ and the per capita consumption $c(t)$ remain constant, so that F_{out} is constant over the time span shown; the product yield per unit area $y(t)$ has a different value in each case. The three cases are:

a) $R(t)$ decreases throughout the time span shown. This is because the yield y_a is low so that $F_{in} < F_{out}$ at all times. The effect of the increase in $A(t)$ is to slow the rate at which $R(t)$ is decreasing. Thus, at time t_2 the value of $R(t)$ is an amount δ greater than it otherwise would have been had $A(t)$ not increased.

b) $R(t)$ decreases until time t_1 and increases thereafter. This happens because the yield y_b is such that $F_{in} < F_{out}$ before t_1 but $F_{in} > F_{out}$ after t_1. The effect of the increase in $A(t)$ is to change the direction of the changes in $R(t)$. But, since the size of the jump in $A(t)$ is the same as it was for Case a, the value of $R(t)$ is once again an amount δ greater at time t_2 than it otherwise would have been.

c) $R(t)$ increases throughout the time span shown. This is because the yield y_c is so high so that $F_{in} > F_{out}$ at all times. The effect of the increase in $A(t)$ is to speed up the rate at which $R(t)$ is increasing. But, the size of the jump in $A(t)$ is the same as it was in the other two cases, and so once again the value of $R(t)$ is the an amount δ greater at time t_2 than it otherwise would have been.

The behaviours shown in Figure 4.7 can be used to precisely define the meaning of causal diagram link polarities (with reference to Figure 4.6):

- Link 1: A positive polarity (+) means that an *increase* in 'rate of replenishment' will cause $R(t)$ to eventually *rise above* the value that it otherwise would have had (all else being equal). Conversely, a *decrease* in 'rate of replenishment' will cause $R(t)$ to eventually *fall below* the value that it otherwise would have had (all else being equal).

- Link 2: A negative polarity (–) means that an *increase* in 'rate of consumption' will cause $R(t)$ to eventually *fall below* the value that it otherwise would have had (all else being equal). Conversely, a *decrease* in 'rate of consumption' will cause $R(t)$ to eventually *rise above* the value that it otherwise would have had (all else being equal).

The phrase "all else being equal" indicates that, while changes in $A(t)$, $N(t)$, $y(t)$, or $c(t)$ can affect the behaviour of $R(t)$, when we assign a polarity to Link 1 (for example) we consider the effect of an increase in *rate of replenishment* alone, and assume that *rate of consumption* is constant. Similarly, when we assign a polarity to Link 2 we consider the effect of an increase in *rate of consumption* alone, and assume that *rate of replenishment* is constant. You will sometimes encounter the Latin version of the phrase "all else being equal", which is *ceteris paribus*.

The above definitions are designed to accommodate the full range of behaviours shown in Figure 4.7. Some systems thinkers label their arrows 's' (indicating a change in the *same* direction) or 'o' (indicating a change in the *opposite* direction) where we would use + and − signs, respectively. Thus, in the example shown in Figure 4.6, they would place an 's' on Link 1. This would be taken to mean that a change in 'rate of replenishment' would cause a change in the same direction in $R(t)$. Similarly, they would place an 'o' on the arrow running from *rate of consumption* to $R(t)$. This would be taken to mean that a change in *rate of consumption* would cause a change in the opposite direction in $R(t)$. While this 'same–opposite' convention does work in some cases, it can be misleading. The problem is that it does not adequately represent the range of behaviours generated by stock-and-flow structures. This is made clear by the examples shown in Figure 4.7; in all three cases the level $A(t)$ increases, but the effect on $R(t)$ differs depending on the relative magnitudes of F_{in} and F_{out}.

A labelling convention based on the notion that a change in $A(t)$ will *always* cause $R(t)$ to change "in the same direction" is inadequate (Sterman 2000: 140).

Finally, a word of caution. Causal diagrams that describe feedback loops and have polarities assigned to the arrows are usually called 'causal-loop diagrams' or 'CLDs' (Figures 5.1 and 5.2). While causal-loop diagrams provide useful ways to explain 'dynamic hypotheses' (proposed explanations of cause and effect), they are highly abstract and can lead an uninitiated viewer to erroneous conclusions about the behaviour of a system-of-interest (Richardson 1986). For example, consider the simple case shown in Figure 4.8. The stock-and-flow structure shown in Figure 4.8(a) has a single stock and a single inflow. The inferential logic is clear. An inflow can only increase the level of a stock. An increase in the rate of inflow will increase the rate at which the level of the stock increases. If the rate of inflow falls to zero, then the level of the stock will stop increasing, and it will remain constant as long as the flow rate remains zero (all else being equal). There is no way that a change in an inflow rate can reduce the level of a stock.

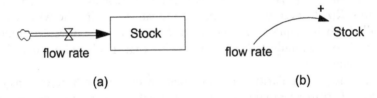

(a)   (b)

Figure 4.8 The limitations of causal diagrams. (a) A simple stock-and-flow structure. (b) A causal diagram representing the same stock-and-flow structure.

The causal diagram shown in Figure 4.8(b) is intended to represent the stock-and-flow structure of Figure 4.8(a). The positive polarity of the link indicates that the flow in question is an inflow. Taken at face value, however, Figure 4.8(b) can be misinterpreted – a person unfamiliar with stock-and-flow principles might infer from it that increasing the flow rate will increase the *level* of the stock (rather than increasing the *rate of increase* of the level of the stock). Worse still, he or she might then infer that decreasing the flow rate will decrease the level of the stock. This inference is erroneous because, even if it is reduced to zero, an inflow can *never* reduce the level of a stock. Errors of this type can be avoided if the limitation of causal diagrams are kept firmly in mind, and inferences about system behaviour are based always on stock-and-flow (bathtub or water tank) logic.

In many cases it is not desirable to assign polarities to the influence links of a causal diagram. A causal diagram without polarities is called an 'influence diagram' (Figures 5.17 and 5.18). Influence diagrams are useful when it is not possible to unambiguously assign link polarities. This can happen in the early stages of an investigation or when the causal structure involved is complex. In such cases it can be useful to sketch out the causal structure, but premature, and potentially misleading, to specify link polarities. An influence diagram can also be valuable in the many situations where there is a need for a simple description of causal structure, rather than an analysis of a system's dynamics.

4.5 Stocks and states

The stock-and-flow idea is powerful because it gives us a down-to-earth way to think and talk about change in complex systems. In system dynamics terminology change is described in terms of variations in the 'levels' of a system's stocks. Because 'stocks' and 'state variables' are just different names for the same thing, the 'level' of the stock can also be referred to as the 'size', 'magnitude', or 'value' of the state variable (Table 4.1). Consider, for example, a water tank that is part of a water-supply system. The tank will have a number of variable characteristics that indicate its condition, or state, at a given time. Different state variables are important to different people at different times. For example, the colour of the tank might remain an important characteristic for its owners – they might decide to repaint the tank if its colour fades over time. In regions where mosquito-borne diseases are prevalent, the condition of the tank's insect screens will be a state variable of continuing importance – typically the screens will require regular maintenance. When looked at from a water-supply point-of-view, however, the most important state variable is the *amount* of water accumulated in the tank – that is, the *level* of the stock.

In this book we follow the scientific convention of using the term 'value' to refer to a numerical amount, magnitude, or quantity. For example, the phrase 'an increase in the value of the state variable' will refer to an increase in the quantity represented by the state variable in question. In discussions of human ecology, of course, we will frequently encounter the use of the term 'value' to refer to the importance or preciousness of something. Provided that we stay alert, these two meanings of the term should not cause confusion – the context will make the meaning clear.

The 'behaviour' of a dynamical system can be specified by describing the way that the levels of its component stocks change over time. Stock-and-flow language provides a bridge between qualitative systems thinking and quantitative dynamical modelling. It does this because it rests on a powerful metaphor that is simultaneously (a) an easily understood abstraction from a vast range of concrete cases where fluids accumulate in and drain from containers (bathtubs, buckets, tanks, or lakes), and (b) an accessible way to think and talk about the fundamental mathematical concepts that are embodied in dynamical systems theory. You do not need to be adept at mathematics to think usefully about stocks and flows, but it is important for you to know that the stock-and-flow approach has a rigorous mathematical basis (Box 4.2).

The distinction between stocks and their related flows is of great practical importance in the context of human–ecological theory. In his book, *The Sciences of the Artificial*, Herbert Simon remarks that:

> It is a familiar proposition that the task of science is to make use of the world's redundancy to describe that world simply. I shall not pursue the general methodological point here, but I shall instead take a closer look at two main types of description that seem to be available to us in seeking an understanding of complex systems. I shall call these *state description* and *process description*, respectively.
>
> (Simon 1981: 222)

According to Simon, state descriptions "characterize the world as sensed" and process descriptions "characterize the world as acted upon". He goes on to say that:

The distinction between the world as sensed and the world as acted upon defines the basic conditions for the survival of adaptive organisms. The organism must develop correlations between goals in the sensed world and actions in the world of process ... Thus problem solving requires continual translations between the state and process descriptions of the same complex reality.

(Simon 1981: 223)

In describing the WATER TANK metaphor (Table 4.1) we identified 'stocks' with 'state variables', and 'flows' with 'state-change processes'. Thus, a listing of the levels of the stocks in a system-of-interest meets Simon's definition of a state description, and a listing of the related flows and flow rates meets his definition of a process description. It follows that stock-and-flow analyses automatically integrate "state and process descriptions of the same complex reality". For this reason, a stock-and-flow approach can provide strong support for efforts to tackle sustainability problems in social–ecological systems, and can help to guide the development of robust adaptive plans and sustainable management policies.

4.6 Conclusion

A comprehensive approach to human ecology requires a foundation of powerful ideas – metaphorical concepts that are simple yet generic (Chapter 3). This criterion is satisfied by the concept-cluster that the system dynamics community refers to as 'accumulation' or 'stocks-and-flows'. Accumulation can be understood on the basis of experiences with the flow of liquids into and out of containers. The everyday nature of these experiences increases the chances that metaphorical concepts built upon them will be thought about in much the same way by all the members of a collaborative group. The resultant common understanding can help the group to develop genuine, shared causal explanations.

We began with the WATER TANK metaphor, which provides the required concrete basis for a deep understanding of the nature of stocks and flows. In addition, water-tank logic can be projected, via the underlying metaphor, to support reasoning about the behaviour of many kinds of dynamical system. We discussed the way that flows change stock levels, and stock levels control flow rates. These stock-flow feedback interactions are the basis of the dynamically complex behaviour that can be exhibited by even very simple stock-and-flow systems (Chapter 5). We also pointed out that stocks can be identified with state variables, and flows with state-change processes – which means that a stock-and-flow approach provides an automatic integration of state and process descriptions of social–ecological systems. Finally, we described one of the basic tools of the system dynamics community – causal diagrams. Such diagrams, if used carefully and with an understanding of their limitations, can provide useful visual description of feedback structures. They can act as a shared visual language to aid group-explorations of system structure (Newell and Proust 2012: 10) and to explain dynamic hypotheses to a wide audience.

In Chapter 5 we take a further step into the conceptual world of system dynamics with an exploration of its quintessential basic concept – the feedback loop.

Note

1   In this example we assume that the outflow-pumping rates are adjusted so that F_{out} is constant, independent of the depth of water in the tank. If the flow rates were controlled by simple taps, and the tap settings were constant, then the $V(t)$ graphs shown in Figures 4.3(b) and 4.3(c) would be curved. This happens because, when simple taps are used, F_{out} will depend on the water pressure at the outlet. The water pressure, and hence F_{out}, increase as the depth increases and decrease as the depth decreases.

References

Axelrod, R. and Cohen, M.D. (1999) *Harnessing Complexity: Organizational Implications of a Scientific Frontier*, New York: The Free Press.

Cronin, M.A., Gonzales, C., and Sterman, J.D. (2009) 'Why don't well-educated adults understand accumulation? A challenge to researchers, educators, and citizens', *Organizational Behavior and Human Decision Processes* 108: 116–130.

Forrester, J.W. (1969; Pegasus edition 1999) *Urban Dynamics*, Waltham, MA: Pegasus.

Forrester, J.W. (1971; Productivity Press edition 1990) *Principles of Systems*, Portland, OR: Productivity Press.

Gleick, J. (1987) *Chaos*, London: Penguin.

Meadows, D.H. (2009) *Thinking in Systems: A Primer*, London: Earthscan.

Mitchell, M. (2009) *Complexity: A Guided Tour*, Oxford: Oxford University Press.

Newell, B., 2012, 'Simple models, powerful ideas: Towards effective integrative practice', *Global Environmental Change* 22 (3): 776–783.

Newell, B. and Proust, K. (2012) Introduction to Collaborative Conceptual Modelling, Working Paper, ANU Open Access Research. *https://digitalcollections.anu.edu.au/handle/1885/9386*

Richardson, G.P. (1986) 'Problems with causal loop diagrams', *System Dynamics Review* 2 (2): 158–170.

Richardson, G.P. (1991) *Feedback Thought in Social Science and Systems Theory*, Waltham, MA: Pegasus Communications.

Scheffer, M. (2009) *Critical Transitions in Nature and Society*, Princeton, NJ: Princeton University Press.

Simon, H.A. (1981) *The Sciences of the Artificial*, Cambridge, MA: The MIT Press.

Sterman, J.D. (2000) *Business Dynamics: Systems Thinking and Modeling for a Complex World*, Boston, MA: Irwin McGraw-Hill.

Walker, B. and Salt, D. (2006) *Resilience Thinking: Sustaining Ecosystems and People in a Changing World*, Washington, DC: Island Press.

5 System dynamics II
Feedback

The feedback loop is the fundamental building block of system dynamics models, and is the basic unit of analysis and communication of system behaviour. Moreover, it is the feedback notion pressed to an extreme that leads to the endogenous point of view that is perhaps the single most characteristic and significant feature of the field. I believe that an essential step in understanding the potential of the system dynamics approach is the illumination of the deep meaning and significance of the feedback concept within the field and within the social sciences at large.

(Richardson 1991)

5.1 Introduction

Feedback is the second of our fundamental system dynamics concepts. It is hard to overstate its importance. Feedback loops play a dominant role in the behaviour of dynamical systems of all types and at all scales. As expressed by Richardson, in the quotation above, feedback loops are the defining feature of system dynamics models, leading to the "endogenous point of view that is perhaps the single most characteristic and significant feature of the field". A focus on endogenous forces, generated within the system boundary, is what gives system dynamics its ability to provide a fresh view of system behaviour and management (Richardson 2011). Yet, just as is the case for the concept of accumulation, feedback thinking is rare in human society (Richardson 1991: ix):

> The seeds of this work were planted almost twenty years ago when I first became aware of the feedback concept. I wondered then, and still ponder, how my education could have missed it. A powerful way of thinking—linking concepts of control and self-reinforcement, stability and instability, structure and behaviour, mutual causality, interdependence, and uncounted numbers of the deepest ideas in the natural, social, and behavioural sciences—yet the concept was never mentioned in my undergraduate years.

An awareness of the nature of feedback dynamics, and its potential to support the development of comprehensive theory and practice, is essential in human ecology. It is not necessary, of course, for all human ecologists to become system dynamics modellers. But it is necessary for human ecologists to at least understand the basic concepts, and to have a good grasp of what types of behaviour are typical of feedback systems, and when a system dynamics approach is likely to be useful. We begin with an example of behaviour that is counterintuitive – until seen from a feedback perspective.

Annual ragweed (*Ambrosia artemisiifolia*) is a flowering plant that belongs to the sunflower family. It is wind pollinated, each plant producing in the vicinity of a billion grains of pollen during the flowering season. Ragweed pollen is highly allergenic and is believed to be the main cause of hay fever in North America. Its reputation has led communities to seek its eradication – early efforts often involved spraying with broad-spectrum herbicides. In her classic 1962 book, *Silent Spring*, Rachael Carson wrote (p. 80):

> Ragweed, the bane of hay fever sufferers, offers an interesting example of the way efforts to control nature sometimes boomerang. Many thousands of gallons of chemicals have been discharged along roadsides in the name of ragweed control. But the unfortunate truth is that blanket spraying is resulting in more ragweed, not less.

What causes this behaviour? Ragweed is a fast-growing annual plant that colonises disturbed landscapes. It emerges from last year's seed in early spring, sets a prodigious amount of new seed in late summer, and then dies. Ragweed needs open soil in which to establish itself. It cannot do this where there is a dense, continuous cover of perennial plants that prevents its seeds from reaching the ground. When broad-spectrum sprays are used in an attempt to control ragweed, the perennial plants die, exposing the soil and providing an opportunity for ragweed to spread. The ragweed then crowds out young perennial plants and slows their growth. The net result is an expanding loss of the slow-growing perennial plants and a corresponding increase in ragweed infestation. Further spraying serves only to exacerbate the situation (Figure 5.1).

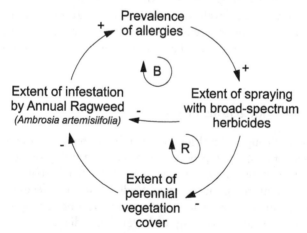

Figure 5.1 The Ragweed Boomerang. In this causal-loop diagram there is a balancing feedback loop (labelled B) that represents the community's efforts to reduce the prevalence of allergies by spraying ragweed. But ragweed thrives where soils are poor and perennial cover is patchy. A ragweed infestation is a *symptom* of these deeper problems. Spraying reduces the symptom temporarily, but it also reduces the cover provided by perennial plants and so amplifies the underlying problem. This amplification process is represented by the reinforcing feedback loop (labelled R).

Problems of this nature do not yield to narrow, silo-based approaches. The way that a social–ecological system will respond to a management intervention cannot be anticipated on the basis of studies of the behaviour of the system's individual parts taken in isolation from one another. The aphorism that "the whole is more than the sum of the parts" refers to the differences that exist between (a) the behaviour of separate bits and pieces, and (b) the behaviour of the fully assembled entity that is made up of those same bits and pieces. The ragweed-eradication policies described above failed initially because the community focused exclusively on the effect of herbicides on ragweed, and did not take into account the crucial feedback interactions that occur in the ragweed-perennial plant system. Some years later, as botanists learned more about the system, the community took advantage of the natural competition that occurs between perennial plants and ragweed. This led to effective control policies that focused primarily on the re-establishment and nurturing of perennial plants, and the careful use of selective sprays (Goodwin and Niering 1959).[1]

Here, in microcosm, is the type of challenge that human ecologists face when they seek to understand the way that social–ecological systems change over time. Of course, the challenges facing humanity are vastly more complicated than that posed by ragweed infestations. Nevertheless, the basic issues are the same. Management actions taken in complex social–ecological systems inevitably have more than one outcome. These outcomes *sometimes* include those intended by the policy makers, but the mix will *always* include unintended outcomes. In the vast majority of cases the unintended outcomes will be unexpected and undesirable, even catastrophic. Furthermore, they are often delayed, or occur at places distant from the centre of management activity, making it difficult to identify cause–effect links. Indeed, there is a strong tendency for delayed or distant outcomes to be blamed on 'proximal events' (events that occur close by in space and time), rather than on the management actions that actually caused them. If we want to develop robust policies, that are sustainable in the long term, we need to take account of endogenous behaviour – that is, behaviour that is driven by the feedback interactions that occur between the parts of our systems-of-interest.

5.2 Feedback and endogenous behaviour

Feedback operates through causal loops, whereby a change in the level of a system variable influences state-change processes that act to amplify or oppose the original change. There are just two types of feedback. A feedback structure that amplifies change is called a 'reinforcing' or 'positive' feedback loop. A feedback structure that opposes change is called a 'balancing' or 'negative' feedback loop (Figure 5.2).

The dynamical story corresponding to the left-hand diagram in Figure 5.2 is that, all else being equal, an increase in the amount of exercise undertaken by an individual will trigger physiological processes (Link 1) that result in an increased physical fitness. Increased physical fitness then causes physiological and psychological changes (Link 2) that increase the extent to which the individual values and enjoys exercise, resulting in an increased amount of exercise (Link 3). The encircled R indicates that this is a 'reinforcing' feedback loop that will amplify a change in the level of any of its variables. Note that a reinforcing loop can drive the level of its variables up or down.

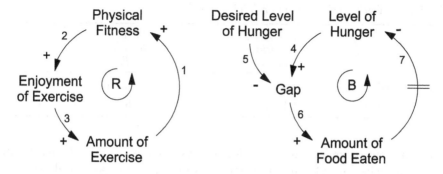

Figure 5.2 Reinforcing and balancing feedback structures. In these causal-loop diagrams (CLDs) the blocks of text represent system variables and the arrows represent causal links. The arrows are numbered for ease of reference. The plus signs and the minus signs show the 'polarity' of each link (Section 4.4). The encircled R signals a 'reinforcing' loop and the encircled B signals a 'balancing' loop.

Thus, a *decrease* in the amount of exercise will cause a *decrease* in the level of physical fitness, which will then lead to a further *decrease* in amount of exercise.

The dynamical story corresponding to the right-hand diagram in Figure 5.2 is that, all else being equal, an increase in an individual's level of hunger will lead to an increase in the discrepancy(s) between the actual level of hunger and the desired level of hunger (Links 4 and 5). An increase in the gap brings into play processes that increase the amount of food eaten (Link 6). An increase in the amount of food eaten will then act to reduce the level of hunger (Link 7). The encircled B indicates that this is a 'balancing' feedback loop that works to maintain the individual's hunger at an acceptable level (provided, of course, that food is available). The short parallel lines drawn across Link 7 indicate a delayed response – it is this delay that allows the eater to over-indulge. Note that balancing loops are always 'goal seeking', with their behaviour driven by the 'gap' between a 'goal state' and the actual state of the system. In the interests of clarity we will sometimes omit the goal and the gap when we draw influence and causal-loop diagrams.

Note that the labels 'positive' and 'negative' feedback can be misleading. They do not signal 'good' or 'bad' feedback. The desirability (or otherwise) of a feedback effect depends on the context in which it is encountered. As shown in Table 5.1, reinforcing (positive) feedback acts to amplify change can be helpful in situations where you want change, but unhelpful when you do not want change. Conversely, balancing (negative) feedback acts to oppose or dampen change, which can be helpful when you do not want change, but unhelpful when you do want change. In this book, to minimise the chance of confusion, positive feedback will usually be referred to as 'reinforcing' feedback, and negative feedback will usually be referred to as 'balancing' feedback. Nevertheless, you do need to be familiar with the terms 'positive feedback' and 'negative feedback' because you will encounter them in many technical contexts.

System dynamicists are particularly interested in observed behaviours that can be explained as *endogenously* generated within relatively simple, self-contained feedback structures. Indeed, it can be argued that a focus on endogenous behaviour can be considered to be *the* defining characteristic of system dynamics (Richardson 2011). There are several reasons for the importance of this approach.

Table 5.1 Feedback – helpful and unhelpful

	Reinforcing (or positive) feedback	Balancing (or negative) feedback
Change wanted	Helpful	Unhelpful
Change unwanted	Unhelpful	Helpful

First, a focus on endogenous behaviour draws attention to the role that feedback plays in the behaviour of real-world systems. Consider the hypothetical cause–effect structures shown in Figure 5.3. If the structure shown in Figure 5.3(a) represents your mental model of causation in a situation to be managed, and if you make the assumption that the cause–effect processes are linear, then you will expect that a change in X will cause a proportional change in Y. But, as is often the case, the reality might be different. One possibility is shown in Figure 5.3(b), where levels X and Y interact to form a reinforcing feedback system. A change in X can now trigger a runaway change in *both* Y and X. Another possibility is shown in Figure 5.3(c), where levels X and Y interact to form a balancing feedback system. In this case any change in Y will be resisted and so it is possible that an attempt to change X will have no effect at all on Y.

Thus, depending on the actual causal structure involved, a moderate change in X can cause (a) a matching change in Y, (b) a runaway change in Y, or (c) no change in Y. The behaviours generated in Cases *b* and *c* will be counterintuitive to those whose mental models are restricted to Case *a* alone. Because it focuses on such feedback effects, the endogenous approach can guard against simplistic thinking. At the same time, it can provide relatively simple explanations of unexpected behaviour.

Second, a focus on endogenous behaviour provides a way to deal with complexity. There are two types of complexity – 'detail complexity' (also called 'combinatorial complexity') and 'dynamic complexity' (Senge 1990: 71). Detail complexity arises, for example, in large-scale scheduling and timetabling problems where there are many variables and possible combinations. The challenge in such situations is to select an optimal arrangement from a very large number of possibilities. Dynamic complexity, however, is caused by feedback interactions, and can emerge in systems with few variables (Sterman 2000: 21). Dynamically complex systems behave in counterintuitive ways and display non-linear behaviour such as oscillation and overshoot and collapse (Figure 6.7). They are sources of 'policy resistance' where efforts to solve a problem give rise to endogenous forces that counteract those efforts. Apparently good policies, formulated without taking feedback into account, can even act to exacerbate the target problem. An awareness of dynamic complexity motivates the search for relatively simple, self-contained feedback systems that have the potential to cause the counterintuitive behaviour. In seeking to understand a particular aspect of observed real-world behaviour, system dynamicists do not try to take account of all the potentially relevant variables and cause–effect links. Instead, they seek an explanation that involves feedback interactions between the smallest possible set of variables. The relatively simple feedback structures that emerge from their endeavours must be regarded as dynamic hypotheses proposed to explain the dominant features of observed behaviours. In every respect, this is an application of Occam's Razor, the

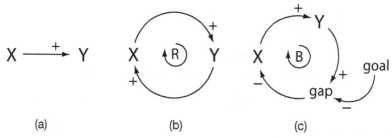

(a)   (b)   (c)

Figure 5.3 Counterintuitive behaviour. In these diagrams the symbols A and B represent the levels of two stocks. Diagram (a) shows a simple causal chain where a change in X causes a corresponding change in Y. In Diagram (b) X and Y interact via a reinforcing feedback loop, so that a change in X will cause a runaway change in both Y and X. In Diagram (c) X and Y interact via a balancing loop embedded in the chain. In this case, as the balancing loop reacts to maintain Y close to its goal, a change in X will have no lasting effect on Y.

basic principle that one should always seek the simplest theory that has the required explanatory power.

Third, the possibility that powerful endogenous explanations can be found is demonstrated by the discovery of 'system archetypes' (Section 5.4). System archetypes are simple *generic* feedback structures that occur in many guises, and in many situations, and that give rise to commonly observed patterns of behaviour. The existence of such archetypical feedback structures was first popularised by Meadows (1982) and Senge (1990). Senge points out that these basic structures, which he calls "nature's templates" (1990: 93), reoccur in many fields of knowledge – "in biology, psychology, and family therapy; in economics, political science, and ecology; as well as in management" (1990: 94) – and thus offer the promise of knowledge unification. This is precisely the kind of invariance, across disciplinary boundaries, that can provide the foundations for an integrative theoretical framework for human ecology (Chapter 7).

5.3 Basic feedback dynamics

The simplest feedback behaviours are those that arise when a stock influences its own rate of change via a single feedback loop. We discuss three fundamentally important cases here: exponential growth, goal seeking, and exponential decay. In Chapter 6 we will go on to consider S-shaped growth (caused by changing loop dominance in a simple two-loop structure), and the oscillations caused by delays in balancing feedback loops.

Exponential growth

Exponential growth is a case of reinforcing feedback. The simplest structure that drives this type of behaviour is shown in Figure 5.4. The parameter *fractional growth rate* sets the speed of growth – it is often called the gain of the feedback loop. The rate of inflow F_{in} is related to the level $S(t)$ of the stock by the equation:

$$F_{in} = \text{fractional growth rate} \times S(t). \tag{5.1}$$

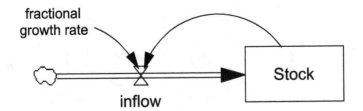

Figure 5.4 Exponential growth. The stock-and-flow structure shown in this diagram has one accumulation, labelled *Stock*, and one state-change process, labelled *inflow*. The influence link that runs from *Stock* to *inflow* establishes a reinforcing feedback loop. The parameter labelled *fractional growth rate* represents the gain of the feedback loop. That is, as shown in Figure 5.5, it is the sensitivity of F_{in} to changes in $S(t)$.

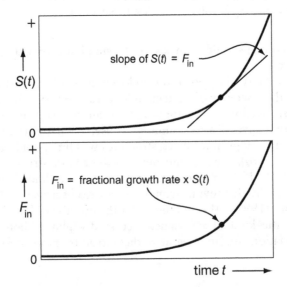

Figure 5.5 Exponential growth. The horizontal axis represents time. The vertical axes, which run from zero toward positive numbers, represent the level $S(t)$ of the stock (upper panel) and the inflow rate F_{in} (lower panel). The filled circles indicate corresponding points on the F_{in} and $S(t)$ graphs.

The growth of the balance of an interest-bearing bank account (where the interest paid by the bank is reinvested and there are no withdrawals) is a good example. When we are dealing with an interest-bearing bank account the fractional growth rate corresponds to the interest rate paid by the bank. The interest rate is usually expressed as a percentage of the balance.

The time-series graphs of Figure 5.5 illustrate the characteristic form of exponential growth (see also Box 5.1). Note that the graphs of $S(t)$ and F_{in} have identical shapes (in accordance with Equation 5.1). Growth is very slow at first and then speeds up as time progresses. Why does this happen? For this discussion we can assume that *fractional growth rate* remains constant. When $S(t)$ is low F_{in} will also be low and $S(t)$ will increase only slowly. That is, the graph of $S(t)$ will be almost horizontal.

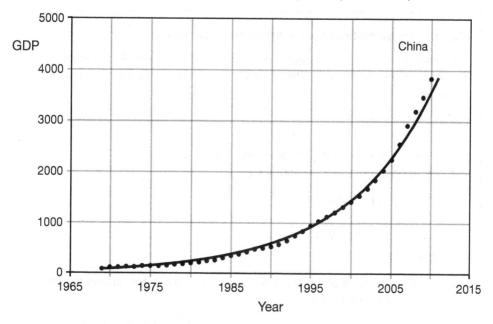

Figure 5.6 The growth of China's Gross Domestic Product (GDP) from 1969 to 2011. The horizontal axis is year of measurement and the vertical axis is GDP expressed in billions of 2005 US dollars. The points show the measured GDP time series, and the solid line is an exponential function fitted to the observational data (Box 5.1).

Sources: Data from the United States Department of Agriculture (USDA). Data from www.ers.usda.gov/data/macroeconomics. World Bank World Development Indicators, International Financial Statistics of the IMF, IHS Global Insight, and Oxford Economic Forecasting, as well as estimated and projected values developed by the Economic Research Service, all converted to a 2005 base year.

But as $S(t)$ rises F_{in} will increase, causing $S(t)$ to rise faster. As $S(t)$ speeds up, F_{in} grows more rapidly, and $S(t)$ speeds up even more. The growth continues to accelerate, with the graphs of $S(t)$ and F_{in} becoming steeper and steeper, until some limit is reached. Exponential growth cannot continue indefinitely in a finite world. An example where the growth limit is not yet in sight is shown in Figure 5.6.

Goal seeking

Balancing (negative) feedback loops are called 'goal seeking' because they operate to maintain the level of a stock close to a specific target value. The simplest structure that drives this type of behaviour is shown in Figure 5.7. The parameter *gap* represents the difference between the system *goal* and the level $S(t)$ of the stock. That is, *gap* = *goal* − $S(t)$. Thus, the rate of inflow F_{in} is related to $S(t)$ by the equation:

$$F_{in} = \text{fractional growth rate} \times (\text{goal} - S(t)). \tag{5.2}$$

The growth of a well-established tree provides a good example. In this case the goal is the mature size of the tree and, as the tree approaches this size, its growth rate

---

Box 5.1 Mathematical note – exponential behaviour

Exponential growth occurs when the rate of change of a stock S is proportional to the level of the stock itself. This situation can be described by the differential equation

$$\frac{dS(t)}{dt} = g\,S(t),$$

where $S(t)$ is the level of the stock at time t and g is a constant. The variation of $S(t)$ over time is given by the integral equation

$$S(t) = S_0 + g \int_{\tau=0}^{t} S(\tau)\, d\tau,$$

which can be solved to yield

$$S(t) = S_0\, e^{gt},$$

where is S_0 is the level of the stock at time $\tau = 0$, and e is the base of the natural logarithms (Euler's constant).

---

slows. As a result the tree approaches its maximum size asymptotically, growing ever more slowly as the gap, between its actual size and its eventual mature size, decreases. 'Regulation' of all types (mechanical, biophysical, social) involves goal-seeking structures. In all cases, the level of a stock is to be held close to a desired level. Corrective action is taken when the gap between the level and the goal becomes too large.

The time-series graphs of Figure 5.8 illustrate characteristic goal-seeking behaviour. In accordance with Equation 5.2, the graph of F_{in} mirrors that of $S(t)$. When $S(t)$ is low, so that there is a big gap between it and its goal, F_{in} will also be high and

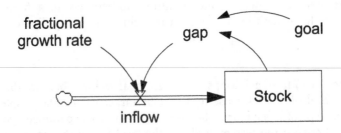

Figure 5.7 Goal seeking. The stock-and-flow structure shown in this diagram has one accumulation, labelled *Stock*, and one state-change process, labelled *inflow*. The variable *gap* represents the difference between *goal* and the current level $S(t)$ of the stock. The influence link that runs from *Stock*, via *gap*, to *inflow* establishes a balancing feedback loop. The parameter labelled *fractional growth rate* represents the sensitivity of F_{in} to changes in *gap* and hence to changes in $S(t)$.

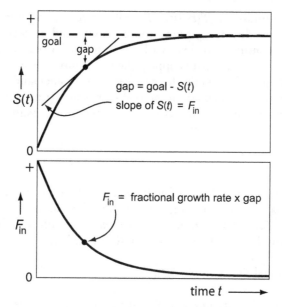

Figure 5.8 Goal seeking. The horizontal axis represents time. The vertical axes represent the level $S(t)$ of the stock (upper panel) and the inflow rate F_{in} (lower panel). The filled circles indicate corresponding points on the F_{in} and $S(t)$ graphs.

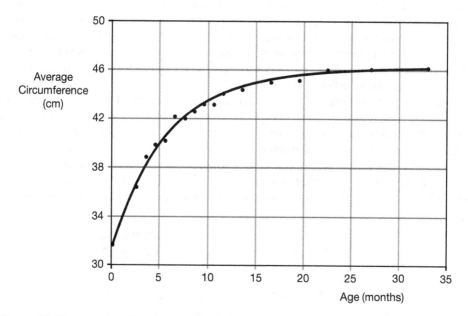

Figure 5.9 The growth of head circumference in young boys from birth to 33 months. The horizontal axis represents age in months and the vertical axis represents average head circumference measured in centimetres.

Sources: Data from the National Center for Health Statistics, USA. Data from Kuczmarski, R.J., Ogden, C.L., Guo, S.S., *et al.* (2002) '2000 CDC growth charts for the United States: Methods and development', *Vital and Health Statistics*, Series 11, Number 246 (National Center for Health Statistics), Table 12, column 4. Average head circumference for boys from national surveys, 3rd percentile.

$S(t)$ will increase rapidly. As $S(t)$ rises F_{in} will decrease, causing $S(t)$ to rise more slowly. As $S(t)$ slows down, F_{in} grows more slowly, and so $S(t)$ slows down even more. The growth continues to slow, with the graphs of $S(t)$ and F_{in} becoming more and more horizontal, as the goal is approached ever more closely. In abstract terms this is asymptotic growth – while the gap becomes smaller and smaller over time, $S(t)$ never actually reaches its goal. In the real world such growth limits are achieved in a finite time; very often, they are passed (Section 6.4). An example of goal-seeking behaviour is shown in Figure 5.9.

Exponential decay

Exponential decay is a special case of goal seeking, where the initial level of the stock is high and the goal is zero. The simplest structure that drives this type of behaviour is shown in Figure 5.10. The parameter *fractional decay rate* sets the speed of decay. The rate of outflow F_{out} is related to $S(t)$ by the equation:

$$F_{out} = - \text{fractional decay rate} \times S(t), \tag{5.3}$$

where both *fractional decay rate* and $S(t)$ are positive quantities.

Why is there a minus sign in this equation? In the discussion so far inflows and outflows have been distinguished by the use of the subscripts 'in' and 'out', respectively. Thus, we have used F_{in} to represent the rate of an inflow, and F_{out} to represent the rate of an outflow. In stock-and-flow diagrams the direction of the flow arrows is used for the same purpose. A flow arrow pointing into a stock indicates an inflow (Figure 5.4), and a flow arrow emerging from a stock indicates an outflow (Figure 5.10). When we come to the *quantitative* assessment of stocks and flows, however, these naming and graphical conventions are inadequate. We need a mathematical way of distinguishing inflows and outflows. From the mathematical point-of-view, an inflow is a *positive* flow because it increases (*adds to*) the level of a stock, and an outflow is a *negative* flow because it reduces (*subtracts from*) the level of a stock. There is a minus sign in Equation 5.3 because the quantity that we have named F_{out} is the rate of an outflow that reduces the level of $S(t)$. The minus sign tells us that, in cases of exponential decay, large stocks will decay faster than small stocks.

The leakage of water from a tank exemplifies the exponential-decay process. Consider a tank with a hole in its side near the bottom. When the water level in the

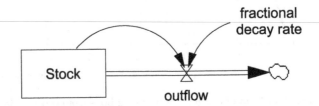

Figure 5.10 Exponential decay. The stock-and-flow structure shown in this diagram has one accumulation, labelled *Stock*, and one state-change process, labelled *outflow*. The influence link that runs from *Stock* to *outflow* establishes a balancing feedback loop. The parameter labelled *fractional decay rate* represents the sensitivity of F_{in} to changes in $S(t)$.

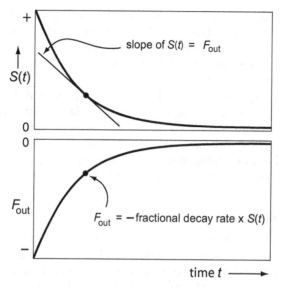

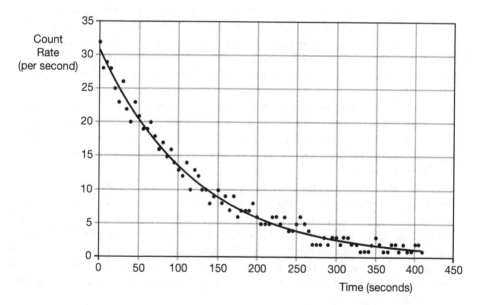

Figure 5.11 Exponential decay. The horizontal axis represents time. In the upper panel the vertical axis represents the level $S(t)$ of the stock. In the lower panel the vertical axis, which runs upwards from negative numbers towards zero, represents the outflow rate F_{out}. The filled circles indicate corresponding points on the F_{out} and $S(t)$ graphs.

Figure 5.12 A time series showing the exponential decay of the radioactivity of a sample of ^{234}Pa (Protactinium). The horizontal axis represents time measured in seconds. The vertical axis represents the number of β particles per second emitted by a small ^{234}Pa source. The data points show the experimentally measured count-rates, and the curved line is an exponential function fitted to the experimental data.

Source: Data from the *Integrated Science Through Experiments* course developed by the Faculty of Natural Sciences at Matej Bel University, Banska Bystrica, Slovak Republic.

tank is high, the water pressure at the hole will be correspondingly high, the outflow will be rapid, and the water level will drop quickly. As the water level in the tank drops, the pressure at the hole reduces, the flow slows, and the water level falls more slowly. Eventually, when the water level falls to zero, the water pressure at the hole reaches zero, and the flow ceases.

The time-series graphs of Figure 5.11 illustrate exponential decay. The graphs of $S(t)$ and F_{out} are mirror images of each other (in accordance with Equation 5.3). When $S(t)$ is high, F_{out} will also be high and $S(t)$ will decrease rapidly. As $S(t)$ falls F_{out} decreases, causing $S(t)$ to fall more slowly. The growth continues to slow, with the graphs of $S(t)$ and F_{out} becoming more and more horizontal, as $S(t)$ approaches zero. An example of exponential decay is shown in Figure 5.12.

5.4 System archetypes

The basic feedback structures described in Section 5.3 are examples of simple generic structures with characteristic patterns of behaviour. In this book we consider these structures to be the simplest system archetypes. The double-loop structure that gives rise to S-shaped growth (Figure 6.4) is a particularly important example. This structure plays a central role in discussions of sustainability – where it is usually called the Limits to Growth system archetype.

Another key example is illustrated by the CLDs shown in Figures 5.1 and 5.13. For reasons that should be clear from our discussion of the Ragweed Boomerang (Section 5.1), the causal structure shown in these figures is known as the Fixes that Fail archetype. This archetype describes any situation where there is a basic problem, with unwelcome symptoms. The individuals or communities involved attempt to 'fix' the symptoms, rather than the underlying problem, but (with a delay) their fix makes the underlying problem worse. In Figure 5.13(a) there are two feedback loops:

- loop B – the fix and the symptom interact in a balancing loop. As the symptom grows stronger, more of the fix is applied, and the symptom is reduced. As the symptom decreases, the amount of the fix is reduced, and the symptom grows stronger. In the presence of response delays this goal-seeking system will tend to oscillate (Figure 6.7);
- loop R – the basic problem, the symptom, and the fix interact in a reinforcing loop. The extent of the symptom depends on the extent of the problem. So, if the problem gets worse, then the symptom will become worse. This will lead to a more extensive application of the fix. In a Fixes that Fail situation, the increased application of the fix works to make the basic problem worse. This worsens the symptom, leading to a more extensive application of the fix, and making the problem worse still. This runaway situation will continue until some natural limit is reached.

The characteristic behaviour of this Fixes that Fail system is illustrated in Figure 5.13(b). At the start of the time period shown in the graph the problem and its symptom are at moderate levels. Concern about the symptom leads to a moderate application of the chosen fix. This action leads, after a delay, to a reduction of the symptom. As the symptom become less of a worry so too the extent of the fix is reduced. This causes the symptom to rise and, eventually, leads to an increased

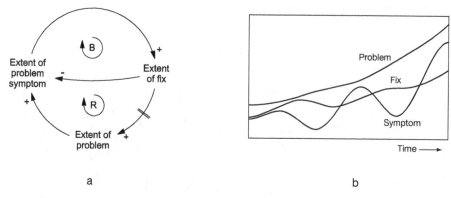

a   b

Figure 5.13 Structure and behaviour of the Fixes that Fail system archetype. These CLDs illustrate (a) the generic Fixes that Fail feedback structure, and (b) the characteristic behaviour of the archetype.

application of the fix. The symptom and fix continue to oscillate about each other as time passes (Loop B). At the same time, application of the fix leads to an increase in the severity of the problem. As the problem increases in severity so too both the level of the symptom and the amount of fix increase, leading to further increases in the severity of the problem (Loop R). As the problem becomes more severe, the average levels of all three variables will continue to increase over time, until something catastrophic occurs, or direct actions are taken to reduce the severity of the problem.

The diagram shown in Figure 5.14 represents a Fixes that Fail situation that can be encountered in minority communities. The members of such communities are commonly subject to discrimination. In such circumstances it is natural for an individual to become depressed and, if his or her resources are limited, seek relief in substance abuse. While this response does relieve the depression, at least temporarily, it can also lead to behaviour that is socially unacceptable. This behaviour leads to a greater level of discrimination and so the situation becomes steadily worse. The limit

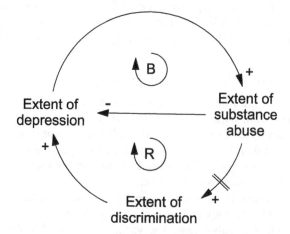

Figure 5.14 The relationship between discrimination, depression, and substance abuse. A Fixes that Fail system of this form can operate in minority communities.

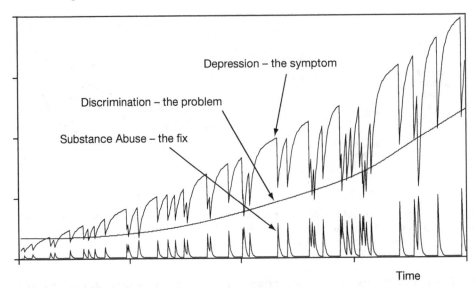

Figure 5.15 This graph shows the Fixes that Fail behaviour that might be generated by the discrimination example shown in Figure 5.14. The horizontal axis represents time. The vertical axis represents the levels of the variables that measure the extent of discrimination, depression, and substance abuse. These time series were computed using Stella®.

is reached when the individual dies from substance abuse or, in the best cases, seeks and receives help to escape his or her personal Fixes that Fail situation. This behaviour is illustrated in Figure 5.15.

A study of the structure and behaviour of system archetypes is an excellent way to develop an appreciation of the power of the endogenous worldview. Senge's archetypes include feedback structures named Limits to Growth, Tragedy of the Commons, Success to the Successful, Fixes that Fail, Accidental Adversaries, Shifting the Burden, Escalation, Drifting Goals, and Growth and Underinvestment. Each archetype displays a characteristic pattern of behaviour. Observation of one of these patterns in the real world indicates that study of the corresponding archetype may provide useful insights into the structure and dynamics of the system-of-interest.

5.5 Cross-sector feedback – an invisible force

A major challenge facing human ecologists is to develop a deeper understanding of the feedback dynamics of social–ecological systems. The causal links of such a system cut across the boundaries of traditional disciplines, institutions and sectors. Thus, management action taken in one sector can produce significant changes in a second sector, and then the changes in this second sector can feedback into the first sector to undercut the aims of the original action.

Consider, for example, the annual ragweed problem introduced in Section 5.1. As shown in Figure 5.16, the ragweed system can be thought of as a social subsystem overlapping an ecological subsystem. The variables assigned to the social subsystem are those related to management action taken by a human community, and those assigned to the ecological subsystem are those related to the reaction of the plant

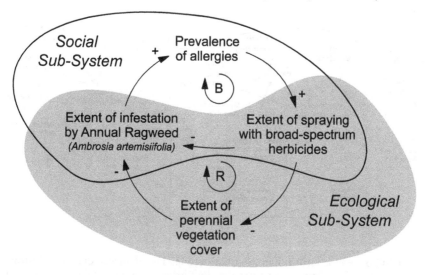

Figure 5.16 Cross-sector feedback and the ragweed problem. In this diagram the variables
of Figure 5.1 are assigned to two overlapping subsystems. The ecological
subsystem is indicated by the shaded area, and the social subsystem by the
closed outline.

community. The Fixes that Fail feedback structure that drives Rachel Carson's
'Ragweed Boomerang' problem (Figure 5.1), simply cannot be seen by anyone who
confines their attention to either of these subsystems alone. Only those who look for
cross-sector feedback have a chance of seeing this structure, and so identifying an
increase in perennial vegetation cover as a sustainable solution to the ragweed
problem. A more complex urban example is displayed in Figure 5.17.

Cross-sector feedback effects can undermine management initiatives, causing
serious unexpected and unwanted outcomes, but such effects are rarely taken into
account in human decision making. One of the main causes of this oversight is the
general 'invisibility' of feedback loops. A number of factors can contribute to peoples'
inability to see cross-sector feedback structures:

- Most people understand causation on the basis of their concrete experiences in
  the real world (Section 3.3). The vast bulk of these experiences appear to be
  driven by simple causal chains, where effect follows cause without delay. You
  pour water into a glass and the level of the water in the glass rises. Even if
  feedback enters the equation (for example, when the person filling the glass
  watches the water level rise and turns off the tap when the glass is full), the
  process is not usually noticed and thought about consciously as 'feedback'. At
  the level of immediate experience, therefore, feedback explanations are not widely
  used and, as a result, few people are inclined to look for feedback loops.
- Feedback effects in complex systems are usually delayed by accumulation –
  stocks take time to fill and drain. Timescales can be very long, in many cases of
  policy making they can range from decades to hundreds of years. When unwanted
  behaviours do finally emerge there is a natural tendency for policy makers and
  managers to seek proximal causes, overlooking the earlier triggering events, and

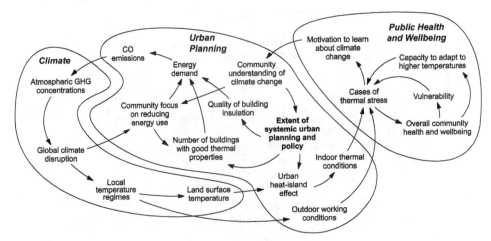

Figure 5.17 Cross-sector feedback in an urban setting. This influence diagram illustrates some of the causal structures that link urban planning, global climate, and public health and wellbeing. The diagram includes important cross-sector feedback loops that will be invisible to research or planning efforts that focus exclusively on variables confined to one or other of the sectors (K. Proust 2013, private communication).

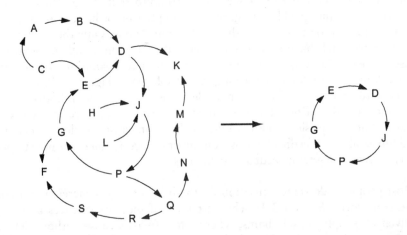

Figure 5.18 Seeing the invisible. In this influence diagram the letters represent variable stock levels, and the arrows represent cause–effect links. Levels E, D, J, P, and G are the only variables involved in a feedback loop and so, together with their associated causal links, they constitute a feedback system. These variables are endogenous to the feedback system. The other variables form a part of the wider causal context. They are classed as exogenous variables that lie outside the feedback-system boundary. Exogenous variables can affect, or be affected by, the state of the system, but by definition they are not parts of the feedback system.

thereby failing to see the feedback connections. It is not possible to fully understand the dynamics of a social–ecological system without historical studies.

- The management of social–ecological systems is usually fragmented. The complexity of such systems drives the establishment of sector-based management 'silos', thereby hiding cross-sector feedback loops that can have a dominant effect on the system's behaviour.
- Feedback structures are not always easy to identify, even when you know that they exist. They can be hidden in a complicated network of causal links. A hypothetical case is shown in Figure 5.18. The diagram shows a single feedback loop embedded in a moderately complicated causal context. In cases like these it can be difficult to 'see' the embedded feedback structure. One good way to begin the search is to examine the behaviour-over-time of selected variables. In particular, the observation of archetype behaviours can signal the presence of well-known feedback structures.

The identification of dominant cross-sector feedback structures requires collaborations and investigations that mesh the knowledge and mental models of people with widely different worldviews. This requirement underlines the importance of the powerful ideas discussed in Chapter 3.

5.6 Conclusion

In this chapter we have outlined some basic aspects of the system dynamicist's view of feedback. This concept is of central importance in human ecology because many aspects of the behaviour of social–ecological systems are most easily explained as feedback effects. In particular, feedback loops can have causal impacts that lead even very simple systems to behave in unexpected and complicated ways.

We began by introducing the two basic causal structures, reinforcing (or positive) feedback and balancing (or negative) feedback, and discussed the key notion of endogenous behaviour. A focus on endogenous (or internally generated) behaviour, which is a defining characteristic of the system dynamics approach, can lead to powerful new insights. The commonly observed behaviours of exponential growth, goal seeking, and exponential decay can all be explained endogenously. We argue that the existence of system archetypes, generic feedback structures with characteristic patterns of behaviour, provides evidence for the validity and explanatory power of an endogenous point of view.

Finally, we discuss the 'invisibility' of cross-sector feedback effects. This 'loop blindness', which is widespread in modern communities, is due in part to individuals' lack of perceived experience of feedback. Feedback loops can be hard to identify in complex systems, particularly because their effects often lag well behind the triggering actions. The situation is not helped by the fragmented approach that is often taken to policy making and management. While it may not be seen, cross-sector feedback is real and can undermine promising initiatives. The inclusion of feedback concepts in a theoretical framework for human ecology can help overcome such problems by promoting a wider awareness of the need for strong cross-discipline, cross-sector collaboration between researchers, policy makers, and managers.

The system dynamics concepts outlined in this chapter, and in Chapter 4, provide a powerful metaphorical foundation for effective cross-disciplinary dialogue. Because they are context-free, however, these concepts do not themselves constitute an understanding of any specific human situation. Can they, in fact, contribute to the theoretical foundations of human ecology? We turn to this question in Chapters 6 and 7.

Note

1   We are grateful to Glenn Dreyer, Director of the Connecticut College Arboretum, and Executive Director of the Goodwin-Niering Center, for providing a copy of this early publication.

References

Carson, R. (1962; Mariner Books Edition 2002) *Silent Spring*, Boston, MA: Mariner Books.

Goodwin, R.H. and Niering, W.A. (1959) 'The management of roadside vegetation by selective herbicide techniques', *The Connecticut Arboretum Bulletin* 11: 4–10.

Meadows, D.H. (1982) 'Whole earth models and systems', *Coevolution Quarterly*, 34, Summer: 98–108.

Richardson, G.P. (1991) *Feedback Thought in Social Science and Systems Theory*, Waltham, MA: Pegasus Communications.

Richardson, G.P. (2011) 'Reflections on the foundations of system dynamics', *System Dynamics Review* 27 (3): 219–243.

Senge, P.M. (1990) *The Fifth Discipline: The Art and Practice of the Learning Organization*, Sydney: Random House.

Sterman, J.D. (2000) *Business Dynamics: Systems Thinking and Modeling for a Complex World*, Boston, MA: Irwin McGraw-Hill.

6 Systems and sustainability

The Seventh Law of Ecological Bloodymindedness: If any species of animal should develop the mental and physical capacity consciously to manage the ecosystem of which it is a part, and proceeds to do so, then the long-term survival of that species will require, as a minimum, that it understands the rate limits of all processes essential to the functioning of that ecosystem and that it operates within those limits.

(Brown 2003)

6.1 Introduction

The sustainability of social–ecological systems is of central concern in human ecology. At a superficial level there is general agreement that a sustainable system is one that continues to function adequately throughout time. But different people have different ideas about what 'to function adequately' means, and different beliefs about what must be done to ensure that adequate functionality is maintained in a given system. Consider, for example, the notions of 'sustainable growth' and 'sustainable development'. Those who believe that continued economic growth is necessary, despite planetary limits, talk about sustainable growth. They rely in part on the argument that new technologies will help societies to 'do more with less', thus enabling them to operate within planetary limits despite continued growth in consumption. Those who promote sustainable development disagree. They argue that there is an absolute limit to what can be achieved technologically, and that continued growth is not possible on a finite planet – human consumption of energy and matter must eventually be stabilised at rates that can be accommodated indefinitely by the planet.[1] They stress the practical ethical and equity issues that lie at the heart of social sustainability, and point out that many of these issues cannot be 'solved' by techno-fixes or continued economic growth.

A more comprehensive approach can be developed if an 'operational definition' of sustainability is adopted. An operational definition is one that is expressed in terms of what a society has to *do* to be sustainable – how it must *act*. Seen from a system dynamics perspective, the actions in question are those that influence the rates of critical social and biophysical processes. This suggests that sustainability is fundamentally a matter of flow management – of controlling the rates of processes that alter the levels of resource and pollution stocks. This perspective is expressed well by Duncan Brown in his *Seventh Law of Ecological Bloodymindedness*. This law, as seen in the quotation above, captures the motivation behind the process-oriented (or flow-oriented) sustainability principles that we develop in Section 6.2.

6.2 Sustainable processes

All human activities consume resources and generate waste. Each activity drives a set of resource-consumption and pollution-generation processes. In Figure 6.1 we use basic stock-and-flow structures to define three cases that illustrate our operational definition of sustainability. While the processes discussed, and the related sustainability principles, may seem to apply most naturally to biophysical variables, we stress that they apply just as well to social stocks and flows as they do to biophysical stocks and flows (see Box 6.1). The three cases are:

a) *A process that consumes a non-renewable resource*. In Figure 6.1(a) the rectangle represents the stock of a non-renewable resource, such as coal or oil.[2] The flow labelled *consume* represents the effect of a resource-consuming process that runs at rate R_c (units of resource consumed per unit time). Such a process is not sustainable. It is 'stock limited' rather than 'flow-rate limited'. That is, while the resource can be consumed at any flow rate that is technically possible, the process will cease when the stock is exhausted. The time period Dt over which the process can be maintained is given by the equation $Dt = $ (initial level of stock)$/R_c$.

b) *A process that consumes a renewable resource*. In Figure 6.1(b) the rectangle represents the stock of a renewable resource, such as a population of fish, the trees of a forest, or social capital. Once again, the flow labelled *consume* represents the effect of a resource-consuming process that runs at rate R_c (resource units consumed per unit time). The flow labelled *replenish* represents the effect of a resource-building process that runs at rate R_r (units of resource generated per unit time). From a sustainability point-of-view such a process is 'flow-rate limited' rather than 'stock limited'. That is, the process can be made sustainable by ensuring that the rate of consumption is less than the rate of replenishment ($R_c < R_r$).

c) *A process that generates pollution*. In Figure 6.1(c) the rectangle represents the stock of a pollutant, such as sulphur dioxide, a heavy metal, or employee stress. The flow labelled *generate* represents the effect of a polluting process that runs at rate R_p (units of pollutant generated per unit time). The flow labelled *neutralise* represents the effect of a natural process that renders the pollutant harmless and that runs at rate R_n (units of pollutant rendered harmless per unit time). This is another flow-rate limited process. It can be made sustainable by ensuring that the rate of pollution generation is less than the rate of neutralisation ($R_p < R_n$).

We use the stock-and-flow structures illustrated in Figure 6.1 as the basis for three sustainability principles (adapted from Daly 1990). These are process-oriented principles that are expressed in terms of *relative flow rates*:

> A process that consumes a *non-renewable resource* is sustainable as long as the rate at which it uses that resource does not exceed the rate at which a renewable resource (used sustainably) is substituted.
>
> A process that consumes a *renewable resource* is sustainable as long as the rate at which it uses that resource does not exceed the rate of regeneration of the resource.
>
> A process is sustainable as long as the rate at which it generates a *pollutant* does not exceed the rate at which that pollutant can be recycled, absorbed, or rendered harmless in the environment.

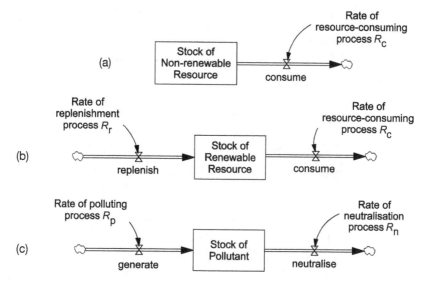

Figure 6.1 These stock-and-flow diagrams show the elements of a process-rate approach to defining sustainability. Three cases are illustrated: (a) a process that consumes non-renewable resources, (b) a process that consumes renewable resources, and (c) a process that generates pollution.

These principles are 'operational' in that they provide useful guides for management action. As mentioned above, managers cannot change stocks directly – all they can do is change the rates of existing processes or change net flow rates by introducing new processes. Nevertheless, it is common for managers to assess the sustainability of a resource-consumption process by watching the level of the resource stock, rather than by looking at the net rate of replenishment of that stock (Meadows 2009: 22). This is a risky procedure.

Consider, for example, the situation depicted in Figure 6.2. This diagram illustrates, in essence, what happens when a resource is replenished at a constant rate R_r while the resource-consumption rate R_c increases steadily from a value that is less than R_r to a value that exceeds R_r (the symbols are defined in Figure 6.1(b)). The net flow rate $F_{net} = R_r - R_c$ is positive at the start of the time period shown, but decreases as R_c increases. F_{net} passes through zero at time t^* (the time when $R_c = R_r$) and becomes increasingly negative during the remainder of the time period. The level $S(t)$ of the stock increases during the first half of the time period, but at a slower and slower rate as F_{net} approaches zero. When F_{net} equals zero, so too the slope of the $S(t)$ curve equals zero – at this instant of time $S(t)$ is momentarily in a state of dynamic equilibrium (Figure 4.3(d)). $S(t)$ then begins to fall as F_{net} becomes negative. The rate at which $S(t)$ decreases accelerates as F_{net} becomes more and more negative. The resource-consumption process is sustainable for times $t \leq t^*$ and unsustainable when $t > t^*$.

Because $S(t)$ changes only slowly around its maximum at t^* it can be difficult for resource managers to notice that the rate of consumption has grown to the point where it now exceeds the rate of replenishment. This is particularly the case when $S(t)$ varies about its average value, or measurements of $S(t)$ are prone to error, and

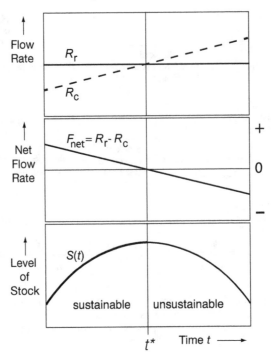

Figure 6.2 The sustainability of a process that consumes a renewable resource. In all panels the horizontal axis represents time. *Upper panel*: the vertical axis represents flow rates. The solid horizontal line labelled R_r represents a constant replenishment rate. The dashed line labelled R_c represents a steadily increasing rate of consumption. *Middle panel*: the heavy line represents the net flow rate $F_{net} = R_r - R_c$ and the vertical scale shown on the right-hand side indicates that F_{net} runs from positive values (inflow), through zero, to negative values (outflow). *Lower panel*: The vertical axis represents the level of a biophysical or social stock. The solid line labelled $S(t)$ represents the way that the level of the stock changes in response to the net flow-rate changes shown in the middle panel. The vertical line at time t^* represents the point where R_2 and R_r are momentarily equal. The process is sustainable before time t^* and unsustainable after that time.

so the manager's estimates of $S(t)$ fluctuate about the true values. In such circumstances valuable time can be lost before managers realise that R_c exceeds R_r and their operation is no longer sustainable. By then it is often too late. The community has become so dependent on high (and increasing) consumption rates that a reduction can seem close to impossible. Such situations can be avoided if attention is paid to the identification and careful monitoring of process rates.

6.3 Limits to growth

While a flow-rate view of sustainability has many practical advantages, it must always be remembered that flows are ultimately controlled by the levels of their associated stocks. The phenomenon of 'S-shaped growth' (also called 'sigmoidal growth') provides an important example of the dynamical effects of such stock-flow feedback. S-shaped growth occurs in many different contexts. The classic case involves

Box 6.1 Social capital is a stock

While it is relatively easy to think of sustainability in terms of material stocks and flows, the principles presented above apply equally well to the more intangible, social dimensions of social–ecological systems. For example, the stock depicted in Figure 6.2 might well be *social capital, optimism,* or *political will. Capital value,* while measured in dollar terms, is an intangible stock and the *depreciation* that erodes it is an intangible flow. Such stocks can be thought of as resources – the social or psychological processes that consume or erode them are in many cases counter-acted by processes that replenish them. It should be obvious that it is not possible to understand the behaviour of a social–ecological system without accounting for interactions that involve such stocks. Intangible social stocks may be difficult to define and assess. Indeed, efforts to devise a way to measure such stocks, to take a quantitative approach, can divert attention away from essential cultural and ethical questions. But an analysis that ignores intangible stocks and flows has little chance of generating reliable insights into system behaviour (Meadows 2009: 176).

population growth. Initially, when population levels are well below the carrying capacity of the region, resources are plentiful and growth can be rapid – often it is exponential. Then, as the population level approaches the local carrying capacity, competition for resources intensifies and growth slows. In the long run population levels can become essentially constant (Figure 6.4). The diffusion of technical innovations follows a similar pattern (Rogers 1995; 23; Sterman 2000: 295). Furthermore, as shown in Figure 6.3, the feedback structure that causes S-shaped growth is relatively simple. Because it is simple, yet generates generic behaviour, this structure can be considered to be a Limits to Growth system archetype.

S-shaped growth reflects competition between two feedback loops. The loop that has the greatest effect on system behaviour can change over time. It is a general systems principle that such changes in 'loop dominance' can complicate the behaviour of even relatively simple systems. In Figure 6.3 the influence link that runs from the stock labelled *Fish* directly to *net growth* establishes a reinforcing feedback loop, with its gain equal to *fractional growth rate*. This part of the structure is essentially the same as the exponential-growth structure illustrated in Figure 5.4 (the only difference being the presence of a bi-flow in Figure 6.3).

The second influence link, which includes the variable labelled gap, establishes a balancing feedback loop. The parameter labelled *carrying capacity* (and represented by the symbol K) is the number of fish that can be supported sustainably by the local ecosystem – it is the goal of the balancing loop. This balancing loop is essentially the same as the goal-seeking structure illustrated in Figure 5.7.

Consider two extremes. First, when the number of fish $N(t)$ is much smaller than carrying capacity K, the reinforcing feedback loop dominates and population can be expected to grow exponentially. This behaviour corresponds to the segment of the $N(t)$ graph that is labelled a in Figure 6.4. Second, when $N(t)$ approaches the carrying capacity, the balancing loop dominates and growth slows. This goal-seeking behaviour is seen in the segment of the $N(t)$ graph that is labelled b in Figure 6.4. When loop

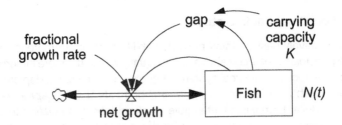

Figure 6.3 The Limits to Growth system archetype. The stock-and-flow structure shown in this diagram is a combination of the exponential-growth structure shown in Figure 5.4 and the goal-seeking structure shown in Figure 5.7. The stock labelled *Fish* has two influence paths to the state-change process labelled *net growth*. The direct path creates a reinforcing feedback loop, and the other creates a balancing loop. The parameter *carrying capacity* is the goal of the balancing loop. The state-change process *net growth* is shown as a bi-flow (Box 4.1) to accommodate the possibility that it can act to increase (inflow) or decrease (outflow) the level N(t) of the stock of fish.

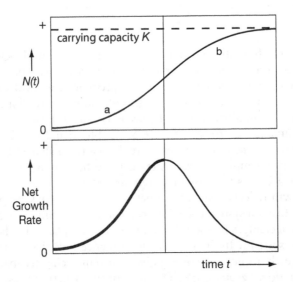

Figure 6.4 S-shaped growth. In both panels the horizontal axis represents time. The vertical axes represent the number N(t) of fish in a hypothetical population (upper panel) and the net growth rate of the population (lower panel). The horizontal dashed line shown in the upper panel represents the carrying capacity K. Elapsed time is divided into two segments. Reinforcing feedback dominates in the time segment labelled *a*, and balancing feedback dominates in the time segment labelled *b*.

dominance changes from reinforcing to balancing, the curvature of the N(t) graph changes from upward curving to downward curving. The point where this happens is called a 'point of inflection'. At the point of inflection the net growth rate, and the corresponding slope of N(t), are at their maxima. At the beginning and end of the time span shown in Figure 6.4 the net growth rate is small and the slope of N(t) is approximately zero (i.e., the graph is close to horizontal). An example is shown in Figure 6.5, and a brief mathematical description is presented in Box 6.2.

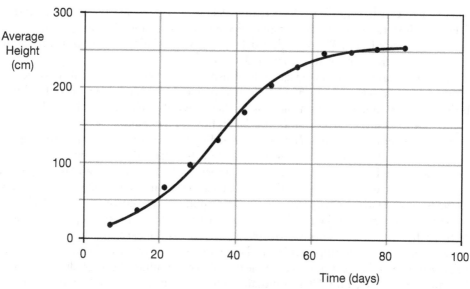

Figure 6.5 A time series showing the characteristic S-shaped growth of a group of sunflower plants (*Helianthus*). The horizontal axis shows time since planting, and the vertical axis shows average plant height measured as elongation above a reference mark drawn on the plant stem. The solid circles show the experimental data (Reed and Holland 1919) and the smooth curve was computed using the logistic growth model (Box 6.2).

Box 6.2 Mathematical note – the logistic growth model

The logistic model, first published by Pierre Verhulst in 1845, provides a useful approximation to S-shaped growth. The logistic model can be expressed as a differential equation of the following form

$$\frac{dN(t)}{dt} = \frac{rN(t)\big(K - N(t)\big)}{K},$$

where $N(t)$ represents the level of the population at time t, r represents the maximum possible growth rate (achieved when $N(t) \ll K$), and K represents the carrying capacity. The population level has two equilibrium points, at $N(t) = 0$ (unstable equilibrium) and $N(t) = K$ (stable equilibrium). There is an inflection point at $N(t) = K/2$.

6.4 Delays, oscillation, overshoot, and collapse

In our discussions of goal-seeking systems we tacitly assumed that flow rates respond immediately to changes in stock levels. When this condition is satisfied such systems can accurately adjust flow rates so that stock levels approach their goals smoothly, without significant overshoot or undershoot. In reality, however, changes in flow rates tend to lag behind changes in stock levels. This is particularly true in managed systems where there can be significant 'perception delays' (Sterman 2000: 426). Perception delays are inevitable in complex systems because it takes time for managers to notice changes in stock levels. When such a delay occurs in a balancing loop, it can cause oscillations in the level of the associated stock.

Consider again the S-shaped growth of fish stocks. The stock-and-flow structure shown in Figure 6.6 is the same as that of Figure 6.3, except for the delay marking. If there is no response delay in the system then it would behave exactly as shown in Figure 6.4. When there is a significant delay, however, the net growth rate does not change fast enough to prevent $N(t)$ from exceeding the carrying capacity of the region. Eventually, at a time depending on the extent of the delay, the net growth rate drops to zero and then becomes negative. As this happens, $N(t)$ grows more and more slowly, reaches a maximum when growth rate equals zero, and then begins to fall back towards the carrying capacity. Because of the response delay, however, $N(t)$ falls below the carrying capacity. When it does so the net growth rate becomes positive again, $N(t)$ reaches a minimum, begins to rise again, exceeds the carrying capacity, and the cycle repeats. The resulting oscillatory behaviour is illustrated in Figure 6.7(a). The behaviour shown in the graph, where the overshoot and undershoot gradually become less and less severe, and $N(t)$ eventually settles down at the level of the carrying capacity, is called 'damped oscillation'.

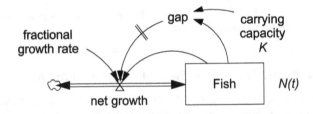

Figure 6.6 Oscillation. The overall structure shown in this diagram is identical to that displayed in Figure 6.3. The pair of parallel lines drawn across the influence link running from *gap* to *net growth* represents a response delay. It indicates that, in this system, changes in net-growth rate will lag behind changes in $N(t)$. If the delay is large enough, $N(t)$ will oscillate around the carrying capacity.

The behaviour shown in Figure 6.7(a) can occur when the carrying capacity of the region is not sensitive to $N(t)$. In such cases the limit to population growth is set by competitive factors, such as those produced by overcrowding. The situation is different when the carrying capacity is sensitive to the rate at which the corresponding resources are consumed. A stock-and-flow structure that illustrates this case is shown in Figure 6.8. This diagram represents a simplified predator–prey system where the carrying capacity for the predator depends on the size $n(t)$ of the prey population, and the rate of consumption of the prey depends on the size $N(t)$ of the predator population.

The graphs displayed in Figures 6.7(b) and 6.7(c) illustrate the type of behaviour generated when the carrying capacity of the region is set by the available resource. In the hypothetical case shown in Figure 6.8, the carrying capacity K for big fish depends on the population $n(t)$ of small fish. In such idealised circumstances the rate at which the small fish are consumed will just equal their replenishment rate when

$N(t)$ equals the carrying capacity; and $n(t)$ will decrease (thus reducing the carrying capacity) whenever $N(t)$ exceeds the carrying capacity. If the rate at which the small fish population is replenished returns to normal when $N(t) < K$, and if system delays are relatively short, then the type of behaviour shown in Figure 6.7(b) will be generated. If, however, the replenishment rate is strongly affected by increasing consumption rates, and system delays are long, then there is a chance that $n(t)$ will be driven down below its collapse threshold. If this happens, the population of large fish will itself collapse. Such 'overshoot and collapse' behaviour is illustrated in Figure 6.7(c).

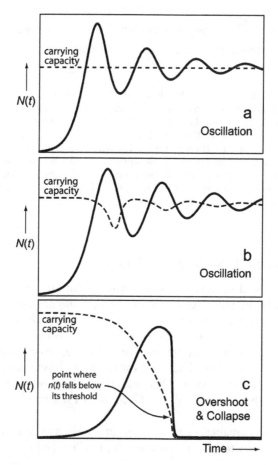

Figure 6.7 The impact of delays. This diagram shows the effect of delays in the balancing loop of a goal-seeking system. In all panels the horizontal axis represents time, and the vertical axes represent the number $N(t)$ of individuals in a hypothetical population. The solid lines represent the time-dependence of $N(t)$ and the dashed lines show the time-dependence of the carrying capacity. Panel *a*: overshoot and damped oscillation where the carrying capacity is not affected by the overshoot. Panel *b*: overshoot and damped oscillation where the carrying capacity is affected by the overshoot. Panel *c*: overshoot and collapse of the carrying capacity and then the population. The variable $n(t)$, defined in Figure 6.8, represents the population of a prey species that determines the carrying capacity of the region for the individuals in population $N(t)$. These graphs were computed using a stock-and-flow model created in Stella®.

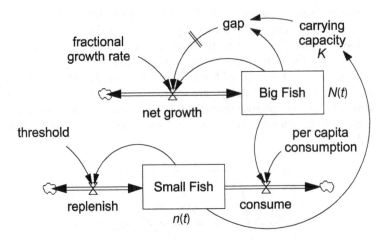

Figure 6.8 Big fish, small fish. A simplified predator–prey system involving a population of big fish and its food supply (represented by the stock labelled *Small Fish*). $N(t)$ represents the number of big fish and $n(t)$ represents the number of small fish. The upper part of the structure is identical to that shown in Figure 6.6, with one exception – there is now a link showing that carrying capacity K depends on $n(t)$. The rate of consumption of small fish depends on the product of $N(t)$ and *per capita consumption*. The variable labelled *threshold* represents the minimum sustainable population of small fish. If $n(t)$ falls below the threshold, the community of small fish will collapse, dragging down K and then $N(t)$.

6.5 Extending the Ehrlich–Holdren relation

So far we have confined our discussion of sustainability to the need for societies to impose *upper limits* on the rates of processes that impact the viability of social–ecological systems. From the perspective of human ecology, however, it is necessary to consider also the *lower limits* to the rates of such processes (Raworth 2013). An obvious example is the basic requirement for individuals to consume sufficient food each day in order to stay alive. The need for the world community to be aware of, and operate between, these upper and lower limits can be expressed as a sustainability-focused version of what we will call the *Goldilocks Principle*:[3]

> In order to be sustainable a society must maintain its resource and waste flows at rates that are not too high, not too low, but just right.

A theoretical framework for human ecology must incorporate the Goldilocks Principle. This principle raises essential questions of equity and ethics, and its inclusion can help ensure that key social issues are not overlooked in sustainability discussions. In the form presented above, however, the principle is too vague to support anything more than hand-waving. A more useful version requires, as a minimum, a clear definition of the meaning of 'just right'. In this section we work towards such a definition, beginning with an examination of the *Ehrlich–Holdren relation*.

Many decades ago Paul Ehrlich and John Holdren published a seminal paper concerning the contribution of population growth to "man's predicament" (Ehrlich and Holdren 1971). They organised their discussion around the simple algebraic equation

$$I = PF, \tag{6.1}$$

where I represents the total negative impact that a society has on its environment, P represents the population of the society, and F represents the average environmental impact of an individual within that society. Ehrlich and Holdren made it clear that they considered the function F to be influenced by two factors – affluence and technology. In later work these factors were included explicitly to give the relation

$$I = PAT, \tag{6.2}$$

where A represents the average per capita consumption of resources and production of wastes, and T represents the average technology-dependent impact per unit consumption (Ehrlich and Ehrlich 1990, 1991; Daily and Ehrlich 1992). The product AT measures the social–environmental impact of an individual, which is scaled by the multiplier P to give the total impact of the community in question. Equation 6.2 expresses Ehrlich and Holdren's essential insight that humanity's impact on the planet is not driven by population, or consumption, or technology acting alone, but by all three acting together. Given that A tends to increase over time, and that it is not possible to reduce T to zero, the relation $I = PAT$ makes it clear why accelerating population growth is unsustainable on a finite planet.

The Goldilocks Principle expresses the idea that there are both upper and lower limits to sustainable resource flows. As a first step towards formalising this idea, we extend the Ehrlich–Holdren relation to include a lower limit to consumption. Our extended relation is

$$I = P(A + B)T. \tag{6.3}$$

We define the variables in this equation as follows:

- I represents the social–ecological *impact* of a resource-consuming or pollution-generating process. In system dynamics terms I is a flow. It is a measure of the *rate* of the process in question. For example, if the situation of concern is the rate at which CO_2 is released into the atmosphere during the process of heating water, then the dimensions of I might be kilograms of CO_2 emitted per annum. The units employed will depend on the scale of the investigation.
- P represents *population*. In system dynamics terms P is a stock. It is a measure of the number of individuals engaged in activities that contribute to I. In the case of water heating, P might be the size of a population subgroup that has moved from electrical heating to passive solar-thermal heating. Because P always represents a simple number, it is said to be 'dimensionless'.
- A represents *affluent consumption*. A is a flow. It measures the rate of that part of an individual's consumption that exceeds his or her minimum requirements. We intend the term 'consumption' to be interpreted broadly to include the use of energy and materials, the use of ecosystem services (such as pollination of crops or waste detoxification), and the use of social stocks such as goodwill.

In our water-heating example, consumption is measured as the rate at which an individual uses the energy embodied in hot water – it can have the dimensions of kilowatts per person per annum. Because A represents *affluent* consumption, in our example it represents the amount of energy used during profligate or wasteful use of hot water.

- B represents *base consumption*. It measures the rate of that part of an individual's consumption that is the *minimum* required for him or her to maintain a dignified existence. B is a flow of the same type as A, and it has the same dimensions as A. In the case of water heating, B represents the amount of energy used during frugal use of hot water.

- T represents the *technology impact factor*. It is a measure of the amount of resources consumed, or waste generated, for each unit of consumption. The value of T depends on the technology used. In the water-heating example the technological possibilities include open fires, natural gas, direct solar heating, electricity from coal-fired power stations, and electricity from renewables. In this case, the value of T will also depend on the efficiency of energy conversion – for consistency with A and B its dimensions would be kilograms of CO_2 emitted per kilowatt of energy used.

When we do not need to consider affluent and base consumption separately, it will be convenient to use a more compact form of Equation 6.3, namely

$$I = PCT, \tag{6.4}$$

where $C = A + B$ represents an individual's total consumption. We will call this 'the extended Ehrlich–Holdren relation', and will assume that it relates to social as well as ecological impacts.

The extended Ehrlich–Holdren relation can be applied to a community of any size. The broadest view of their implications can be obtained by considering the global community. A *lower limit* to global consumption I_{global} can be derived from Equation 6.4 by setting A to zero. This represents the situation where everyone consumes at their base rate B. The minimum *safe* flow rate, required for sustainable human health and wellbeing, is then

$$I_{min} = PBT. \tag{6.5}$$

An *upper limit* to global consumption depends on the planet's carrying capacity K for humans. Note that K is less than Earth's overall carrying capacity, because planetary resources and ecosystem services must be shared with all other organisms, the survival of which, in many cases, is essential for human survival. The maximum *safe* flow rate that the global social-ecological system can support is

$$I_{max} = K - \delta, \tag{6.6}$$

where δ represents a carrying-capacity buffer zone. Given that both I and K can vary independently over time, a buffer zone is necessary to avoid unsustainable situations where I exceeds K.

As shown in Figure 6.9, the condition $I_{min} \leq I_{global} \leq I_{max}$ defines an operating zone that is both safe and equitable – a zone where conditions are 'just right'. At the bottom

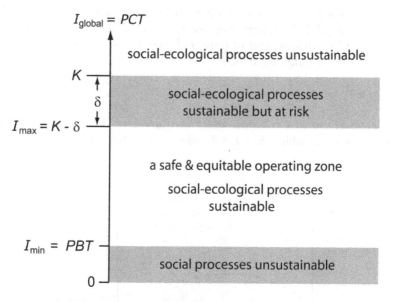

Figure 6.9 Just right. The vertical axis represents the global community's social-ecological impact $I_{global} = PCT$. The equation $I_{max} = K - \delta$ represents the maximum impact that can be maintained indefinitely – here K represents the carrying capacity of the planet, and δ is a buffer zone that allows for unavoidable fluctuations in K and I_{global}. The equation $Imin = PBT$ represents the minimum impact that can be achieved under conditions where all members of the global community are able to maintain a dignified existence.

of the scale, where $I_{global} < I_{min}$, resource use is insufficient to maintain a dignified life for all. The ecological subsystem is able to cope easily with the light demands placed upon it, but basic social processes cannot be sustained. In the zone from $K - \delta$ to K social–ecological processes are sustainable, but at risk if I_{global} and K vary significantly. If I_{global} increases while K decreases then the system can become, at least temporarily, unsustainable. At the top of the scale, I_{global} exceeds the planetary carrying capacity K. In this upper zone both social and ecological resources are eroded over time, and neither social nor ecological processes can be sustained.

Studies of humanity's ecological footprint indicate that I_{global} already exceeds K (Wackernagel and Rees 1996). Does that mean that a just-right status can no longer be achieved? Not necessarily. Among the persistent problems faced by the world community are massive inequalities in per capita resource-consumption rates (with many communities forced to operate below I_{min}), and wasteful use of essential ecological and social resources. It is conceivable that efforts to reduce inequality and waste can lead to a society that satisfies the Goldilocks Principle.

The challenge of moving humanity into a safe and equitable operating zone cannot be understood on the basis of planet-wide averages. What matters, in this context, is the *distribution* of consumption, and the associated environmental impact, generated by individual communities spread around the planet. In the discussion that follows we use the relation $i = pct$ to represent the impact of a local community with population p, consuming a specific resource at rate $c = a + b$, using a technology with impact factor t (the lower-case letters indicate that we are dealing with only a small part of the global impact). We use the symbol k to represent the carrying capacity affected by this element of impact (k may be determined by both local and global conditions). Finally, we define

$$\lambda = pct/k \qquad\qquad (6.7)$$

to be the 'load-to-capacity' ratio that characterises the element of impact – consumption is sustainable when $\lambda \leq 1$, and unsustainable when $\lambda > 1$.

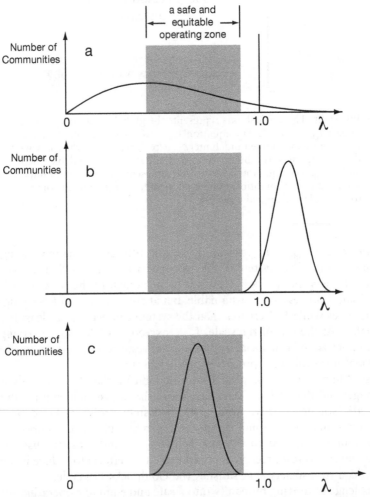

Figure 6.10 Convergence. In all three panels the horizontal axis represents the load-to-capacity ratio λ (Equation 6.7), and the vertical axis represents the number of local communities that operate at each value of λ. The curves show the distribution of λ aggregated over all of the communities that make up the global population. The grey rectangles represent the safe and equitable operating zone defined in Figure 6.9.

In Figure 6.10 we use load-to-capacity distributions to illustrate the convergence that is required for humanity to achieve a balance of consumption that is 'just right'. The distribution shown in Figure 6.10(a) represents the status quo, where many communities are impoverished, some seriously, while a wealthy few consume well above the sustainable limit ($\lambda = 1$). Figure 6.10(b) shows the unsustainable distribution that will result if humanity endeavours to reach the level of consumption currently achieved by the privileged few. This is the situation that will be reached if wealthy communities continue to consume at unsustainable levels while the rest of humanity works hard to achieve the same high levels of consumption. Figure 6.10(c) shows the distribution that will result if humanity manages to converge on the safe and equitable operating zone. The evolution required in this case involves increasing the impact of impoverished communities while reducing the impact of wealthy communities. How and when this might be achieved, in the face of rising global population and growing consumption world-wide, are crucial questions for humanity.

Consider the illustrative stock-and-flow map displayed in Figure 6.11. While far from complete, the feedback structure shown in this diagram indicates the kind of interactions that need to be considered by users of the extended Ehrlich–Holdren relation. The heavy curved arrows represent the simple cause–effect structure suggested by the surface appearance of the relation. That is, they show the dependence of social–ecological impact I on the variables P, C, and T acting together. The diagram makes explicit the feedback interactions expected between C and T, and indicates that both of these variables will be affected by changes in P. It shows that carrying capacity K depends on both resource levels and the per capita consumption of those resources. It shows also an outer feedback loop, whereby changes in I, acting through their impact on both resource levels and K, affect the way that P, and so I itself, change over time. The flow labelled *collapse* serves as a reminder that excess consumption can push resource stocks down below their sustainable levels. In the relatively narrow view shown in this diagram, and assuming that substitution is not possible, resource collapse will drag down carrying capacity K, and can lead eventually to population collapse (Figure 6.7(c)).

Even a cursory examination of Figure 6.11 makes it clear why human ecologists must be wary of silo thinking. Approaches to sustainability that focus exclusively on the challenge of stabilising population levels, or reducing per capita consumption, or the development of technologies that can 'save the world' are inadequate. There is no question that each of these challenges is critically important, and must be met in order to build sustainable societies. But, the behaviour characteristic of a social–ecological system emerges from feedback interactions between its parts (Section 3.1). It follows that the behaviour of such a system cannot be optimised by optimising the behaviour of its parts taken separately.

The causal model implicit in the extended Ehrlich–Holdren relation links social and ecological variables, and therefore potentially has great importance in human ecological research. Nevertheless, as pointed out by Ehrlich and Holdren (1971: 1212), "a great deal of complexity is subsumed in this simple relation" and there is always a danger that it will be interpreted simplistically. The adoption of a system dynamics approach, with its strong focus on feedback causation, can help to reduce this danger by countering the widespread 'loop blindness' that is a significant barrier to the development of sustainable social–ecological systems.

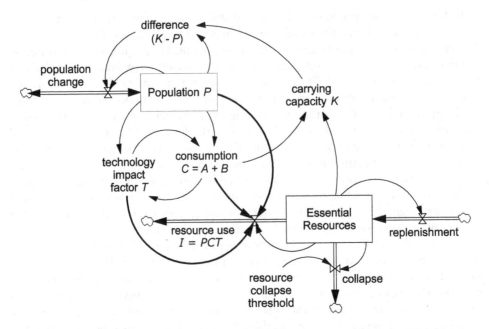

Figure 6.11 The extended Ehrlich–Holdren relation in a resource-use context. The heavy
arrows represent the causal structure made explicit by the equation $I = PCT$.
The causal structure shown here indicates some of the feedback interactions
that need to be considered in sustainability discussions. The diagram has the
same basic feedback structure as the generic stock-and-flow map shown in
Figure 6.8.

6.6 Conclusion

The global impact of humanity is the sum of many contributions, from many
communities, involved in many activities, drawing down many resources, using many
technologies. And the quest for sustainability is being pursued by many people,
exploiting many methods, guided by many worldviews, attempting to deal with many
challenges, misunderstandings, and conflicts. In the face of such operational complexity, it is obvious that there is a pressing need for diverse individuals and groups
to develop effective ways to 'think together' across cultural and disciplinary divides.
In Chapter 3 we discussed the nature of the required comprehensive conversations,
and outlined some of the barriers to effective communication. We stressed the need
to develop a priori shared contexts for cross-sector, cross-discipline communication
and, in Section 3.6, introduced the notion of 'powerful ideas' that can support the
development processes.

As outlined in Chapters 4 and 5, some of the required powerful ideas can be derived
from system dynamics, in the form of conceptual building blocks (stocks, flows, and
feedback) that are both simple and generic. The process of theory-building for human
ecology involves placing these context-free building blocks into social–ecological
contexts. One approach to doing this involves constructing stock-and-flow models
of basic feedback structures that are of importance in human ecology. Such models
include system archetypes such as Fixes that Fail (Section 5.4) and Limits to Growth

(Sections 6.3 and 6.4). Such a procedure has the added benefit of drawing attention to the dynamic complexity that can be generated by even simple feedback systems.

The process-oriented sustainability principles developed in Section 6.2 provide an example of the practicality of stock-and-flow thinking. These principles provide an operational definition of sustainability – a definition that can be easily understood and readily converted into prescriptions for action. A definition of sustainability based on process rates does not, of course, indicate that the monitoring of resource and pollution stock levels is unimportant. Significant changes in the levels of social and biophysical stocks are always signals of potential problems. For example, continued inequality can cause social unrest and rebellion; animal species can collapse if local population levels decrease to the point where average birth rates fall below average death rates; communities are in trouble when water reservoirs dry out. But managers cannot control stocks directly. The most that they can do, to paraphrase Brown's words in the epigraph, is to work to understand the rate limits of all processes essential to the functioning of their systems-of-interest and to attempt to operate within those limits.

Our discussion of the *Limits to Growth* system archetype sets the scene for a discussion of the original Ehrlich–Holdren relation and our extension of this relation to include a lower limit to human consumption. The Ehrlich–Holdren relation captures one of the essential invariances that are needed in a theoretical framework for human ecology. It is invariant in the sense that it can be used, without change of basic form, at different scales and different levels of aggregation. It can be used to think about the impacts of a community of any size, from an individual consumer ($P = 1$) to everyone on the planet; it is not resource or technology specific; it makes explicit the critical cross-scale links between individual actions and global impacts. The stock-and-flow version of the extended Ehrlich–Holdren relation, shown in Figure 6.11, gives a glimpse of the feedback structure that causes the dynamically complex behaviour observed in social–ecological systems, and indicates the key role that the relation can play in discussions of sustainability.

In this chapter we have put system dynamics to work in the context of a crucial challenge for human ecologists – namely, the development of a shared understanding of the nature of sustainable societies. We have done this to illustrate some of the ways in which ideas about stocks, flows, and feedback can support discussions of specific human situations. In Chapter 7 we extend our exploration to consider the strong resonance that exists between the aims of system dynamics and human ecology.

Notes

1 The notion of sustainable development was introduced by the World Commission on Environment and Development (1987). The Commission's publication, *Our Common Future*, is often referred to as the *Brundland Report*, after Gro Harlem Brundland who was chair of the Commission. Sustainable development was defined to be "development that meets the needs of the present without compromising the ability of future generations to meet their own needs". A more specific definition is: "A sustainable society is one that is far-seeing enough, flexible enough, and wise enough not to undermine either its physical or its social systems of support" (Meadows *et al.*, 1992, p. 209). These definitions are a step in the right direction, but they are too general to provide practical guidance for managers and policy makers.

2 A resource that has an immensely long regeneration time can be considered to be non-renewable. Coal, oil, and some groundwater stocks are examples.

3   This principle draws its name from a traditional children's story entitled *Goldilocks and the Three Bears*. One day young Goldilocks was wandering in the woods and came upon a cottage where three bears lived. The bears were not home, so she went inside. She finds three bowls of porridge on a table – a large bowl for Father Bear, a middle-sized bowl for Mother Bear, and a small bowl for Baby Bear. Goldilocks tastes the porridge in the large bowl, but it is too hot. Then she tastes the porridge in the middle-sized bowl, but it is too cold. Finally, she tries the porridge in the small bowl, and it is 'just right'. So she eats it all. As the story continues, Goldilocks tries the bears' chairs. She choses the baby bear's chair because it is 'just right' – but she is too heavy and the chair breaks. Then she goes upstairs and tries the bears' beds, finally selecting the baby bear's bed because it is 'just right'. She falls asleep, and that is where the bears find her after they return home. The baby bear complains so loudly about his empty bowl and broken chair that Goldilocks wakes, jumps out the window (yes, it's a second storey window), and runs home.

References

Brown, A.D. (2003) *Feed or Feedback: Agriculture, Population Dynamics and the State of the Planet*, Utrecht: International Books.

Daily, G.C. and Ehrlich, P.R. (1992) 'Population, sustainability and, Earth's carrying capacity', *Bioscience* 42 (10): 761–771.

Daly, H. (1990) 'Toward some operational principles of sustainable development', *Ecological Economics* 2: 1–6.

Ehrlich, P.R. and Ehrlich, A.H. (1990) *The Population Explosion*, New York, NY: Simon & Schuster.

Ehrlich, P.R. and Ehrlich, A.H. (1991) *Healing the Planet: Strategies for Resolving the Environmental Crisis*, Reading, MA: Addison-Wesley.

Ehrlich, P.R. and Holdren, J.P. (1971) 'Impact of population growth', *Science* 171 (3977): 1212–1217.

Meadows, D.H. (2009) *Thinking in Systems: A Primer*, London: Earthscan.

Meadows, D.H., Meadows, D.L. and Randers, J. (1992) *Beyond the Limits: Global Collapse or a Sustainable Future*, London: Earthscan.

Raworth, K. (2013) *A Safe and Just Space for Humanity: Can we live within the doughnut?* Oxfam Discussion Papers 2013. www.oxfam.org/en/grow/policy/safe-and-just-space-humanity.

Reed, H.S. and Holland, R.H. (1919) 'The growth rate of an annual plant *Helianthus*', *Proceedings of the National Academy of Sciences of the United States of America* 5 (4): 135–144.

Rogers, E.M. (1995) *Diffusion of Innovations*, 4th edition, New York: The Free Press.

Sterman, J.D. (2000) *Business Dynamics: Systems Thinking and Modeling for a Complex World*, Boston, MA: Irwin McGraw-Hill.

Wackernagle, M. and Rees, W. (1996) *Our Ecological Footprint: Reducing Human Impact on the Earth*, Cabriola Island, BC: New Society Publishers.

7 Towards a shared theoretical framework

[T]he term 'Human Ecology' has been around for at least sixty years, we have to admit that the subject is still characterised by considerable confusion and misunderstanding. ... it is high time that we made a deliberate effort to assess the state of our art ... and to move towards the development of a generally acceptable theoretical framework and methodology which will improve understanding of, and communication about the ecology of human situations.

(Boyden 1986)

7.1 Introduction

In the quotation above Boyden calls for "a generally acceptable theoretical framework and methodology which will improve understanding of, and communication about the ecology of human situations". This is a formidable and multifaceted challenge. A theoretical framework for human ecology must draw together foundational concepts and principles from a wide range of disciplines, cultures, and life experiences. It must help to define the nature of human ecology itself, clarify its relationship to other areas of inquiry, and guide the design of research projects. The construction of such a framework is clearly a major undertaking. Indeed, some practitioners believe that it is not possible to do so – that human behaviour is so complex and contingent, and the conceptual gaps between the required areas of knowledge and experience so wide, that human ecologists must inevitably labour under the weight of multiple, incompatible theories.

We take a more optimistic stance. All theories describe what are believed to be *invariant* aspects of the world. At the formal end of the scale, physics provides perhaps the best-known examples of explanations that capture invariance – powerful theorems such as Newton's Laws of Motion and the Second Law of Thermodynamics. At the informal end of the scale, every individual has private 'theories' (mental models) that embody their experience-based beliefs about the unchanging, and therefore reliable, aspects of the world. Early in life young children come to expect the Sun to rise and set each day, hot surfaces to burn their fingers, and to get wet if they run around in the rain. Adults add generalised beliefs about such things as human nature, the effect of political systems on the actions of politicians, and the behaviour of the stock market. It is true that 'theoretical frameworks' usually are more formal and organised than an individual's personal conceptual frameworks. But both kinds of framework serve the same function. That is, they summarise ideas about the things that can be relied upon to be more-or-less constant over space and time – invariant things that you can depend on to help you in your efforts to anticipate the future. These things include the basic cause-and-effect relationships, processes, and behaviours that you encounter over and over again as you move from one context to another, and from one day to the next. It follows that progress towards a theoretical framework for human ecology depends, in large part, on efforts to identify basic concepts that are held to be fundamental by researchers in more than one discipline – that is, on efforts to identify powerful ideas (Section 3.6). And there are many powerful ideas that are relevant to human ecologists. System dynamics is a rich source. Consider, for example, the system archetypes introduced in Section 5.4. These simple feedback structures can be described as 'invariances of organization' that can be relied upon to produce 'invariances of behaviour' across many different contexts.

Boyden's challenge is one that must be addressed if human ecology is to provide insights and guidance that can support efforts to build sustainable communities. In this chapter we take up his challenge and explore theoretical ideas that have the potential to support the development of a truly comprehensive human ecology.

7.2 System dynamics and human ecology

Boyden (1986: 8) describes six attributes of a theoretical framework capable of helping human ecologists to develop a comprehensive approach. Here we use his list to structure a brief discussion of the ability of system dynamics to play a key role in the development of such a framework:

> *[The framework] should provide a rational basis for organising information relating to different aspects of the culture–nature system under consideration.*

A social–ecological system can be looked at from many disciplinary points of view – the list includes physical, biological, ecological, technological, economic, institutional, and cultural perspectives. Information generated by people concerned with these different aspects of reality usually reflects the influence of different (sometimes incompatible) conceptual frameworks, and typically concerns different variables expressed in different currencies. The extent to which a theoretical framework can help to establish a rational basis for organising disparate data depends on its ability to establish an a priori shared context that links the disciplines involved (Section 3.6). System dynamics satisfies this criterion. It deals in conceptual 'building blocks' (stocks and flows and feedback loops) that are simple, low-level, and 'context free' (Box 7.1). Such building blocks can be identified with entities and processes that are of fundamental concern in a wide range of contexts, from the physical to the cultural. This identification, or 'instantiation', is a process wherein an abstract entity (for example, a stock) is given a context-specific name (examples include: amount of water in the tank, personal stress, population, and atmospheric CO_2 concentration). Once such identifications have been made, the named building blocks can be combined (like Lego® bricks) in a variety of ways to produce a huge range of more-complex, context-specific structures. Because of their versatility and focus on change processes, system dynamics concepts and methods can support efforts to develop a shared 'language of causation' – a language that will improve the communication between and within groups from different disciplines and sectors, and so help them to coordinate and blend information "relating to different aspects of the culture–nature system under consideration".

[The framework] should provide a structure for analysing, visualising and communicating about the interactions between the different aspects (natural and cultural) of human situations.

System dynamics methods are designed specifically to support the analysis of the interactions between the variables of feedback systems. The analytic processes involved in constructing influence diagrams, causal-loop diagrams, and stock-and-flow maps and models are intended to support the development of insights into the feedback dynamics of complex systems, and the formulation of dynamic (cause–effect) hypotheses to explain observed behaviour. The simulation of stock-and-flow models can bring the analyses to life, opening the door to exploration of the effects of changes in system structure and policy settings. System dynamics methods involve the use of visual representations to explain analytic thinking and dynamic hypotheses. These graphic representations, together with the use of simulation to explore the implications of dynamic hypotheses, provide a powerful basis for communication and the generation of shared understanding of causation (Chapter 3).

[The framework] should facilitate recognition and consideration of fundamental principles relating to the interactions between variables of different kinds.

System dynamics theory embodies fundamental principles relating to the interactions between variables. Many of these principles are expressed in the language of stocks, flows, and feedback (Chapters 4 and 5). For example, it is a fundamental principle of system dynamics that feedback loops must be accounted for in attempts to explain the behaviour of complex systems. A study of system dynamics theory and methods can help human ecologists become familiar with fundamental causal principles and adept in their application. Furthermore, the generic nature of system dynamics concepts means that these principles apply to variables of many different kinds. This generality is illustrated in Figure 5.17, which draws attention to selected interactions between key social, physiological, psychological, and biophysical variables. In this case the selected variables include atmospheric GHG concentrations, quality of building insulation, community focus on reducing energy use, extent of systemic urban planning and policy, capacity to adapt to higher temperatures, and motivation to learn about climate change.

[The framework] should encourage consideration of the full spectrum of variables which may be relevant in any particular situation under investigation. In particular it should (a) ensure that when a situation or a planning option is being assessed or analysed, consideration be given both to the state of ecosystems of the biosphere and to the actual life experience of human beings; (b) ensure that full consideration be given not only to variables of a tangible and easily quantifiable kind but also to psychosocial and intangible aspects of reality.

A system dynamics study typically begins with an attempt to identify the full spectrum of variables that may be relevant to the situation of interest. The variables identified are then sorted into those that will be included in the study and those that will be excluded. The included variables are further subdivided into those that are endogenous to the feedback structure under consideration, and those that are exogenous (Sterman

2000: 97). Dynamical systems theory deals with the relationships between stocks (state variables) and flows (state-change processes), and does so in a context-free manner. Thus, while a system dynamics study can easily encompass both human and ecological variables, it does not do so automatically. Boyden's criterion *a* (above) will be met by a theoretical framework only if it includes additional principles that mandate the inclusion of human and ecological variables (for example, as is done in Figure 6.11). Criterion *b*, on the other hand, is satisfied by the system dynamics framework as it stands. System dynamics was formulated explicitly to handle both tangible and intangible variables (Box 6.1). For example, any state variable (such as psychological stress or political will) that can be thought of as accumulating and draining can be discussed usefully in stock-and-flow terms.

> *[The framework] must encourage consideration of changes over time in the system under investigation as well as a sense of perspective with respect to rates of change and the scale of societal activities and impacts.*

The primary focus of a system dynamics study is the description and explanation of changes over time. Analyses of relative rates of change (including the size and dynamical impact of delays) are fundamental to such causal descriptions and explanations. In addition, because system dynamics building blocks are context-free, they can be applied at any scale. For this reason, systems dynamics methods provide an effective way to investigate cross-scale interactions.

> *[The framework] must be flexible. That is to say, while it must be useful in the organization of information and in communication, it should also encourage speculation and the formulation of new ideas; it must never dictate our way of thinking about human situations.*

We have already referred to the flexibility of the theoretical framework underlying system dynamics practice. This flexibility arises naturally from the fundamental, context-free nature of its conceptual building blocks. These building blocks can be combined in an unlimited number of ways to construct diagrams and models that support "speculation and the formulation of new ideas". We agree with Boyden, that a satisfactory theoretical framework "must never dictate our way of thinking about human situations", but we qualify this statement. A theoretical framework must, to a significant extent, dictate ways of thinking – otherwise it cannot guide research and planning and be tested for usefulness. What matters is that the theory does not dictate rigid approaches to the issues to which it is applied. The system dynamics framework satisfies these criteria. It specifies basic conceptual building blocks, and ways of combining them to build more-or-less complex structures, but places no limits on the actual form of those structures. Thus, it can provide a coherent, *general* approach to thinking about causation in complex systems, without dictating ways of thinking about the ecology of *particular* human situations.

7.3 Feedback-guided analysis – unravelling complexity

Anyone who tries to explain the behaviour of a social–ecological system faces a complexity dilemma. Such explanations must take account of the interactions between

Box 7.1 Context-free concepts

A theoretical framework's ability to support the development of shared under-standing depends on the extent to which its conceptual building blocks are seen as fundamental by people who work in different disciplines and sectors. Buildings blocks that satisfy this condition can be developed by identifying those entities and processes that are encountered in a number of different contexts and expressing their common properties in a generic, 'context-free' manner.

To clarify what we mean by a context-free concept, consider the difference between Figures 4.3 and 4.4. The explanation of stocks and flows built around Figure 4.3 is couched in terms of a concrete example – the accumulation of water in a tank and the flows that can change the amount of water accumulated. In other words, it is set in a specific context. On the other hand, the explanation presented in Figure 4.4 is presented in abstract terms. It involves flows and accumulation, but what is flowing and accumulating is not specified. In this sense, an explanation based on Figure 4.4 is 'context-free' and can be applied in any situation where it makes sense.

Consider two human ecologists, one of whom uses the abstract ideas conveyed by Figure 4.4 to discuss the effect of sales on an inventory of manufactured goods, and the other of whom applies the same ideas to discuss the effect of exercise on children's body weight. In the first case, $S(t)$ represents the manufacturer's warehouse inventory, F_{in} represents the rate of production, and F_{out} represents the rate of distribution to retailers. In the second case, $S(t)$ represents a child's stored energy (in the form of adipose tissue), F_{in} represents the rate at which food energy is ingested, and F_{out} represents the rate of dissipation of energy through exercise and autonomous physiological processes. While their interests and professional backgrounds may be quite different, these two people can use their shared familiarity with the context-free, stock-and-flow language of Figure 4.4 to build an under-standing of each other's basic thinking about cause-and-effect in complex systems. This, in essence, is the way that context-free building blocks can work to support the cross-disciplinary collaborations that are necessary in human ecology.

the parts of the system, but any attempt to account for all of the interactions will soon be defeated by the immense number of causal connections (Box 7.2). Indeed, it is often said that "in a complex system everything is connected to everything else", which seems to indicate that it is not possible to escape the complexity dilemma. But, in reality everything is not *significantly* connected to everything else. Experience suggests exactly the opposite. That is, the most important behaviours of even very complex systems can often be explained in terms of feedback interactions between a relatively small number of key variables (Walker *et al.* 2006; Richardson 2011). The discovery of system archetypes (Section 5.4) provides strong evidence for the existence of such dynamically dominant subsystems. From the point-of-view of policy makers and managers the challenge is to find ways to identify simple structures that, despite having few variables, can provide useful insights into the behaviour of systems with literally thousands of variables.

Box 7.2 The complexity dilemma

1   A feedback system is a set of parts (elements, actors) that interact to constrain each other's behaviour.

2   The behaviour of such a system emerges from the interactions between its parts.

3   This means that you cannot understand the behaviour of a complex system by studying the behaviour of the parts taken in isolation from each other.

4   You have to study the system as a whole.

5   But, when you try to do this, you become overwhelmed by complexity. It is then likely that you will either (a) study a small part of the system in isolation, and so miss critical cross-sector feedback effects, or (b) completely abandon your attempt to be systemic.

As a part of their exploration of ways to meet this fundamentalal challenge, Newell and Proust (2012: 13) have developed a three-stage modelling protocol that they call 'feedback-guided analysis'. Feedback-guided analysis can be thought of as a form of 'holistic reduction', a label that many will consider to be an oxymoron (a contradiction of terms). In system analysis there is always a tension between the need to be reductive and holistic at the same time. Feedback-guided analysis uses this tension to reduce the possibility that those working to create sustainable communities will lose sight of the real-world context of their endeavours, and become lost in a maze of details. Newell and Proust's basic idea is that, while the identification of simple feedback structures is necessarily a reductive process, this reduction is less likely to be misleading if it is carried out in a way that preserves the dominant interactions between the main subsystems of the wider system. Their process involves the following three steps:

Step 1 – Develop an overview template

An overview template is an influence diagram that describes a proposed mental separation of a complex system into component parts or subsystems. The way that system variables are grouped into subsystems depends on the particular aims of the analysis, and so will change as those aims change. The template diagram specifies (a) a set of high-level state variables, each of which is used to label a major subsystem that needs to be considered in the final analysis, and (b) the main feedback loops that involve these variables.

Consider the abstract representation of a social–ecological system that is shown in Figure 7.1(a). Typically such a system will have thousands of state variables and many more causal links – it will be far too complex to be understood as a whole. It is, however, always possible to separate a complex dynamical system into a set of related subsystems (Figure 7.1(b)). In the hypothetical case shown here it is assumed that three subsystems provide a useful, problem-focused representation of the system being analysed. The number of subsystems encompassed by a template depends on the nature of the overall system and the aim of the research programme. For example,

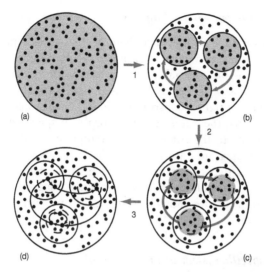

Figure 7.1 Feedback-guided analysis. In these sketches the small solid circles represent the state variables of a social–ecological system. The open circles represent system and subsystem boundaries. The curved arrows represent causal links, at various levels of aggregation, and the numbered heavy arrows represent the three steps of the modelling process. For clarity the causal links between the system state variable have been omitted in Panels *a*, *b*, and *c*. Panel *a* represents the whole of the particular social–ecological system under investigation. Panel *b* shows the template subsystems and feedback structure (as developed in Step 1). Panel *c* shows the problem space (as identified in Step 2). Panel *d* shows a specific system-of-interest (as defined in Step 3). In Panel *d* the solid circles representing the variables of the specific system-of-interest have been enlarged to emphasise the selected causal structure.

we suggest that it is useful, in any human-ecological study, to consider interactions between four major subsystems – culture, community, ecosystem, and human health and wellbeing (Section 7.5). In general, the subsystems will be complex systems in their own right, each with as many as one or two hundred state variables and its own complicated feedback structure. The feedback structure represented by the overview template is maintained throughout the analysis, thus ensuring that a broad cross-sector perspective is preserved, even as the focus of the analysis shifts to specific state variables.

It is essential to recognise that each of the overview-template variables stands for a cluster of system variables. Similarly, the causal links that are shown in a template diagram represent a bundle of specific links between a selection of the system variables. Given that some of the specific links in the bundle will have positive polarity and some will have negative polarity, it is not usually possible to assign a single polarity to the causal links of the template diagram. It follows that overview templates cannot be expressed as causal-loop diagrams or stock-and-flow models – their feedback structures can be presented as influence diagrams only. For this reason, plus the fact that each of their variables aggregates a cluster of system variables, overview templates can never be used directly to explain social–ecological system behaviour or to build quantitative models. They can, however, be used to constrain the diagrams produced in Steps 2 and 3 of the analysis.

Step 2 – Develop a problem-space diagram

A problem-space diagram is an influence diagram that gives a more focused view of the feedback structure specified by an overview template (Figure 7.1(c)). As the name indicates, the problem-space variables are selected for relevance to a particular problem situation or issue. They are still aggregate variables, but they represent subsystems that are more tightly constrained than the subsystems represented by the template variables. Thus, the names given to problem-space variables can be more specific than those given to the corresponding template variables.

The problem-space diagram must maintain the feedback structure of the overview template. This imposes two constraints: (1) each of the template subsystems must contribute at least one variable to the problem-space diagram, and (2) each causal link of the template structure must have at least one corresponding link in the problem-space diagram.

Step 3 – Isolate a specific system-of-interest (SSoI)

The final step in feedback-guided analysis is to project the problem-space diagram down into the domain of a specific system-of-interest (SSoI). An SSoI diagram is a causal-loop diagram that embodies at least one variable selected from each of the problem-space subsystems (Figure 7.1(d)). It must also have at least one causal link that matches each link of the problem-space diagram. Like its parent problem-space diagram, an SSoI maintains the feedback structure specified by the overview template, but may include additional system state variables and causal links.

The state variables of an SSoI diagram are not aggregates. They must be single, well-defined state variables whose behaviour over time can be observed and, ideally, quantified. Furthermore, the arrows linking the variables must represent separate, well-defined causal processes. An SSoI feedback structure that meets these conditions can be expressed as a causal-loop diagram (i.e., polarities can be assigned to its causal links). A well-defined feedback structure of this kind can guide the formulation of working stock-and-flow models, and so support investigations of the system behaviours implied by high-level dynamic hypotheses.

Unravelling complexity

The value of feedback-guided analysis lies in its ability to produce insights that meet the practical needs of researchers, policy makers, and managers. It is particularly effective when the subsystems identified in the overview template and the problem-space diagram are closely related to the sectors (or silos) recognised by a policy-making and management community. But, to what extent does it provide an escape from the complexity dilemma? After all, the progression from overview template, through problem space, to specific system-of-interest steadily narrows the focus of the analysis, and thus reduces its explanatory reach. This is an inevitable outcome of any reductive process. Feedback-guided analysis, however, has a number of characteristics that are designed to maximise its usefulness in practical management situations:

First, the use of an overview template creates a focus on endogenous dynamics, and overcomes the all-too-common invisibility of cross-sector feedback (Section 5.5). Such a template captures the sector-to-sector interactions that are hypothesised to play a dominant role in the behaviour of a particular social–ecological system. As long as this structure is preserved in the specific systems-of-interest, it ensures that cross-sector effects are taken into account in the detailed analysis. This means that, even if the SSoI models have very simple structures, it is always possible to use them to develop insights that are potentially valuable in the wider domain of real-world management.

Second, the use of a problem-space diagram ensures that the final analyses remain relevant to real-world management issues. In operations research it is recognised that an effective way to discover weak points in a commercial company's internal arrangements is to begin with a customer's complaint and track its causes back into the organization. In feedback-guided analysis, the process of developing a problem-space diagram plays much the same role. It focuses attention on management problems that, in many cases, prove to be symptomatic of more serious, underlying issues.

Third, the isolation of specific systems-of-interest facilitates the development of working system dynamics models. The construction of such models is possible only if state variables and state-change processes are unambiguously defined. A properly configured SSoI meets this criterion. While a tightly defined model typically provides a limited view of system behaviour, it does enable simulation experiments that can yield important, often surprising, insights into the potential impacts of policy and management initiatives. The relevance of such experiments is enhanced when the working models are problem-focused, yet manage to preserve the cross-sector feedback structures of the wider system.

Finally, as shown in Figure 7.2, there can be more than one problem space associated with a given overview template, and more than one specific system-of-interest associated with a given problem space. Thus, a thorough application of feedback-guided analysis can produce a set of related SSoIs. While experiments with each of these small subsystems may throw only limited light on the behaviour of the wider system, together they can lead to a fuller understanding of the whole. In particular, a search for similarities between the individual SSoIs can reveal the presence of feedback structures that are both simple and generic. Such structures,

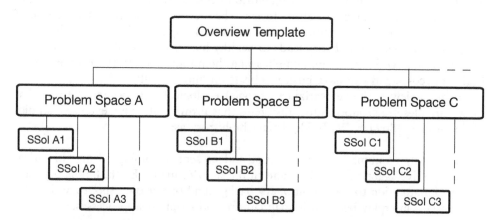

Figure 7.2 Hierarchical relationship between the diagrams produced by the process of feedback-guided analysis. This figure shows the progression from overview template diagram, to problem-space diagrams, to specific system-of-interest (SSoI) diagrams. This progression is one of increasingly tight analysis.

such as the system archetypes, have the potential to dominate the behaviour of the wider system. They therefore provide the basis for the formulation of powerful ideas, and so can lead to significant improvements in cross-sector dialogue and understanding (Chapter 3).

Crucial dynamical insights, about system stability and sustainability, can flow from the application of an approach that allows focused dynamical modelling to be carried out within a broad cross-sector framework. If your aim is to develop a fully detailed model of a social–ecological system, then feedback-guided analysis may not help. If, however, your aim is to promote dialogue and the growth of shared understanding between a group of people drawn from many disciplines and many walks of life, then the development of a set of specific systems-of-interest can be a powerful stimulant.

7.4 Boyden's transition framework

Feedback-guided analysis can help human ecologists to unravel the complexity of social–ecological systems. An indication of how this might work in practice will occupy us for the remainder of this chapter. Our approach builds on the 'transition framework' presented by Stephen Boyden in his booklet, *Our Place in Nature: Past, present and future* (Boyden 2011: Figure 2). Boyden's framework provides strong support for efforts to think and communicate about the behavioural changes that are needed if human communities are to survive in a rapidly changing world. In particular, it provides a useful classification of the state variables of social–ecological systems, and so can guide the separation of such systems into the subsystems required for feedback-guided analysis. Boyden also takes a first step towards useful dynamic hypotheses by specifying some of the main causal links that operate between these subsystems.

We start with Boyden's biosensitivity triangle (Figure 7.3). A 'biosensitive society' is one whose activities and societal arrangements are designed, first and foremost, to promote the health of all humans and of the ecosystems on which all life depends. By definition, the members of such a society understand the evolution of life on Earth, are attuned to the biology of the living world (including the biology of humans), and have a deep respect for life in all its forms. They recognise the utter dependence of humans on the continued, healthy functioning of the biosphere. The diagram illustrates the basic idea that biosensitivity leads to healthy humans and healthy ecosystems. It includes also a 'co-benefits' link, emphasising the notion that efforts to improve the health of ecosystems can have positive effects on human health.

Boyden's view of the key variables of social–ecological systems, and the way that these variables are grouped into subsystems, has grown out of his extensive studies of 'biohistory' (Boyden 1987). He defines biohistory as:

> The study of human situations, past and present, in biological and historical perspective against the background of the story of life on Earth. Biohistory pays special attention to the evolutionary background of our own species and to the constant interplay between human culture and biophysical processes.

Among the useful products of these earlier studies is Boyden's understanding of the health needs of humans and ecosystems. His working lists are reproduced here in Tables 7.1 and 7.2. The 'needs' listed in these tables are not state variables. Rather,

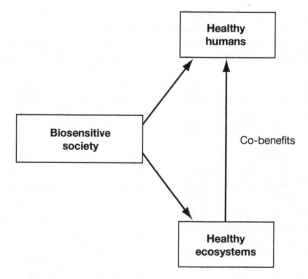

Figure 7.3 The biosensitivity triangle. "This diagram emphasises the fact that the ultimate objective in planning for a biosensitive society is the health of both humans and of the ecosystems on which they depend" (Boyden 2011: 43).

they are goals that a biosensitive society will strive to reach. The corresponding state variables must be expressed as quantities that can increase or decrease – that is, as stocks whose levels can be less than, equal to, or greater than their respective goals (Section 4.2). So, for example, the state variable corresponding to the need for clean air (Table 7.1) could be labelled *air quality*. *Air quality* is obviously an aggregate of a number of lower-level variables, such as *concentration of carbon monoxide,*

Table 7.1 Human health needs

Physical	*Psychosocial*
• Clean air	• Emotional support networks
• Clean water	• Conviviality
• Healthy (natural) diet	• Cooperative small-group interaction
• Healthy (natural) physical activity	• Creative behaviour
• Noise levels within the natural range	• Learning and practising manual skills
• Minimal contact with microbial or metazoan parasites and pathogens	• Recreational activities
• Natural contact with environmental non-pathogenic microbes	• Variety in daily experience
• Electromagnetic radiation at natural levels	• Sense of personal involvement
• Protection from extremes of weather	• Sense of purpose
	• Sense of belonging
	• Sense of responsibility
	• Sense of challenge and achievement
	• Sense of comradeship, affection, and love
	• Sense of security

Source: Reproduced from Boyden (2011: 47). See also Boyden (1987), Table 4.1.

Table 7.2 The health needs of ecosystems

• The absence of polluting gases or particles in the atmosphere that change the climate	• No ionizing radiation that can interfere with the normal processes of life and photosynthesis
• The absence of polluting gases or particles in the atmosphere which interfere with living processes (e.g. particulate hydrocarbons from combustion of diesel fuel, sulphur oxides, ozone)	• The absence of chemical compounds in the soil that can interfere with the normal processes of life (e.g. persistent organic pollutants, heavy metals)
• The absence of substances in the atmosphere (e.g. CFCs) that result in destruction of the stratospheric ozone layer that protects living organisms from the ultraviolet radiation from the sun	• Soil loss no greater than soil formation (i.e. no net soil erosion) • No increase in soil salinity • The maintenance of the biological integrity of soil (i.e. maintaining a rich content of organic matter)
• The absence of chemical compounds in oceans, lakes, rivers, streams, and reservoirs in concentrations harmful to living organisms (e.g. persistent organic pollutants, drugs and certain nanoparticles)	• Intact nutrient cycles in agricultural ecosystems involving the return of nutrients to farmland • The maintenance of biodiversity in regional ecosystems (including aquatic ecosystems)

Source: Reproduced from Boyden (2011: 48).

concentration of volatile organic compounds (VOC), and *concentration of ground-level ozone*. Thus *air quality* is a composite measure, and the extent to which it meets its target reflects the extent to which its component variables meet their targets. Similarly, the state variable corresponding to no increase in soil salinity (Table 7.2) could be expressed as *level of soil salinity*, with the corresponding goal set equal to the natural level of salinity in the region.

Boyden's lists of universal health needs provide a rich picture of the goals that would motivate a biosensitive society. His transition framework extends this picture, using the biosensitivity triangle as a structural foundation, to encompass the variables that affect a community's ability to meet these goals. As shown in Figure 7.4, these variables are grouped into ten major categories. Starting from the left-hand side of the diagram, the first two columns, under the heading *Human society*, show representative cultural and biophysical variables that can, in principle, be adjusted by a community. The third column shows examples of variables that measure the state of the biosphere. In the Anthropocene the values of these variables are increasingly affected by human activity. Some of the health needs of humans and ecosystems are listed in the final column (representing the variables shown in Tables 7.1 and 7.2). The arrows in the diagram indicate the most important causal pathways whereby human worldviews, decisions, and actions influence the state of human and ecosystem health.

Boyden's transition framework provides an excellent indication of the wide range of variables that are needed to specify the state of a social–ecological system. It must be recognised, however, that the framework is not meant to represent the feedback structure of such a system. As Boyden points out (2011: 43, footnote 14):

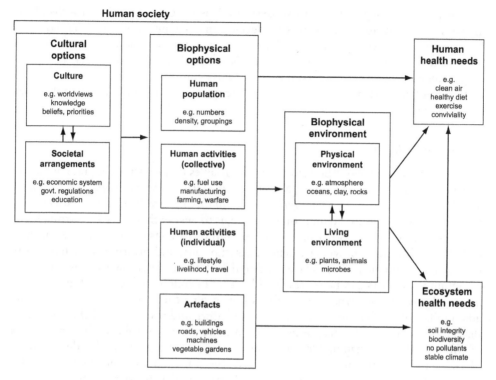

Figure 7.4 Boyden's transition framework.
Source: Based on Boyden 2011: Figure 2.

The fact that some of the arrows in this diagram are pointing only in one direction demands an explanation. It does not mean, of course, that there are no important feed-back loops in the system. However, this is not a 'systems diagram'. The direction of the arrows simply reflects our chief interest – namely, the important factors and pathways of influence, direct and indirect, on the health of humans and ecosystems.

The transition framework is, however, an ideal stepping-off point for the development of an overview template that *is* a systems diagram.

7.5 A cultural adaptation template

Some of the most pressing questions facing human ecologists relate to the evolution of society. A society facing social and environmental pressures can respond in a number of different ways. The choices made can have a strong influence on the society's eventual adaptive capacity and ability to survive into the future. In this section we describe an overview template that can support studies of the nature and impact of these critical decisions.

An overview template is an influence diagram that specifies a useful way to separate a complex system into component parts or subsystems (Section 7.3). The way that system variables are grouped into subsystems depends on the particular aims of the analysis. In this chapter our aim is to develop insights into the ways that societies learn from experience, with a particular emphasis on the evolution of human culture. This means that our overview template needs to specify a set of subsystems that will help human ecologists to understand and discuss cultural adaptation. We will refer to this feedback structure as our 'cultural adaptation template'. The template has four subsystems:

Cultural paradigms

In his transition framework Boyden classifies variables that measure the state of human society into boxes labelled *Culture, Societal arrangements, Human population, Human activities (collective), Human activities (individual)*, and *Artefacts*. Our first concern, in setting up our cultural adaptation template, is to ensure that there is a strong focus on 'culture'. Following Boyden, we define culture to consist of the shared mental models, worldviews, knowledge, beliefs, assumptions, and priorities that hold sway in a given community. The relative strengths of the different worldviews held by community members can be represented by a set of state variables that together play a crucial role in the dynamics of the social–ecological system. In particular, the adaptability of a community depends on the nature and robustness of the 'big ideas' that guide its members' perceptions, decisions, and actions. It follows that the success of efforts to develop sustainable communities rests, in large part, on the identification of conventional ways of thinking that have the potential to either help or hinder progress. While not always as formal or well articulated as the paradigms of physical science (Kuhn 1962), these modes of thought are based on powerful belief systems that we will call 'cultural paradigms'. Accordingly, we suggest that it is necessary to include a cultural-paradigms subsystem as part of our cultural adaptation template.

In our cultural adaptation template (Figure 7.5) we use the aggregate variable *State of Cultural Paradigms* to represent the cluster of state variables that measure the relative strengths of competing worldviews. While Boyden includes these cultural variables in the larger set that describes the state of human society, we place them in their own subsystem because of their dominant role in cultural adaptation. These are the variables that change first when a community learns – and learning from experience is the basis of adaptation (Holland 1992).

Community

We assume here that human beings play two key roles in a social–ecological system: as social actors within the community, and as living creatures within the ecosystem. Our second subsystem encompasses variables that relate to the social roles. These are variables of the type included by Boyden in his category *Societal arrangements*. Variables of this kind constitute our community subsystem. Depending on the scale appropriate to a particular investigation, the community referred to can be a small hunter–gatherer band or the whole of humanity. In a globally connected world, the community subsystem can include distant people and places.

The community subsystem encompasses a very large set of social, political, and economic variables. For example, the factors that Boyden considers include economic arrangements, legislation, structure of the workforce, institutions, the political system, and the education system. In Figure 7.5 this cluster of variables is represented by the aggregate variable *State of Community*.

Human health and wellbeing

An emphasis on human health and wellbeing is a defining characteristic of human ecology. Accordingly, our overview template must emphasise variables that measure the physiological and psychological state of the members of a given community, and their overall level of security, comfort, and happiness. This is another large set of variables. Examples include incidence of specific diseases, average levels of physical fitness, ability to acclimatise to weather extremes, stress levels, level of mental health, sense of purpose, sense of belonging, sense of security, and level of conviviality.

In Figure 7.5 this cluster of variables is represented by the aggregate variable *State of Human Health and Wellbeing*. The inclusion of a human health and wellbeing subsystem ensures that (a) a focus on the human condition is maintained throughout the analysis, and (b) the co-effects structure of the biosensitivity triangle is retained. Note that the variables included among Boyden's *Human Health Needs* (Table 7.1) are not state variables – ideally they are community goals.

Ecosystem

Our final subsystem is assumed to encompasses state variables of the kinds listed in the boxes labelled *Human population*, *Artefacts*, and *Biophysical environment* in Boyden's transition framework. These variables measure the state of the ecosystem that affects, and is affected by, a given community. Our inclusion of demographic and infrastructure variables in this subsystem requires explanation. As stated above, we assume that the ecosystem includes human beings in their role as living creatures. We take a community's ecosystem to consist of its 'natural environment' plus its 'built environment'. Our classification of the built environment as a component of the ecosystem follows the convention used in other-species ecology. For example, the ecosystem of the North American beaver (*Castor canadensis*) is considered to include the dams and lodges built by the beaver community (Jones *et al.* 1994; Moore 2006; Jones *et al.* 2010).

Once again we are dealing with a large set of variables. Boyden's list includes human population numbers, density, and groupings; buildings, roads, vehicles, machines, and vegetable gardens; atmosphere, oceans, clay, and rocks; soil, plants, animals, microbes, biodiversity, pollutants, and climate. The category can include variables that measure the extent of such landscape-altering artefacts as dams, sea walls, canals, levees, and swales. At small scales this subsystem will represent local ecosystems, at the largest scale it can represent the whole planet. The ecosystem of concern to a given community can include key components that are geographically outside the local area – examples include distant electricity-generation facilities and water storages that are part of irrigation schemes. This large cluster of variables is represented in Figure 7.5 by the aggregate variable *State of Ecosystem*.

Two notes in conclusion: first, Boyden's list of *Ecosystem health needs* (Table 7.2) refers to the natural environment only – the notion of 'health' is not useful in discussions of non-living entities. For example, concepts such as 'sick-building syndrome' refer to the impact of the built environment on human health and wellbeing, not to the health of the building itself. Second, the factors listed in the *Human activities (collective)* and *Human activities (individual)* boxes in Figure 7.4 are not state variables (stocks). They are state-change processes (flows) whose intensities (flow rates) determine the time it takes for human actions to impact the health of community members and their natural environment. These flows are represented by the arrows in Figure 7.5.

The cultural adaptation template

Our overview template is presented in Figure 7.5. It shows the four aggregate variables described above, and specifies the high-level causal links whose influence needs to be taken into account in studies of system evolution. The state-change processes associated with each link in the template are outlined in Table 7.3. The structure has four feedback loops, labelled *Social Effects*, *Health Effects*, *Environmental Effects*, and *Co-Effects*. The loops are identified and described briefly in Table 7.4.

Paradigm shifts

Links L2, L4, and L6 represent learning activities – that is, processes that result in paradigm shifts. Not all learning is beneficial – the processes represented by these links can be adaptive or maladaptive. Furthermore, it is important to recognise that the learning process is influenced by the paradigms themselves. As shown in

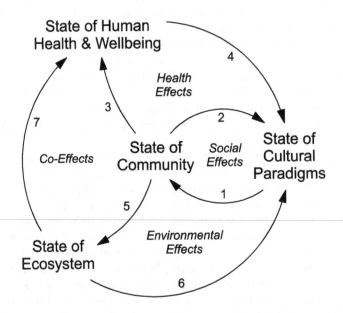

Figure 7.5 The cultural adaptation template. In this influence diagram the blocks of text represent groups of variables that measure the state of the major subsystems. The curved arrows represent influence links. Numerals are attached to the influence links for ease of reference – these numerals are distinguished in the text by prefacing them with a capital L.

Table 7.3 State-change processes of the cultural adaptation template

Link	Processes represented by the link
L1	Planning and goal-setting activities, driven by the community's cultural paradigms, that include the design and implementation of social policies and practices.
L2	Learning activities. Observation and assessment of the state and evolution of the community, and the modification of cultural paradigms to take these observations and assessments into account.
L3	Individual and collective activities, influenced by the state of the community, that directly affect an individual's physiological, psychological, and social functioning. Examples are listed in Figure 7.4 in the boxes labelled *Human activities (collective)* and *Human activities (individual)*.
L4	Learning activities. Observation and assessment of the state and evolution of population health and wellbeing, and the modification of cultural paradigms to take these observations and assessments into account.
L5	Individual and collective activities, influenced by the state of the community, that directly affect the structure and functioning of the impacted ecosystem. Examples are listed in Figure 7.4 in the boxes labelled *Human activities (collective)* and *Human activities (individual)*.
L6	Learning activities. Observation and assessment of the state and evolution of the relevant ecosystems, and the modification of cultural paradigms to take these observations and assessments into account.
L7	Natural processes whereby environmental conditions directly affect human physiological, psychological, and social states.

Table 7.4 Feedback loops of the cultural adaptation template

Loop	Links	Description
Social Effects	1–2	Links worldviews and community outcomes. A loop within society that can lead to cultural evolution as long as L2 is strong. This evolution can be either adaptive or maladaptive.
Health Effects	1–3–4	A loop within society that can lead to cultural evolution as long as L4 is strong. This evolution can be either adaptive or maladaptive.
Environmental Effects	1–5–6	A cross-sector loop that can lead to cultural evolution as long as L6 is strong. This evolution can be either adaptive or maladaptive.
Co-Effects	1–5–7–4	A cross-sector loop that can lead to cultural evolution as long as L4 is strong. This evolution can be either adaptive or maladaptive. The dynamical effects generated by this loop correspond to Boyden's 'co-benefits', but the use of the more general term 'co-effects' allows for co-costs as well as co-benefits.

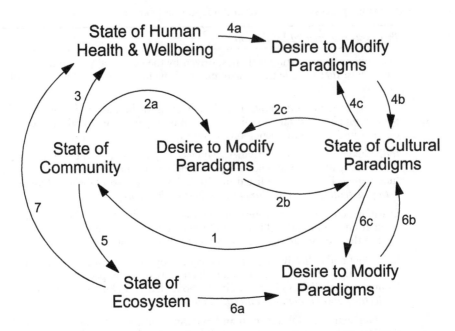

Figure 7.6 The learning links. This diagram is a version of Figure 7.5 modified to show additional structure in L2, L4, and L6. An intermediate variable *Desire to Modify Paradigms* has been inserted into all of these links, dividing them into 'a' and 'b' segments. Additional links, running from *State of Cultural Paradigms* back to *Desire to Modify Paradigms* have been added to allow for the influence of the paradigms on the learning process. These additional links are labelled 'c'.

Figure 7.6, the desire to modify a paradigm depends (among many other things) on both the assessments made of the relevant subsystem (via L2a, L4a, and L6a) and the community's attitudes toward those assessments. These attitudes are set by the paradigms themselves (via L2c, L4c, and L6c). When people are trusting, non-defensive, and receptive of new ideas, then the detection of unwanted situations in one or other of the major subsystems can lead to a modification (via L2b, L4b, and L6b) of the idea–action combinations that led to these situations. If people are, on the whole, suspicious of each other, defensive, and closed to new ideas, then it is unlikely that significant paradigm shifts will be made. Indeed, in many cases, unwanted outcomes will be unobserved or ignored.

Finally, a practical note. Paradigm shifts are essential mechanisms of cultural adaptation. This implies that cultural adaptation can be tracked through time by measuring the changing state of a community's cultural paradigms. But, how can this be done? How can one represent the state of a community's cultural paradigms? While 'idea stocks' are hard to visualise, one practical approach is to think of paradigms as pairs of stocks, where the level of each stock measures the number of community members committed to one of a pair of opposing beliefs. In the example shown in Figure 7.7, the left-hand stock represents the number of people who believe that unlimited growth is both possible and necessary, expressed as a fraction of the total population. The right-hand stock represents the number of people who reject the possibility of unlimited growth in a finite world, also expressed as a fraction of the total population.

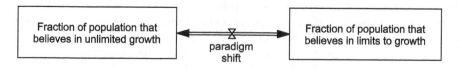

Figure 7.7 Paradigm shift. This stock-and-flow diagram shows a pair of stocks that together measure the relative strength of alternative paradigms. The bi-flow arrow represents the movement of people between the paradigms.

The sum of these two fractions is always ≤ 1 (the sum will be less than 1 if there are more than two dominant beliefs). The bi-flow labelled *paradigm shift* represents the evolution of community attitudes as people repudiate their old belief and embrace the alternative.

7.6 An example – technology choice and population health

An example of the way that feedback-guided analysis works is shown in Figure 7.8. We begin with our cultural adaptation template (Figure 7.5). The template is reproduced here as Figure 7.8(a). Once the template has been selected a problem-space diagram can be created. This process serves to focus the analysis on the particular challenge or issue facing the research or policy-making group.

In this example we develop a single problem-space diagram, which is displayed in Figure 7.8(b). We assume that the analysis is being carried out in the context of an investigation of the potential impacts of technology choice on population health. By 'population health' we mean "the health outcomes of a group of individuals, including the distribution of such outcomes within the group" (Kindig and Stoddart 2003). The use of this term signals a focus on diseases and situations that affect an entire society. Population health practitioners are concerned with chronic diseases caused by poverty, environmental conditions, and lifestyle. Their areas of concern include infectious diseases, malnutrition, respiratory disease, cardiovascular disease, obesity, diabetes, cancer, workplace injuries, environmental stress, and depression. To anchor our analysis on these broad aspects of human health and wellbeing, we replace the template variable *State of Human Health and Wellbeing* with the more-focused variable *Population Health*. This is our first step towards a useful problem-space diagram.

Technological innovation can have significant negative, as well as positive, effects on population health. This is why technology choice is a crucial population-health issue (Proust *et al.* 2012). The technology mix adopted by a community reflects a large number of individual choices. While some of the chosen technologies are bio-compatible (i.e., have beneficial effects both for human and ecological health), others are bio-incompatible. We therefore replace the template variable *State of the Community* with the problem-space variable *Bio-compatibility of Chosen Technologies*. This is our second step towards a useful problem-space diagram.

The technology mix affects population health via the processes represented by link L3. The cultural adaptation template tells us that, in turn, population health has the potential to affect technology mix via L4 and L1. To establish this connection we need to replace the template variable *State of Cultural Paradigms* with a variable that is commensurate with our chosen problem-space focus. We suggest that, in the context of our hypothetical study, a community's mindset can be represented usefully by the variable *Level of Techno-optimism*. Techno-optimism has become a basic cultural paradigm of modern society (Marx 2010). The more the members of a community believe that technology can solve all of their problems, the less likely they are to be concerned about whether or not a given technology has a negative impact on either humans or the environment. From the techno-optimist's point of view, it is always possible to counter such impacts with yet more technology (Huesemann and Huesemann 2011).

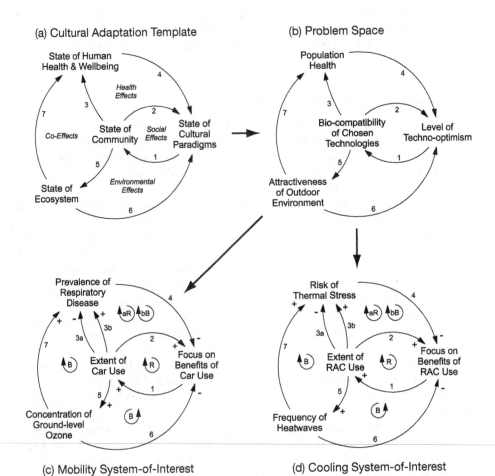

Figure 7.8 Technology choice and population health. An example of the kind of diagrams produced using feedback-guided analysis. The process ensures that the feedback structure of the cultural adaptation template is preserved down into the specific systems-of-interest. In the case shown, it also maintains the focus on the interaction between technology choice and population health that is established in the problem space. In diagrams (c) and (d) L3 has two components (L3a and L3b) with opposite polarities, causing the feedback loop L1–L3–L4 to be reinforcing if L3a dominates or balancing if L3b dominates. The acronym 'RAC' in diagram (d) stands for 'refrigerated air-conditioning'.

Techno-optimism introduces a bias into a community's assessment of potential innovations. It leads people to emphasise immediate benefits, and to downplay the possibility that the innovation will prove to be unsustainable in the long run. Widely adopted innovations can be extremely difficult to abandon in cases where they turn out to be unsustainable. Indeed, in cases of high dependence, it is not uncommon for negative impacts to be ignored or even denied. In adopting *Level of Techno-optimism* as our cultural variable we have taken our third step towards a useful problem-space diagram.

We have now established a problem-space version of the *Health Effects* loop. This loop runs from technology mix, to population health, to techno-optimism, and then back to technology mix (via links L3, L4, and L1). The cultural adaptation template indicates that there is a second causal path by which technology mix can affect population health. This path operates via L5 and L7 by way of a variable that stands for the template variable *State of Ecosystem*, and that is commensurate with the other three problem-space variables. It has long been recognised that human beings need regular contact with nature (Wilson 1984). Indeed, Louv (2011) has suggested that excessive separation from nature can cause a spectrum of unhelpful psychosocial impacts that he groups together under the non-medical term 'nature-deficit disorder'. Healthy ecosystems are pleasant places to be, even if they are highly modified urban green-spaces, and it is likely that time spent in them can have positive impacts on population health, social capital, and community biosensitivity. Accordingly, we have chosen *Attractiveness of Outdoor Environment* to correspond to the template variable *State of Ecosystem*. This is our fourth, and final, step towards a useful problem-space diagram.

Figures 7.8(c) and 7.8(d) are CLDs that represent two of the many specific systems-of-interest that could be derived from the problem space of Figure 7.8(b). The variables in each diagram map out a specific instance of the interactions between technology choice and population health.

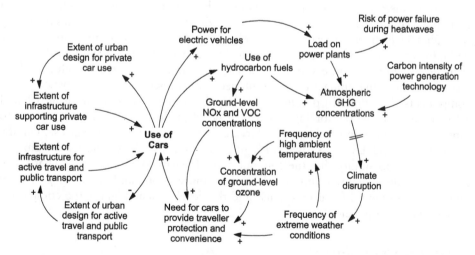

Figure 7.9 Some impacts of the widespread use of private motor vehicles. This causal-loop diagram should be compared with the mobility system-of-interest shown in Figure 7.8(c).

The mobility system-of-interest

The extent to which feedback-guided analysis is beneficial depends on how well the SSoI state variables are chosen. In practice, it is not possible to identify feedback structures that are both simple and dominant without first wrestling with the complexity of the wider system. A glimpse of what this might involve, in the case of urban mobility, is given in Figure 7.9. This causal-loop diagram illustrates a part of the complex web of interactions that characterise the use of cars in urban situations (see also Proust *et al.* 2012: Figure 3). The generation of a useful diagram of this kind requires a wide range of knowledge and significant cross-sector and cross-discipline collaboration.

The bi-lobed feedback structure shown on the left-hand side of Figure 7.9 is an instance of the Success to the Successful system archetype (Senge 1990: 385). The competition here is between urban designs that assume car use and those that support active travel and public transport. The structure shown on the right-hand side of the diagram shows some of the impacts that car use can have on air quality. All of the feedback loops shown in this diagram are reinforcing – a situation that drives a strong lock-in effect that works to promote (or amplify) the *status quo*.

The mobility system-of-interest shown in Figure 7.8(c) has been derived from a consideration of feedback structures such as that displayed in Figure 7.9. The relationship between the two diagrams is clear. The Figure 7.9 state variable *Use of Cars* corresponds to the SSoI variable *Extent of Car Use*. The variable *Concentration of Ground-level Ozone* is common to both diagrams. While Figure 7.9 includes competition between alternative cultural paradigms (represented by the Success to the Successful structure), it does not include interactions that impact population health. One of the advantages of feedback-guided analysis is that its rules ensure that these essential cross-sector interactions are maintained in the SSoI.

The SSoI shown in Figure 7.8(c) represents a strong dynamic hypothesis. First, it is assumed that increased car use will increase the concentration of ground-level ozone (L5) and that an increase in ozone concentration will increase the prevalence of respiratory disease (L7). Second, we assume that car use can exert both good and bad influences on the prevalence of respiratory disease. The good influences operating through L3a include protection of travellers from the effects of air pollution. The bad influences that operate through L3b include a lack of exercise, with a subsequent reduction in physical fitness and an increase in vulnerability to air pollution. In a given case the actual impact of the combined L3 processes depends on which of the components (L3a or L3b) dominates. Third, the feedback loop comprising L1 and L2 is assumed to be reinforcing – that is, a belief in the benefits of car use leads to more car use which, in turn, leads to a greater belief in the benefits of car use. Finally, the links L4 and L6 are shown with negative polarity. This polarity assignment expresses the possibility that the community will learn from experience. That is, an increase in the unwanted impacts of car use (more ozone and respiratory disease) will lead to a reduced focus on car use and the development of more bio-compatible technologies and policies.

The cooling system-of-interest

Figure 7.10 illustrates some of the feedback loops that characterise community dependence on 'refrigerated air-conditioning' (RAC).[1] Once again the bi-lobed

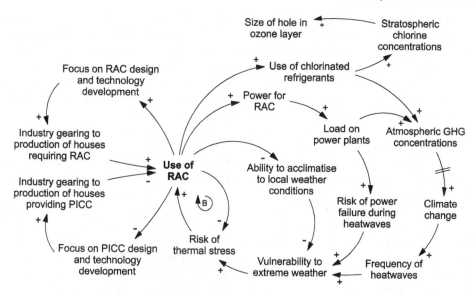

Figure 7.10 Some impacts of the widespread use of refrigerated air-conditioning (RAC) according to Katrina Proust (2012, private communication). There is a tight relationship between this diagram and Figure 7.8(d). The state variable *Use of RAC* corresponds to the SSoI variable *Extent of RAC Use*. The variables *Frequency of heatwaves* and *Risk of thermal stress* are common to both diagrams.

structure shown on the left-hand side of the diagram conforms to the Success to the Successful archetype. The competition in this case is between building designs that assume RAC use and those that support the use of 'passive indoor-climate control' (PICC).[2] The impacts of RAC use, shown on the right-hand side of the diagram, include a balancing loop that represents the health-enhancing effects of RAC use, plus a number of reinforcing loops that illustrate three of its negative effects. Once again, the dominance of reinforcing feedback effects leads to what we can call '*status quo* lock-in'. Taken together, the negative impacts of RAC are extensive enough to suggest that its use can be classified as maladaptive in the context of climate-change adaptation. By now, however, in many developed countries RAC dependence has grown to the point where it will be difficult to reverse. The same pattern of dependence is emerging rapidly in many developing countries (Isaac and van Vuuren 2009; Indraganti 2010; Winter 2013).

The SSoI shown in Figure 7.8(d) represents a dynamic hypothesis similar to that represented by Figure 7.8(c). First, it is assumed that increased RAC use will increase the frequency of heatwaves (L5). The extent to which this is true depends on the carbon intensity of electricity generation, and on the contribution that global RAC use makes to atmospheric greenhouse-gas concentrations. Second, we assume that an increase in the frequency of heatwaves inevitably will increase the risk of thermal stress (L7). Third, as in the mobility system-of-interest, we assume that RAC use can exert both good and bad influences on the risk of thermal stress. The good influences operating through L3a include processes that protect people from temperature extremes. The bad influences that operate through L3b include a loss of ability to acclimatise to local weather extremes, coupled with an increased risk of exposure to high ambient temperatures in the event of power failure caused by increased peak loads. Normally L3a will dominate, but there is always the possibility that the balance will shift dramatically to L3b during heatwaves, with catastrophic results. Fourth, the feedback loop comprising L1 and L2 is again assumed to be reinforcing, as RAC use leads to more RAC use. Finally, the learning links are again shown with negative polarity, expressing the assumption that the community will eventually recognise the dangers of RAC dependence and will decide to move to PICC.

The SSoI state variables (stocks) and state-change processes (flows) that are represented in Figures 7.8(c) and 7.8(d) are tightly defined. They can, therefore, be measured and represented in working system dynamics models. The development and simulation of such models provides a way to explore the implications of the underlying dynamic hypotheses and the possible impact of competing policy choices.

Crucial dynamical insights, about system stability and sustainability, can flow from the application of an approach that allows focused dynamical modelling to be carried out within a broad cross-sector framework. If your aim is to develop a fully detailed model of a social–ecological system, then feedback-guided analysis may not help. If, however, your aim is to promote dialogue and the growth of shared understanding between a group of people drawn from many disciplines and many walks of life, then the development of a set of specific systems-of-interest can be a powerful stimulant.

7.7 Conclusion

In this chapter we have explored the strong resonance that exists between the insights needed by human ecologists and those provided by dynamical systems theory. System dynamics provides a basic set of abstract, context-free, building blocks (stocks, flows, and feedback loops) from which to build a wide variety of causal structures and explanations. These building blocks, and the procedures required to assemble them into useful diagrams and models, constitute a shared language that can unite investigators from different backgrounds and intellectual traditions.

Collaboration across discipline and sector boundaries is necessary in any attempt to develop sustainable communities. As we have stressed, the characteristic behaviour of a complex social–ecological system emerges from the interactions between its parts. It is not possible to understand this behaviour, and thus anticipate how such a system might react to specific management interventions, on the basis of studies of the behaviour of its parts taken one-by-one in isolation. While detailed understanding of the parts is necessary, it is not enough. Studies of how the parts interact with each other are also essential in any effort to generate comprehensive approaches to policy making and management. It follows that such efforts require close collaboration between people with a wide range of experiences and worldviews. Such collaborations, in turn, require the shared understanding and clear communications that are made possible by an integrative theoretical framework.

In the five chapters of Part II we have collected a set of ideas, from cognitive science, system dynamics, and human ecology, that we believe have key roles to play in the development of the required theoretical framework. By themselves these ideas do not, of course, constitute such a framework – much work needs to be done to craft a properly structured approach. But, even in its preliminary form, the collection should provide a useful guide for human ecologists. This is our focus in Part III.

Notes

1 Here we are concerned with the use of refrigeration equipment to cool the interior of buildings and vehicles. We use the term *refrigerated* air conditioning (RAC) to emphasise this narrow focus, and to make it clear that we are not considering the use of reverse-cycle air-conditioners to heat building interiors.

2 We use the term *passive* indoor-climate control (PICC) to refer to the use of technologies that do not consume extrasomatic energy. Such technologies differ from *active* technologies, such as RAC, that do consume extrasomatic energy. Passive approaches to indoor-climate control include siting buildings to maximise opportunities for solar heating and cooling; building designs that include window shutters, louvers, wide eaves, porches, heavy insulation, and windows with multiple glazing; the use of breeze-ways and window designs for cross-ventilation to take advantage of prevailing winds; the use of vegetation, including lawns, trees, and roof-top gardens, to cool buildings and their surrounds. In Figure 7.10 we are concerned specifically with the use of PICC technologies to cool building interiors.

References

Boyden, S. (1986) 'An integrative approach to the study of human ecology', in R.J. Borden, J. Jacobs, and G.L. Young (eds), *Human Ecology: A Gathering of Perspectives*, College Park, Maryland, MD: Society for Human Ecology, 3–25.

Boyden, S. (1987) *Western Civilization in Biological Perspective: Patterns in Biohistory*, Oxford: Oxford University Press.

Boyden, S. (2011) *Our Place in Nature: Past, Present and Future*, Canberra: Nature and Society Forum.

Holland, J.H. (1992) *Adaptation in Natural and Artificial Systems*, Cambridge, MA: MIT Press.

Huesemann, M. and Huesemann, J. (2011) *Techno-fix: Why Technology Won't Save Us or the Environment*, Gabriola Island, BC: New Society Publishers.

Indraganti, M. (2010) 'Behavioural adaptation and the use of environmental controls in summer for thermal comfort in apartments in India', *Energy and Buildings* 42: 1019–1025.

Isaac, M. and van Vuuren, D.P. (2009) 'Modeling global residential sector energy demand for heating and air conditioning in the context of climate change', *Energy Policy* 37: 507–521.

Jones, C.G., Lawton, J.H., and Shachak, M. (1994) 'Organisms as ecosystem engineers', *Oikos* 69: 373–386.

Jones, C.G., Gutiérrez, J.L., Byers, J.E., Crooks, J.A., Lambrinos, J.G., and Talley, T.S. (2010) 'A framework for understanding physical ecosystem engineering by organisms', *Oikos* 119: 1862–1869.

Kindig, D. and Stoddart, G. (2003) 'What is Population Health?', *American Journal of Public Health* 93 (3): 380–383.

Kuhn, T.S. (1962) *The Structure of Scientific Revolutions*, Chicago, IL: University of Chicago Press.

Louv, R. (2011) *The Nature Principle: Reconnecting with Life in a Virtual Age*, Chapel Hill, NC: Algonquin Books.

Marx, L. (2010) 'Technology: The emergence of a hazardous concept', *Technology and Culture* 51 (3): 561–577.

Moore, J.W. (2006) 'Animal ecosystem engineers in streams', *BioScience* 56 (3): 237–246.

Newell, B. and Proust, K. (2012) *Introduction to Collaborative Conceptual Modelling*, Working Paper, ANU Open Access Research. https://digitalcollections.anu.edu.au/handle/1885/9386

Proust, K., Newell, B., Brown, H., Capon, A., Browne, C., Burton, A., Dixon, J., Mu, L., and Zarafu, M. (2012) 'Human Health and Climate Change: Leverage Points for Adaptation in Urban Environments', *International Journal of Environmental Research and Public Health* 9 (6): 2134–2158.

Richardson, G.P. (2011) 'Reflections on the foundations of system dynamics', *System Dynamics Review* 27 (3): 219–243.

Senge, P.M. (1990) *The Fifth Discipline: The Art and Practice of the Learning Organization*, Sydney: Random House.

Sterman, J.D. (2000) *Business Dynamics: Systems Thinking and Modeling for a Complex World*, Boston, MA: Irwin McGraw-Hill.

Walker, B.H., Gunderson, L.H., Kinzig, A.P., Folke, C., Carpenter, S.R., and Schultz, L. (2006) 'A handful of heuristics and some propositions for understanding resilience in social–ecological systems', *Ecology and Society* 11 (1): 13.

Wilson, E.O. (1984) *Biophilia*, Boston, MA: Harvard University Press.

Winter, T. (2013) 'An uncomfortable truth: Air-conditioning and sustainability in Asia', *Environment and Planning A* 45 (3): 517–531.

Part III

Living in the Anthropocene

Robert Dyball

In Part II we blended concepts from the natural, social, cognitive, and system sciences to propose elements of a unifying theoretical framework for human ecology. In particular, we developed a 'cultural adaptation template' that describes our view of the major subsystems that must be considered in any attempt to understand the culture-driven evolution of social–ecological systems.

In this final section of the book we adopt these theoretical ideas and make some preliminary application of them to complex modern society. This process helps us to explain how shifts in dominant cultural paradigms have brought humanity as a whole to the social and environmental conditions of the Anthropocene. These conditions are both unjust and unsustainable. The cultural adaptation template helps us identify the many interacting subsystems – social and environmental – that we are part of, and the influence that the dominant paradigms have in framing how we understand, and attempt to resolve, the problems that we face. However, core beliefs embedded in the paradigms that currently dominate the Anthropocene are wildly incompatible with environmental reality and social justice. Consequently, it is impossible for humanity to live well while these out-of-date paradigms continue to exert their influence. A shift to a new Paradigm of Biosensitivity is required if the ethical and environmental imperatives of living well are to be realized. With human cultures reinvented to produce a humane, sustainable, and worthwhile world, the Anthropocene becomes an era that we can celebrate.

8 Paradigms
Ideas that change the world

The first man who, having enclosed a piece of land, thought of saying 'This is mine' and found people simple enough to believe him, was the true founder of civil society.
(Jean-Jacques Rousseau 1754)

8.1 Introduction

In 1903, a skeleton of a 23-year-old male was discovered in the caves of Cheddar Gorge, Somerset, south-west England. Nicknamed 'Cheddar Man', the remains were dated to 9,000 years ago. At that time, the environment was dominated by dense birch woodland. Cheddar Man would have been part of a small community of hunter–gatherers, whose daily routine revolved around foraging for edible plants such as nuts, berries, and mushrooms, and hunting deer and other animals. These resources, with the intangible resources drawn from his community membership, were sufficient to sustain his physical and psychosocial needs.

In the late 1990s a direct descendent of Cheddar Man was identified by DNA matching. Amazingly, this individual was living barely a kilometre away from where the bones of his ancestor had been found. The implication was that closely related members of this family had lived in the same area for each of the 500 or so generations that separate the two individuals. Yet, although they are closely related, and lived in essentially the same environment with the same basic requirements for their health and wellbeing, neither would be able to survive for long in the other's world.

Culturally, Cheddar Man and his 1990s descendant are worlds apart. They are the product of very different cultural paradigms (as defined in Chapter 7). We cannot know the details of Cheddar Man's worldview, for no records survive from these prehistoric times. However, we do know that, whatever it was, it normalized an everyday lifestyle compatible with hunting and gathering in the particular environment in which he lived. Even though he would be perfectly adequate physically, his belief system would not enable him to function in modern society with its very different attributes of normal, everyday life.

Changing the environment is an inevitable consequence of being part of one, and all living things do it. Humans, however, legitimize how and why they act to change their environment in the way that they do by reference to the knowledge, beliefs, and values of their dominant paradigm. Paradigms and the societal arrangements that they influence are mutually reinforcing, so most community members will consider the state of affairs existing at any one time to be reasonably normal. Current social arrangements will appear to be the unchanging and unchangeable natural order of things. Undesirable aspects of those social arrangements, particularly those that do not directly affect the individual and their immediate peers, will often be seen as regrettable but unavoidable consequences of 'how things are'.

In reality, however, paradigms are evolving social constructs, and paradigms that are wildly incompatible with the health of ecosystems, or are ethically indefensible, or both, will have to change if we are to have a worthwhile, just, and sustainable future. This chapter explores changes in dominant paradigms across time by imagining Cheddar Man and his descendants at a series of time slices. Following Boyden (1987), we set these time slices as hunter–gatherer, early farming, and early urban. The Anthropocene – the world we live in today – is discussed in Chapter 9.

8.2 The original human condition: hunting and gathering

Paradigm of Respect for Nature

Our understanding of the paradigms of pre-literate peoples is based on what we can interpret from the few artefacts that remain from their time, including pictorial and physical representations of certain activities. To this we can add reasonably plausible ethnographic inferences drawn from what we know of recent hunter–gatherer communities. Cheddar Man would have held beliefs that helped him and his community make sense of, and find some order in, the world around him. These beliefs would have included explanations of what happens after death, as suggested by the respect all human groups seem to accord their dead. Artefacts and cave paintings from Western Europe of a similar era have been interpreted as evidence for belief in the power of magic to intervene in daily life. Magic rituals were intended to increase hunting success, and to ensure the environment's fertility, so increasing its capacity to support the community.

Whatever the belief system of Cheddar Man's community, we can be fairly certain it would have been compatible with environmental functions, because the health and wellbeing of a hunter–gatherer community depended on the carrying capacity of their immediate environment. If dominant beliefs led to activities that significantly harmed the environment, the community's wellbeing would be directly affected. Failure to learn and adapt their belief system to respect the realities of their environment would erode its carrying capacity and threaten their own survival. Consequently, we can assume the paradigm that dominated this prehistoric foraging community to be one of 'Respect for Nature'.

In labelling the dominant paradigm as being respectful of nature, we do not imply that these people saw themselves as living in 'harmony with nature', or as being 'conservationists', as we understand the term today. There is evidence that hunter–gatherers damaged environments, slaughtered animals in numbers far in excess of their food needs, and almost certainly contributed to the extinction of some species (Ponting 1991: 32–35). However, the hunter–gatherer's world was constrained by the rate at which basic ecosystem processes operated. Hunter–gatherers could not command the energy or technological resources required to significantly change the natural rate of these processes. Instead, they relied on their intimate understanding of how these largely unmodified environments functioned, and tailored their activities to fit the limits the natural processes imposed.

Hunter–gatherer communities

Our prehistoric hunter–gatherer community kept its impacts well below the threshold of the local environmental carrying capacity. There are a number of interrelated reasons. Foremost was their extremely low population numbers and density. Hunter–gatherer communities typically numbered around 20 to 40 individuals. The lower limit was partly a reflection of the increased efficiency of return-on-effort from working in groups (Smil 2008: 142). The upper limit was set by the land area needed to support the group. This limit depended in part upon the environment's natural productivity, but specifically the relative abundance of those essential resources that humans depend on. For food resources, the limit would be the seasonal availability of sufficient edible and culturally appropriate plants and animals to meet daily dietary needs. On average, the energy expended to secure these food resources had to be less than the energy returned from eating them – of necessity, the difference between energy gained to energy expended had to be strongly positive. A typical food procurement strategy was to seek a balance between (a) gathering small, but easily found, plant items such as nuts, berries, and seeds, and (b) targeting large, but less easily caught, animals (Jochim 1976). This basic strategy led to the essentially universal gender-based division of labour in hunter–gatherer communities. Female foragers typically gathered edible plants from an area relatively close to the base camp. As the location and availability of these resources was known with a high degree of certainty, their foraging expeditions were likely to be successful. Males typically explored a larger region, hunting animals. As animals move around, hunting trips were not always successful, but the food energy return would be very high when they succeeded. In both cases, the likelihood of food procurement strategies being successful was greatly enhanced by the group's detailed knowledge of their environment and of the behaviour of target species. The two activities complemented each other to produce a diversity of nutritionally adequate food that yielded considerably more energy than was expended acquiring it.

The community had to survive periods when the availability of essential resources was at a minimum. This led them to maintain stored reserves. The size of these reserves might have been set by the longest, harshest winter in their cultural memory. This focus on minimum stocking levels saw hunter–gatherers set their population size at 20 per cent to 60 per cent of their environment's nominal maximum carrying capacity (Smith 1992: 15). This 'risk averse' strategy created a large buffer that ensured, for the most part, that the inevitable fluctuations in essential resource availability did not manifest as hardship for the community (Equation 6.6 and Figure 6.9). As the abundance of resources in unmodified environments changes from season to season, foraging communities migrated in order to locate themselves where natural carrying capacity was highest. At times they deliberately overharvested resources from one part of the environment, causing localized collapse. They would then abandon that site for as long as it took for it to recover to pre-disturbance levels. This strategy has been termed 'patch disturbance' (Rees 2000), and depended upon the collapsed site not being revisited prematurely, otherwise the resource would eventually collapse irrecoverably.

To illustrate the carrying-capacity constraint an essential resource placed on hunter–gatherer population size, we take the case of deer hunting (Figure 8.1). For this activity to be sustainable, the deer herd had to be large enough for it to regularly

Figure 8.1 Deer hunting in the Mesolithic.
Source: © Museum of London.

lose members to human predation, among other causes, without approaching its collapse threshold (Figure 6.7). Box 8.1 provides discussion of the relative sizes of human and deer populations, assuming a hunter–gatherer band whose key resource was hunting deer in a largely unmodified birch woodland landscape. A population density of around 1 person per 50 square kilometres is in the mid range of hunter–gatherer communities, and typical of communities living in environments with relatively low human carrying capacity (Smil 2008: 140). Changes in human population numbers are suppressed through social rules governing who is eligible to reproduce, prolonged periods of fertility-reducing lactation in women, and infanticide.

Hunter–gatherer communities did not have high levels of material consumption. The social hierarchy was generally flat, with status relating to age, special knowledge, and wisdom, or to particular skill or prowess. Social status was not usually related to the possession of large quantities of material goods. This is one of the reasons that the volumes of resources owned or consumed by different members of society was not high (see also Figure 8.2, Loop B3). The artefacts the community did possess were mostly organic in origin, derived from wood and other plant material, and from the skins and bones of animals. Their manufacture and post-use disposal had only a minor and transitory impact on the environment.

Hunter–gatherer technology helped increase the efficiency of their resource use and expand the range and type of resources that they could access. Appropriate clothing and shelter allowed humans to forage in a wide range of environments, including in climatic conditions that they could not otherwise tolerate. Sealed pots allowed the storage of resources beyond their inherent lifespan. The means of preserving goods, such as smoking and drying, allowed resources to be overharvested when they were plentiful, and consumed in lean periods. Technology also helped overcome procurement limitations. For example, the manufacture of snow shoes enabled foraging at

---

Box 8.1 Deer predation

Consider a group of 20 hunter–gatherers living in a birch woodland. We assume that their diet comprises about 50 per cent ungulate meat, with the balance from hazelnuts, berries, and other gathered plant matter (McMichael 2001). With a daily energy target of about 10 megajoules, this suggests about 500 grams of meat consumption per person per day. However, the key resource is the energy-dense animal fat. Lean meat has a relatively low energy content and requires higher levels of consumption for an equivalent energy intake. Given that an animal's fat reserves will vary with the seasons, the number of animals killed will also vary seasonally. Because 50 per cent of a carcass is inedible – the hides, antlers, and bones were valued for other purposes, but not food – our 20 hunter–gatherers needed to catch 20 kilograms of ungulate a day to deliver the required 10 kilograms of meat.

We further assume that the target species was roe deer (*Capreolus capreolus*). This is a fairly small deer endemic to Europe, and whose remains are commonly associated with archaeological sites of this era. Roe deer weigh around 30 kilograms, so one would provide 15 kilograms of meat, enough for our group for a day and a half. In a year, at least 245 animals would need to be killed to supply the dietary needs of the community. Increasing this number by 10 per cent to compensate for the limited value of lean meat when the creature's fat reserves are low gives a target of around 270 animals a year.

The deer population can lose 5 per cent of its members per year to human predation without reaching its collapse threshold. This suggests a parent herd of 5,400 animals. However, the hunters' 'risk averse' strategy sets a buffer at 50 per cent of this number, so it adjusts to 10,800 animals. Roe deer densities are low in a birch woodland, about seven animals per square kilometre. It follows that 10,800 animals will occupy an area of around 1,500 square kilometres. Our group of 20 humans then needs to hunt in a territory of 1,500 square kilometres (39 × 39 kilometres) in order to sustain themselves. This is an area roughly equivalent to that of modern cities such as London, Beijing, São Paulo, Mexico City, or Los Angeles. These cities host populations in their millions, with densities of thousands of people per square kilometre. Yet as an unmodified environment, the same area has a carrying capacity for a population density of around one person per 50 square kilometres (Adapted from Cordain *et al.* 2000).

---

times when snow would otherwise make it impossible (Smil 2008: 140). Aids to procurement, such as traps, bows and arrows, and digging sticks, extended the range of access to resources. In some cases, the development of a new technology could turn an aspect of the environment into a resource for the first time. For example, a dugout canoe and a barbed spear could make a fish species catchable, which might have been impossible for swimmers with bare hands. All these technological benefits came at a cost of manufacturing time, material, and energy. Such benefits could be delivered only if the community had both the required manufacturing and artefact-use knowledge and skills.

Fire might be thought of as a special category of technology available to humans. Fire was the main source of extrasomatic energy available to foraging communities. Extrasomatic energy is energy derived from processes external to the human body, as distinct from energy derived from the metabolism of food (the source of muscle power). Fire gave the community a source of light, the means of heating and cooking, and a degree of protection against predators. Hunter–gatherers also used fire to manipulate plant and animal communities. This included creating or extending habitats required by certain target species, such as deer. Hazel trees are fire resistant, so over time would tend to benefit (compared with more fire-sensitive plants) from the deliberate use of fire – consequently burning increased the availability of hazelnuts. Using fire to clear undergrowth would help ease movement through the forest, and the hunter's ability to detect prey, with the added advantage that the regrowth would be attractive as food for that prey. Fire was the one source of energy that was available to hunter–gatherers to at least semi-permanently alter the state of their environments. Consequently, the impacts that hunter–gatherers had on the environment was their own consumption of food and materials, multiplied by the energy of the fire they employed. In terms of the extended Ehrlich–Holdren relation, $I = PCT$ (Section 6.5), the use of fire increases T (the technology impact factor). This increases environmental impact (I) both directly and via its effect on consumption (Figure 6.11).

State of ecosystem health

The prehistoric hunter–gatherer community's low population density, low level of possessions, and basic technology combined to ensure a very low impact on the local environment. Sieferle (2001: 8) summarizes their lifestyle as 'characterised by humans tapping ever more efficiently into energy flows. But in contrast to agricultural society they did not reconfigure these energy flows. Therefore, it is possible to speak of a regime that utilised unmodified and uncontrolled solar energy'. Other than the multiplier of fire, the environmental impacts of our foraging community are similar to those of any large, opportunistic omnivore. In ecological terms their maximum impacts were kept either below the threshold of significant change, or well within the resilience of the ecosystem to recover from their presence.

State of human health and wellbeing

The relative ease with which hunter–gatherers seem to have been able to provision themselves from their environments has seen them termed the 'original affluent society' (Sahlins 1968). With few demands on their time, once their subsistence requirements were met, they are envisaged as having abundant leisure time to engage in important social and cultural pursuits, such as storytelling, ritual and ceremony, and music. This perhaps downplays the potential vulnerability of the community – especially when surviving in strongly seasonal regions, where key resources became unavailable for prolonged, and sometimes unpredictable, periods. However, the non-hierarchical nature of the community would suggest that any hardships that were suffered were suffered reasonably equally by all. If there were periods when an individual was cold, wet, or hungry, then so too would be their peers.

Trauma and subsequent infection would have been a major cause of death, and debilitating, but non-fatal, parasitic infections would have been common. Anything that caused significant incapacitation would likely have been fatal, although there is archaeological evidence of individuals being nursed to recovery. Pragmatic limits may have been placed on how long the infirm or chronically disabled were supported by the community. Average life expectancy was short, around 25 years, although individuals were capable of living to significant old age. Nevertheless, life in prehistoric foraging communities has been described as 'the healthiest time that humans have ever experienced' (Sieferle 2001: 8).

The psychosocial health needs of the community would have been met most of the time (Table 7.1). Community members would have been part of a care giving and receiving network, to which they would have felt a strong sense of belonging. They would definitely have had a wide variety of daily experiences, including a range of interesting challenges – some of which were no doubt dangerous. They would have had regular involvement in creative activities, and practised learned manual skills every day. The near-identical technique for manufacturing flint tools at any one time and place demonstrates that this was a highly refined skill requiring significant training, presumably passed on from the elders. There is no evidence of endemic violence in such communities, although punishment for transgressing rules may have been harsh. Suspicion of strangers seems universal, and raids perhaps occurred, especially during lean periods. However, the very low population densities would limit how often communities unintentionally encountered each other.

Human–environment interactions

The Paradigm of Respect for Nature, a willingness to adapt human activity and numbers to resource availability, and the practice of physically relocating the community to where those resources were most abundant resulted in a series of balancing feedback loops that ensured human impact was well within the seasonal carrying capacity of the ecosystem (Figure 8.2).

The first feedback loop, B1 'Adapt', describes how willingly hunter–gatherers adapted their behaviour to seasonally driven changes to the environment's carrying capacity, in order to avoid the hardship that they would otherwise experience. This adaptation is primarily driven by multi-generational cultural learning that modifies the dominant paradigm so that the community favours practices that limit its impact on the environment. These impacts, whose magnitude can be estimated using the relation $I = PCT$ (Section 6.5), are labelled *Size of extended human metabolism* in Figure 8.2. With small population numbers, levels of affluent consumption barely different to levels of base consumption, and low-impact technology, I (impact) is very small. That is, I is well below $IMAX$ in part due to a risk-averse lifestyle geared to high levels of buffering against long-term fluctuations in levels of carrying capacity (Figure 6.9). Consequently, satisfying the demands of the community's extended metabolism does not erode key resources and so does not reduce future carrying capacity (Figure 6.7).

A second loop, B2, focuses on the historical evolution of the Respect for Nature paradigm. Over time, activities that resulted in hardship led to an increasing understanding of the limits on the rate of resource-use imposed by natural rates of replenishment (Figure 6.1). This understanding would gradually be encoded into individuals' mental models and eventually into cultural traditions of understanding. These modified belief systems resulted in activities that respected environmental

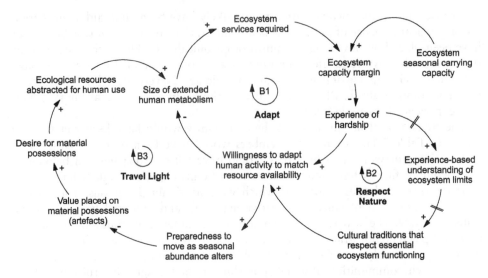

Figure 8.2 Prehistoric hunter–gatherers. Three balancing feedback loops that serve to maintain a stable relationship between a prehistoric hunter–gatherer community and the environment.

limits, and the processes that maintained healthy ecosystem functioning, and so helped the community avoid resource-collapse thresholds. Where generations of hunter–gatherers existed in the same environment, the actual experience of hardship was largely replaced by a knowledge system that allowed them to avoid, or at least minimize, hardship. In some ways the experience of hardship becomes an archaeological relic, while the related understanding and respectful values remain enshrined in the Paradigm of Respect for Nature. In systems terms, hardship became part of a balancing feedback loop that acted to maintain traditional values and understanding, but was itself largely avoided.

The need to move regularly, to fresh areas, also played a key role in a community's behaviour, as illustrated in Loop B3 'Travel Light'. The influence on behaviour flows from a willingness to self-limit, and shows that, as levels of essential resources declined in one location, the community was prepared to migrate away from the area. This need for mobility tended to suppress the value placed on material possessions. The variable *Desire for material possessions* is positively correlated with the amount of resources extracted for human use, which in turn correlates with the material and artefact component of the extended human metabolism. Thus, in the hunter–gatherer community, this self-balancing loop dampened material demand in favour of the ability to 'travel light'. Together, the three balancing feedback loops served to maintain a stable relationship between hunter–gatherer communities and the environment, while they maintained their health and wellbeing at adequate levels.

This generic portrayal of hunter–gatherers captures some of the essential features of a human community that is utterly dependent on local renewable resources. The demands placed on key resources would have necessarily obeyed the principles of sustainability (Section 6.2). If the rate of essential resource use exceeded the rate of resource replenishment, then the consequences for the offending population would have been fairly immediate, and decidedly negative. Evidence from extant hunter–gatherer populations shows that the key mechanisms for maintaining their health and wellbeing within local resource carrying capacity were cultural. That is, knowledge-based understanding of the productive capacity of local environments, coupled with cultural mechanisms that reinforced values, beliefs, and judgements controlled behaviour such that the rate of resource use stayed well below local thresholds for collapse. This does not mean that humans were passive in relation to their environments. Hunter–gatherers typically had elaborate sets of obligations and activities that required them to manage environments in particular ways. But these duties were for the co-benefit of ecosystem and human wellbeing, and did not trade off one for the other.

The total economy of hunter–gatherer bands was very small. However, population density and levels of consumption may well have been as large as could be sustained by hunter–gathering. For the human economy to grow larger, a fundamental change in resource procurement strategies was required. This was delivered by the transition to farming.

8.3 The evolution of agriculture

Paradigm of Ownership and Control of Environments

It has been said that hunters own the animals they kill – farmers own the land the animals live on. Hunter–gatherer and early farming societies represent fundamentally different social–ecological systems. The processes of production, distribution, and consumption by which resources are made available to community members in societies based on agriculture are governed by new social institutions, which generate larger resource demands and significantly alter the environment. Completely new paradigms evolved to explain, legitimize, and normalize these novel practices. Collectively, we label these the 'Paradigm of Ownership and Control of Environments'.

It is impossible to say exactly why there was a shift to this new paradigm. The changes that occurred as a consequence of adopting a farming lifestyle, such as large populations, social hierarchies, work specialization, urbanization, empires, conquering armies, and so forth, could hardly have been foreseen. Nor would members of a hunter–gatherer community have necessarily thought these new arrangements a good idea, even if they could have predicted them. However, for a variety of possible reasons, about 10,000 years ago practices that would ultimately transform humanity's relationship to the earth began to evolve, seemingly independently, at a number of sites across the globe.

The switch, from hunting and gathering to farming, involved a gradual intensification of the extent of human manipulation of the environment. There is no definitive point, no specific time, at which humans became farmers. Indeed, many foraging practices would have continued, and some are still in evidence today – for example, recreational fishing. Hunter–gatherers used fire to maintain clearing, and to encourage certain plants and animals to proliferate at the expense of other species that were of less use to them. At the margins, there is a fine distinction between this kind of activity and the more systematic selection and sowing of seeds, and the enclosure of animals for breeding and eventual domestication that are the hallmarks of agriculture (Jochim 1976). Cheddar Man and his compatriots would have been unaware that the first steps towards these agricultural practices were already being taken while they were still foraging in woodlands. However, the spread of agriculture from the Near East (in what is now Syria), would not reach Cheddar Man's descendants for two to three thousand years. This was in part because the land area they occupied was gradually cut off from the rest of the European continent by rising sea levels.

There is considerable debate about exactly when and how agriculture entered England. However, dates of 5,500 to 5,000 years ago are given for early farming settlements (Wymer 1991: 58). Novel resources, such as cattle, sheep, wheat, and barley were all originally domesticated elsewhere and imported. However, this does not mean that European farmers physically invaded the region to establish agriculture. It is plausible that once one community embarked on the pathway towards agriculture, the increased demand that the practice had for labour would be self-reinforced by the larger populations it could support. Over time, this feedback effect would see areas converted to agriculture as populations, and resource demands, grew. Further growth would require subgroups to split off and colonize new territories within which to establish agriculture. This 'wave of advance' would result in gradual encroachment of farmers into areas that were managed by low-density populations of hunter–gatherers (Pryor 2006: 30). Quite literally, farming communities would eventually be able to 'muscle out' hunter–gatherer communities simply by numerical strength, in a Success to the Successful feedback effect.

It also seems likely that the idea of farming could have spread by observation and copying from one community to another. The unbroken genetic line from Cheddar Man to the present indicates that his descendants were not displaced, but simply adopted new practices. Whatever the mix of 'conquest' and 'copy' mechanisms, the Paradigm of Ownership and Control of Environments gradually displaced the Paradigm of Respect for Nature. To look at the influence of this paradigm on social–environmental systems, we jump forward some 300 generations from Cheddar Man to imagine the everyday life of his descendants, living around 2,500 years ago in an Iron Age farming community.

Agricultural communities

Unlike hunter–gatherers, agricultural communities cannot sustain themselves within the limits of the natural carrying capacity of their local environments. Instead, they must undertake a range of activities in order to increase the replenishment rate of essential resources. The energy of fire continued to be employed for tasks such as clearing and speeding up nutrient recycling by, for example, burning stubble. However, the main additional source of energy available to the community to modify natural flow rates was the somatic energy of its members. Population numbers increased dramatically. These higher population numbers were supported by the increased yields of food and other essential resources obtained from the human-modified landscapes. At the same time the amount of hard, energy-intensive labouring each member undertook increased. In time, the somatic energy of human bodies was augmented by the somatic energy of draught animals.

The efficiency with which somatic energy, both human and animal, could be harnessed depended on what artefacts were used. It is impossible to maintain an ecosystem for agricultural output without tools such as axes, sickles, ards (a primitive kind of plough), and harnesses to yoke animals. With such tools, and the knowledge

Figure 8.3 A reconstruction of an Iron Age farming community (Butser Ancient Farm).
Source: © Peter J. Reynolds by kind permission of Christine Shaw.

and skills to use them, agricultural communities could significantly increase the carrying capacity of the environments that they controlled. The actual carrying capacity would, of course, be strongly influenced by the climate and underlying productivity of the natural environment, but with the technology available to Iron Age farmers, population densities of eight people per square kilometre could be estimated (Mazoyer and Roudart 2006). The 1,500 square kilometres that had a carrying capacity of 20 hunter-gatherers could now support around 600 times that number.

Iron Age communities were based on kinship groups living in relatively small settlements of roundhouses, surrounded by pastures for livestock, fields of cereal, and managed woodlands (Figure 8.3). Ownership of territory was sharply delineated, and neighbouring hamlets were connected by networks of tracks. Trade and social interchange, sufficient to establish strong friendships and inter-hamlet marriage, passed along these routes. But the presence of forts and perimeter defences indicate that relations were not always friendly. Although community structure remained fairly egalitarian, a more complex hierarchy was starting to develop. This is partly because, in order to function, a society based on agriculture must possess social mechanisms that can effectively coordinate the activities required to convert natural environments to agricultural ones, harvest the produce, and apportion resources among members of the community. Crucially, for a sedentary community, this coordination includes ensuring that sufficient food reserves are maintained. Levels of production are high for a few months only, and the community needs reserves to draw upon during the lean months.

Over time the move to farming led to a more complex social hierarchy, and eventually to an agrarian economic system in which wealth, power, and social status ultimately derived from the ability to control the output of agricultural landscapes. Increasing social complexity is in part a response to the administrative challenges of managing farming-based societies, but one that generates additional resource demands of its own (Tainter 1988). Social status and power flowed also to those holding religious office. Members of the community who wanted to demonstrate their status could do so through the greater material possessions that they owned. This included energy and resource-intense possessions, such as jewellery, that had no direct-use value. Specialized skills, such as metalworking, emerged. Consequently, not only were population numbers higher than for hunter–gatherer communities, but average per capita consumption was higher, and started to become less evenly distributed across the community. Once the community became dependent on successful harvests, rituals were undertaken to ensure that every harvest was good. It has been suggested that this marked a change in belief systems from seeing nature as bountiful, if properly respected, to one that saw nature as capricious, unless coerced or dominated.

The basic needs of the community as a whole, including farm animals, and the additional demands of 'affluence', drew upon the productivity of the environment they occupied. This limited the rate at which resources could be extracted, and consequently the rate at which material possessions could be accumulated. For example, the energy required to smelt a tonne of iron could be derived from around 75 tonnes of wood, the sustained output of around 10 hectares of coppiced woodland permanently devoted to that purpose. Consequently, the amount of iron the community produced was tied both to the amount of iron ore in the environment it controlled, and the replenishment rate of the wood needed to produce the energy required for the smelting process (see Box 8.2).

Societies based on agriculture remained bound by the rate at which plants photosynthesize biomass. Agriculturalists can determine what grows in their environments, but they cannot increase solar energy flows or the rate of biometabolism. The rate at which a tree produces new wood depends on the species, the environment, and the prevailing climatic conditions. Early foresters could try to optimize growth conditions, but beyond that they were fundamentally constrained by the natural replenishment rate. Increasing the harvest rate above the replenishment rate would erode the forest's productive capacity, eventually leading to deforestation. More land could be converted to wood production, but this would mean taking it out of other uses, such as food or fibre production.

Consider the production of iron. Improving the efficiency of the furnaces in which wood was burnt could reduce the amount of resources required. Increasing technological efficiency could see the community produce the same amount of metal as before, but with less environmental impact. In this sense, new technologies can be more sustainable than old technologies. Typically, though, new technologies were used to produce more metal than before, using the same amount of wood. Indeed, as metalworking has other environmental impacts (caused by smoke, slag waste, and water pollution), the net result of increased technological efficiency was often increased environmental impacts. Another option is to trade with communities that are better positioned to smelt iron. So a community that had the natural advantage of being located near good deposits of ore with plentiful woodland could devote itself to sustainable charcoal production and exchange metal products for food, fibre, and

Box 8.2 Energy for iron smelting

Assuming you have access to iron ore-bearing rocks, which is a geological rather than ecological issue, you need energy to smelt that ore. This energy comes from a stand of trees you have allocated for the purpose. The wood will be sustainably harvested by coppicing (the selective removal of individual branches). A well-managed forest will yield 5–10 tonnes of hardwood timber per hectare. To minimize moisture the wood will first be air dried, which will give it an energy density of around 15 megajoules per kilogram. This is too low an energy density to reach 1,535°C, the temperature at which iron melts. Consequently, you will need to convert your wood to charcoal, which has an energy density of around 30 megajoules per kilogram. You do this by stacking the wood and covering it with sods of earth to create a largely oxygen-free environment and then slowly burning it over a number of days (the process is called pyrolysis). You now have your charcoal – a moistureless, pure carbon fuel, free of volatile compounds and capable of burning at very high temperatures.

As you are using some of the chemical energy of the wood to create the charcoal there is a net energy loss. Ten kilograms of wood yields about 2 kilograms of charcoal. In energy terms that means 150 megajoules of chemical energy is converted to 60 megajoules of chemical energy; a net energy loss of 60 per cent. However, the denser energy of the charcoal is far more useful to you. A basic smelting process needs approximately 15 kilograms of charcoal per kilogram of melted iron. In terms of the primary resource, this means 75 kilograms of wood per kilogram of metal. Taking the median sustainable yield of 7.5 tonnes of wood per hectare of coppiced forest, this neatly converts to 10 hectares of coppiced forest per tonne of metal. Forging the metal into a useful object would add another 25 per cent to the energy needs of the process, so each tonne of iron tools produced needed the primary energy content of around 12.5 hectares of forest.

NB: All figures derived from Smil 2008: 188–191.

other resources produced outside its area. This trend towards specialisation made economic and environmental sense, but led to an increased outflow of resources. It also heralded what would become much more significant later – that members of a community could obtain environmental resources sufficient to sustain themselves, without having direct contact with the environment.

State of ecosystem health

Although a degree of specialization had emerged in our Iron Age community, most members continued to be involved in the production and acquisition of primary environmental resources. With their villages clustered in and around their fields and pastures, all members of the community would have been keenly aware of local environmental conditions and productivity. At certain times, such as harvest, it is likely that every physically capable member would participate in food procurement activities. No one would have been ignorant of what resources were available in the local environment from season to season. Significant 'wild' environmental resources, such as mushrooms, fish, and berries, could still be accessed from the region, and these would be an important source of nutritional diversity. The gathering of these resources would have been essentially a continuation of hunting and gathering activities. In years of poor harvest, wild foods could help supplement yields from agriculture, although there would be limits to how long they could support the larger population.

Despite the intimate knowledge early farming societies had of environmental realities there was a fundamental difference between their interactions with that environment and the interactions of hunter–gatherer bands. In essence, the farmers laboured to prevent environments returning to their 'natural' condition. By the Iron Age about half the woodlands that had covered the land had been removed through human activity (Rackham 2000: 72). This would have been a massive undertaking, given the rudimentary tools available, played out over many generations. Furthermore, as cut trees typically regenerate vigorously, an ongoing effort would have been required to prevent regrowth of the forests. Deliberate burning, as well as grazing by domesticated animals, probably helped. However, the sheer effort of clearing land, and then maintaining those clearings, meant that settlements had to be permanent. Rather than following cycles of resource abundance, farmers settled in one spot and altered local environments to increase their capacity to support human settlements. These modified environments were much simpler than the ones they replaced, with lower productivity overall, and significantly reduced biodiversity. What agriculture did was to dramatically increase the yields of resources that humans find useful, so that a given area could support more people than was possible in its natural state. However, as carrying capacity increased, so did population levels, which further increased consumption. Consequently, increased carrying capacity did not stay ahead of population changes for long and population levels tended to rise until they were close to the carrying capacity threshold (Figure 6.9).

A consequence of this reinforcing feedback between production and population was to drive food production towards more energy-dense choices. This led to an increasing proportion of land area being devoted to carbohydrate staples. This maximized the human food-energy production per hectare and therefore maximized the number of humans each hectare could support. Unlike risk-averse hunter gatherers, living well below the carrying capacity of their environments, early farming societies frequently found themselves living close to maximum carrying capacities (Figure 6.9). With only small reserves to buffer them against any drop in output, such as a poor harvest, they were relatively more vulnerable. This vulnerability impacted on their health and wellbeing.

State of human health and wellbeing

In order to produce the surpluses that agrarian economies demanded, people worked increasingly harder and longer than their hunter–gathering forebears in the same region. Although farming communities continued to augment their food intake with a range of items gathered from the wild, the switch to farming narrowed dietary variation, as their demand for greater and greater energy yields focused efforts on cropping a limited range of essential resources. For most of the population this resulted in the following interrelated changes:

- herbivorization—the amount of meat in the diet declined. Meat consumption, over time, took on a status value.
- cerealization—the availability of fresh food declined and the use of stored and preserved foods increased. Energy-dense seeds of plants like wheat, which naturally store well, came to dominate.
- standardization—the variety of food declined and diets become more monotonous.
- quality reduction—the narrow diets could be deficient in proteins, vitamins, and trace elements, and subject to periodic shortfalls when harvests were poor

(Sieferle 2001: 13).

Although agriculture delivered a diet that was nutritionally poorer and less secure than foraging could provide, the big payoff was that the much higher energy output per unit area meant that the managed environments could support higher population levels.

The extent to which an early farming society met the health and wellbeing needs of its members was increasingly influenced by an individual's status. For those at the bottom of the social scale, and this may have included slaves, the basic physical needs of a satisfactory diet and adequate clothing and shelter may have been barely met for much of the time. In terms of the modified Ehrlich–Holdren relation, these individuals were frequently below base consumption levels and consequently unable to maintain a dignified existence for extended periods (Section 6.5). However, for the majority of the population, most physical resources were accessible, although with a much greater degree of hard work and effort than affluent societies would be prepared to tolerate today. The adequacy of psychosocial support varied, as strong social capital can characterize the most impoverished communities. We can imagine that in these relatively tight-knit, kinship-based communities a strong sense of belonging and camaraderie would have provided an emotional support network. While work would have been hard for all members of the community, there would have been no sense working for the sake of it. Tasks would be done as needed and, when there was nothing to attend to, more leisurely pursuits would have been possible. We can imagine people gathering around the fire in the centre of their roundhouses and telling stories at the end of the working day. Those few individuals who were higher up the social hierarchy may have been more secure than others, because they had access to greater buffers against hardship. However, in extreme circumstances even a local chieftain would suffer along with the rest of the community.

The health of everyone in the community was negatively affected by the emergence of modern diseases, which arose from organisms that flourished in the novel agricultural environments. These are diseases that occur from living in closer, settled proximity with other humans, and those that cross over to humans from domesticated animals and commensals such as rats. The list includes ailments such as smallpox, measles, chickenpox, tuberculosis, influenza, and the common cold (McMichael 2001).

Human–environment interactions

The Paradigm of Ownership and Control of Environments has at its core a reinforcing feedback effect, wherein a growing population requires increases in the carrying capacity of the farming landscape, but the effort required to increase the carrying capacity demands a larger labour force. There is also pressure to increase the technological efficiency with which a farm's environmental resources are produced and utilized. However, a balancing feedback effect, arising from ecological limits on the extent of modification and production, acts to keep this reinforcing feedback in check. As a growing population puts increasing pressure on the environment, new farming communities break off from the parent community and colonize new territory. This process of 'filling the Earth' is eventually checked by the amount of suitable land available for conversion to agriculture. Consequently, the system as a whole tends towards the diversion of all available environmental resources to human use. This process stops only when it hits what Wrigley (2006) calls the 'land productivity ceiling' of a fully developed organic economy. At this point no further growth is possible. Any consumption in excess of these limits will be brought into balance through hardship and starvation. The system is depicted in Figure 8.4.

In Figure 8.4 the central reinforcing feedback loop R1 ('Modify Nature') works as follows: an increase in the carrying capacity of the farm increases the size of the workforce it can support. A larger workforce increases the amount of somatic energy that can be brought to the task of modifying the environment, initially through the labour of community members, but eventually augmented by draft animals. The more the environment is modified from its natural state, the greater its yield of resources the community needs and values. The extent of these resources determines the number of humans, and livestock, that the farm can support – thus closing the loop. The loop tends to drive population increases and results in the maximum possible modification of the environment. However, as with all reinforcing feedback systems the reverse can also occur. For example, if disease reduced the size of the workforce, the resulting labour shortage could see the amount of resources produced by the farm decline. This could lead to increased death rates, further falls in population, further reduction in production, and so on around the loop. Eventually, the situation could

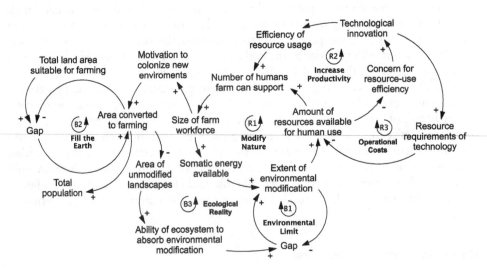

Figure 8.4 Early farming settlements. The central reinforcing loop driving growth is kept in check by a number of environmental balancing loops that limit growth.

reach the point where the farm was abandoned and the landscape allowed to revert to its natural condition.

There is a principal environmental limit (represented by Loop B1) that constrains the growth of the community. This limit is imposed by the ability of the ecosystem to absorb modification. There is a point beyond which the ecosystem can absorb no more modification without its capacity to function being eroded. As the extent of environmental modification increases, the difference (gap), between the amount of modification already undertaken and the amount of modification possible, diminishes. When these two amounts are the same – when the gap is zero – further modification is unsustainable. Ideally, at this point the balancing loop B1 would bring the reinforcing loop R1 to a halt, allowing the ecosystem to retain its resilience. In reality, there are significant delays in the system and it is not uncommon for farming communities to push ecosystems beyond their resilience limits.

As the amount of resources available for human uses hits a ceiling, concern for the efficiency with which those resources are used is stimulated. This triggers the 'Increase Productivity' reinforcing feedback loop R2. This loop drives innovation in farming technology, which in turn drives increasing efficiencies in resource production and use. Farming technology here includes both biotechnology, such as methods for the cultivation of higher yielding plant varieties and the breeding of improved animal characteristics, and engineering technology, such as the development of more efficient harnesses, ploughs, or windmills. These technological innovations serve to increase the number of humans and livestock that the farm can support, within the limits on environmental modification. However, as all technology has resource demands of its own, its production always has an 'Operational Cost' (Loop R3), which draws on the resources available to the farming community. This feedback drives further technological innovation aimed at reducing the resource demands imposed by the farming technologies themselves.

Technological innovation can produce remarkable increases in the human carrying capacity of a given environment. However, it cannot reduce to zero the level of impact of the community. It can reduce the impact per unit of consumption, but as population numbers increase, total consumption increases, and environmental impacts will eventually trend upwards. Eventually, total consumption overwhelms improvements in efficiency, at which point Loop B1 will reassert itself. As the population continues to grow, despite the fact that further production from the same land area is now unsustainable, the environmental limits will tend to stimulate the colonization of new environments. Consequently, some younger members of the original farming community will leave to find new, unmodified environments that can be converted to farming.

The extent to which this process of colonization can continue is itself limited by the balancing loop B2 ('Fill the Earth'). This loop represents the limits imposed by the finite amount of land suitable for farming. Farming communities 'fill the Earth' as the area actually converted to farming approaches the total area that could be converted to farming. When there is no gap between these two amounts – when actual and maximum potential areas being farmed are the same – Earth is 'full' and no further expansion of farming is possible. With few unmodified landscapes left, no further landscape modification can occur and the total environmental limit has been reached. Balancing loop B3 imposes 'ecological reality' on the farming communities, and the total population with its per capita consumption demands will be at its ceiling.

Any further increases in population size, or per capita consumption by some members of the community, will necessarily increase the levels of hardship – for example, starvation – imposed on other members of the community. That is, when Earth is 'full' and no supplementary resources are available, further increases in demand in one place must be offset with reduced satisfaction of demand in another. Conquest and colonization of land areas occupied by other communities is a solution only for the colonizers – it merely imposes hardship on those dispossessed.

Apart from instances where the resources of another community are appropriated, farming communities are directly affected by the realities of environmental limits. They must either work to respect those limits or feel the consequences of transgressing them. Those farming communities that work for generations on landscapes with which they are highly familiar know and respect these limits. Only in communities where this feedback does not exist can a lack of awareness or respect for environmental reality develop without its members feeling the immediate effects of their ignorance. Such overexploitation becomes significant for the first time with the rise of cities and their environmentally disconnected urban communities.

8.4 Urbanism and the rise of the city

Paradigm of environments in the service of remote consumers

Urban communities evolved on sites where agricultural productivity was sufficient to sustain their farming-community precursors and to support the additional demands made by greatly increased populations and complex social and physical structures. Urban populations are inevitably driven to construct and support complex physical and social apparatus in order to manage the conditions that make their cities possible. From the start, such communities sought to circumvent the limitations set by the finite productive capacity of their local landscapes. Extending the total land area a town could draw upon was an obvious strategy. Trade was one way to achieve this physical expansion, but so too was the conquest, colonization, or enslavement of other peoples, in order to access the products of their landscapes. Dependence on distant lands required the means to transport goods across longer distances sufficiently swiftly for them to arrive in good condition. This required not only the design and manufacture of vehicles to carry the goods, but also the construction, maintenance, and often protection of routes along which the vehicles travelled. Imported goods need to be accounted for, stored, and preserved until needed and distributed to the end user. In time, towns would take on distinctive functions, which set them aside from other community arrangements. This included serving as sacred and ceremonial places, providing security to their populations, and hosting markets or centres of commerce and trade (Kotkin 2005). A large, heterogeneous population, with a wide range of work specializations and occupying widely divergent social positions, was needed to perform these core functions. This diversity gave rise to disparities in wealth, status, and power.

Large volumes of environmental resources were utilized to support urban communities. However, the urban dwellers who consumed these resources had little or nothing to do with their production. For the first time in history, human impacts on the environment came from communities that were not physically located within that environment. We call the underlying belief-system the 'Paradigm of Environments in the Service of Remote Consumers'. The evolution of this belief system did not require a paradigm shift from the Paradigm of Ownership and Control of Environments, as the two are not competing. The new paradigm depends utterly on environments being owned and controlled in order to provide essential resources. It is just that the new paradigm holds these resources to be 'services' that a consumer can acquire in a market or by exchange, and need have no knowledge of their means of production. Indeed, under this paradigm, it is entirely reasonable that consumers will play no part in the production of the goods that they consume.

Early urban communities

Imagine that one of Cheddar Man's descendants had migrated 200 kilometres to the east and now is a member of the bustling urban community of London (Figure 8.5). In the Middle Ages, urban communities made up only a tiny percentage of the total population – perhaps 2.5 per cent (Ponting 1991: 295). In the late thirteenth century, London was the largest town in England, with a population of about 80,000 crowded in and around the old Roman-built city walls (Galloway 1995). At a time when the national population was estimated to be about 4.7 million, London was home to just over 1.5 per cent of the total (Broadberry *et al.* 2011a).

An urban population can be sustained only by surpluses produced by a rural population. One reason why urban populations were small at this time was that surplus production was low. On average, a medieval urban community would have had a moderately affluent lifestyle, with more meat and a much more varied dietary intake than that of a peasant (Broadberry *et al.* 2011a: 13). It is estimated that about three-quarters of the daily food needs of the typical urban consumer were obtained from arable landscapes – these products were primarily wheat, rye, and barley

Figure 8.5 Medieval London.
Source: © Museum of London.

(for brewing beer), and one-quarter from pasture landscapes – meat, dairy, and poultry, plus fish (Broadberry *et al.* 2011a: Table 7). The total agricultural land area of England at this time was around 10 million hectares, approximately half arable and half pasture (Broadberry *et al.* 2011b). Not all the food produced from these landscapes was available for trade. Significant amounts of food were consumed by the rural communities that produced it, certain religious orders held rights to tithes (a tax in the form of a tenth of the harvest), and seed had to be retained for the next year's crop. However, feudal landowners would have made about 40 per cent of surplus yields available for trade. Galloway (1995) estimates that the 'grain' portion of London's food demand would have been the annual surplus of production from 202,000 to 364,000 hectares. In principle, London of 1300 could have provisioned itself from its hinterlands – about twice the land area it occupies today. In practice, the cost and challenge of transporting resources by land meant that landscapes near rivers were preferred. Products that commanded lower prices, such as oats, were grown closer to the city than products such as wheat, as the higher-valued commodities were better able to absorb the cost of transport (Galloway 2012).

The influence the urban community exerted on its hinterlands and further afield was primarily through an extensive network of markets. There was now a very large difference in the levels of affluence of different members of the community, and consequently their levels of consumption differed. A very small percentage of the community occupied positions of high status, and enjoyed considerable affluence. Much of their wealth stemmed from their control of extensive land areas, and the environmental resources they contained. Such individuals and families could engage in conspicuous displays of wealth and power. They built grand residences, maintained large retinues, and owned fine furniture, clothing, and jewellery. To meet these desires it was necessary to draw in resources from far away, including exotic imports from abroad.

In these times most of the population performed a range of skilled and semi-skilled tasks, many as servants in the households of the wealthy. While consuming at levels far below the elite, these members of the community would have secured basic levels of consumption, adequate for a frugal but reasonably comfortable lifestyle. At the bottom of the social scale were the unemployable and the outcast – the homeless, the elderly, and the infirm. These people had essentially no support and would have had to beg, steal, or scavenge as best they could. Their levels of consumption were well below minimum basic requirements of a dignified existence. However, from high to low status, the members of the urban community were gaining access to environmental resources by primarily economic means. Those who were wealthy were secure in their access to resources; those who were poor were not. However, for all classes, environmental goods and services had become commodities to be accessed through markets, rather than by engaging directly in production processes in the biophysical environment.

However, despite the proliferation of novel artefacts, and increasing demands for the services that they provided, total national levels of environmental impact were not much increased. Human innovation and ingenuity constantly led to new technologies, and to improvements and adaptation of existing ones. As a result, the efficiency with which resources could service human needs improved, and the material intensity per unit of service went down over time. Also, while the per capita consumption of urban communities was greater than for their agricultural counterparts, urban populations remained small and the far greater proportion of society continued in an agricultural lifestyle.

State of ecosystem health

The basic ecology of early urban communities rests on the same fundamental principles as agricultural ones. Society remained constrained by flows of solar energy through biometabolic pathways that could be manipulated but not increased. The process of land conversion across the country was essentially complete. All land areas capable of some productive output had been converted to that use: woodlands for fuel, timber, and some animal feed such as acorns for pigs; pastures for animals for food, fibre, and power (including farm work and transport); and fields for grains, legumes, root crops, and plant fibres such as flax. Significant land areas would be left fallow – that is, not sown to a crop – from year to year to allow the recovery of soil nutrients. Crop rotation and grazing animals also played a crucial role in conserving soil fertility. However, the export of environmental resources to distant urban settlements (such as London), saw for the first time a significant one-way flow of nutrients away from rural environments. Soil degradation resulted where the rate of outflow of nutrients exceeded their replenishment rates. Conversely, in the crowded streets of London, the inflow of nutrients far exceeded the rate at which they were transported out of the system, and they accumulated in piles of rotting organic waste and human and animal excrement. The presence of this material would have significant health consequences for the inhabitants of urban areas.

The relative wealth of urban populations resulted in urban communities often enjoying a more adequate diet than did the peasants who actually produced the food. That the producers of primary commodities gained the least reward for their efforts was a common pattern, and one that would intensify with time. It is likely that with almost complete conversion of environments to some form of productive output, the maximum carrying capacity of the environment had been reached. Famines at this time are an indication of severe environmental stress. It is possible that, with a population edging towards five million, the system was sitting on the threshold of significant regional environmental and social collapse. However, that tipping point was not reached. Within decades bubonic plague reached England. In a matter of a few years the population was halved, lifting the pressure on the environment. The total population of England would not surpass that of its pre-plague levels until well into the seventeenth century. The total agricultural population would not recover to the same levels (Apostolides *et al.* 2008). The relationship between town and country would never be the same again.

State of human health and wellbeing

Urban communities faced the same range of infectious diseases as their agricultural counterparts, but diseases that arise in areas of very high population density and inadequate sanitation are especially prolific. The most significant diseases included dysentery, enteric fever, typhoid fever, typhus, smallpox, and tuberculosis – a list that would soon be joined by bubonic plague (Boyden 2004). Plague reached England via trade routes from distant locations, exposing populations to diseases for which they had no immunological resistance. With no knowledge of the causes of these diseases, there were no cures and little effective activity to remedy them. Wealth and status provided no special defence, other than perhaps slightly better sanitation. Childbirth was a risky undertaking for women of all classes. Wealth could ensure a more adequate diet than that consumed by the poor, and so provided some protection against nutrient deficiency, but it could not overcome the cultural belief that uncooked fruit and vegetables were a health risk. Wealth also allowed some members of the community to be significantly overweight – an early example of ill-health outcomes from excessive consumption. Psychological impacts of urban living were mixed. Towns were drawcards as centres of excitement, entertainment, and conviviality, but urban conditions also generated stress, violence, and crime. All classes, men and women alike, seem to have consumed vast amounts of alcohol – wine for the rich, beer for the poor. However, the biggest health risk of all was probably being young – a quarter of children died before the age of five. Despite the potential hardships, life in the city offered more opportunities than were available in many rural areas, and urban populations expanded steadily as people migrated from the countryside.

Human–environment interactions

The early growth of cities was driven by reinforcing feedback loops – an illustration is shown in Figure 8.6. This diagram illustrates the hypothesis that an increase in the size of an urban economy increases the attractiveness of urban living, the size of the urban population, and so the size of the urban economy. Urban economies add value to raw commodities through the manufacture of goods and the provision of services. This increases the standard of living of the urban community by producing a diversity of employment opportunities, the generation of wealth, and the provision of a range of social and entertainment opportunities. Consequently, urban living becomes increasingly attractive (Loop B1) – especially in comparison to its rural counterpart. The resulting immigration helps swell the urban population. This in turn increases levels of urban consumption, which are already greater per capita than that of a rural community due to the relative wealth of the former. The wealth of the urban community allows its members to purchase the resources that they need and want, diverting large volumes of these resources to the urban economy, and helping to feed its levels of consumption. Because there are few pathways for these resources to be returned to the landscapes of origin, urban environments become a growing resource sink (Loop R2) – a phenomenon not restricted to the organic products, but including the output of such activities as mining and manufacturing. The urban consumer's interaction with environmental reality is mediated largely through economic exchange, providing little information on the social and environmental consequences of their consumption activities. These impacts are perceived as 'external' if they are known about at all. Likewise, the resources accumulating in the urban environment are perceived as waste, to be removed and disposed of as quickly as possible, before they make urban living less attractive. However, urban consumers are ultimately dependent on agricultural production, as the link 'impact on rural environments and society' connects their system to the farming communities of their agricultural counterparts (Figure 8.4). Having distanced themselves from the processes of resource procurement, urban communities become increasingly ignorant of that dependency. This indicates some of the major problems that arise when feedback signals are lost or ignored – a problem that is acute in modern society.

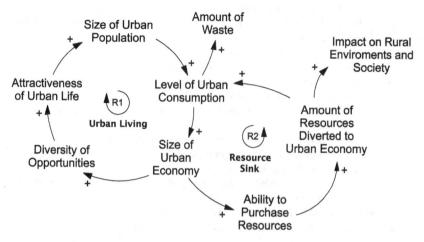

Figure 8.6 The early phase of urbanization. Two complementary reinforcing feedback loops
dominate. Although the growth is welcome to urban dwellers, it produces
negative effects that the urban community is either unaware of or does not care
about. These effects impact on local ecologies and the rural environments and
communities upon which the cities ultimately depend.

Early urban societies were constrained by the limits that constrained the replenishment of essential environmental resources. For most of their history they were small
but influential appendages to an agrarian economy based on agricultural systems of
production. The carrying capacity of the environment for both farming and urban
communities was set by a solar-energy ceiling, being the rate at which photosynthesis
could replenish energy stocks. In the eighteenth century that was to change as, for
the first time, the widespread use of fossil fuel energy allowed production levels, and
subsequent modification of material, energy, and information pathways, quite unlike
anything in human history. This is the story of the Anthropocene – the subject of
the next chapter.

References

Apostolides, A., Broadberry, S., Campbell, B., Overton, M., and van Leeuwen, B. (2008).
   'English agricultural output and labour productivity, 1250–1850: Some preliminary
   estimates'. Unpublished Working Paper, University of Warwick.
Boyden, S. (1987). *Western Civilization in Biological Perspective.* Oxford, Clarendon Press.
Boyden, S. (2004). *The Biology of Civilisation.* Sydney, University NSW Press.
Broadberry, S., Campbell, B. M., and v. Leeuwen, B. (2011a). 'English medieval population:
   Reconciling time series and cross sectional evidence'. *Reconstructing the National Income
   of Britain and Holland, c. 1279/1500 to 1850,* Leverhulme Trust. Reference number
   F/00215AR.
Broadberry, S., Campbell, B. M., and van Leeuwen, B. (2011b). 'Arable acreage in England,
   1270–1871'. Available online at www2.lse.ac.uk/economicHistory/pdf/Broadberry/acreage.
   pdf.
Cordain, L., Miller, J. B., Eaton, S. B., Mann, N., Holt, S., and Speth, J. (2000). 'Plant–animal
   subsistence ratios and macronutrient energy estimations in worldwide hunter–gatherer
   diets'. *The American Journal of Clinical Nutrition* 71(3): 682–692.

Galloway, J. A. (1995). 'London's grain supply: Changes in production, distribution and consumption during the fourteenth century'. *Franco-British Studies: Journal of the British Institute in Paris* 20: 23–34.

Galloway, J. (2012). 'Metropolitan food and fuel supply in medieval England: Regional and international contexts'. *Food Supply, Demand and Trade: Aspects of the economic relationship between town and countryside (Middle Ages – 19th century)*. P. v. Cruyningen and E. Theon. Turnhout, Brepols Publishers, 7–18.

Jochim, M. (1976). *Hunter–Gatherer Subsistence and Settlement: A predictive model*. New York, Academic Press.

Kotkin, J. (2005). *The City: A Global History*. London, Weidenfeld & Nicolson.

McMichael, A. J. (2001). *Human Frontiers, Environments and Disease: Past Patterns, Uncertain Futures*. Cambridge, Cambridge University Press.

Mazoyer, M. and Roudart, L. (2006). *A History of World Agriculture: From the Neolithic age to the current crisis*. London, Earthscan.

Ponting, C. (1991). *A Green History of the World*. London, Sinclair-Stevenson.

Pryor, F. (2006). *Farmers in Prehistoric Britain*. Stroud, Tempus Publishing.

Rackham, O. (2000). *The History of the Countryside*. London, Phoenix Press.

Rees, W. (2000). 'Patch disturbance, ecofootprints, and biological integrity: Revisiting the limits to growth (or why industrial society is inherently unsustainable)'. *Ecological Integrity: Integrating environment, conservation and health*. L. W. David Pimental and Reed F. Noss. Washington, DC, Island, 139–156.

Sahlins, M. (1968). 'Notes on the original affluent society'. *Man the Hunter*. R. B. Lee and I. DeVore. New York, Aldine Publishing Company, 83–95.

Sieferle, R. P. (2001). *The Subterranean Forest: Energy systems and the Industrial Revolution*. Cambridge, White Horse Press.

Smil, V. (2008). *Energy in Nature and Society: General Energetics of Complex Systems*. Cambridge, MA, MIT Press.

Smith, C. (1992). *Late Stone Age Hunters of the British Isles*. London, Routledge.

Tainter, J. A. (1988). *The Collapse of Complex Societies*. Cambridge, Cambridge University Press.

Wrigley, E. A. (2006). 'The transition to an advanced organic economy: Half a millennium of English agriculture'. *Economic History Review* LIX(3): 435–480.

Wymer, J. (1991). *Mesolithic Britain*. Oxford, Shire Publications.

9 Living well in the Anthropocene

Man has been here 32,000 years. That it took a hundred million years to prepare the world for him is proof that that is what it was done for. I suppose it is. I dunno. If the Eiffel tower were now representing the world's age, the skin of paint on the pinnacle-knob at its summit would represent man's share of that age; and anybody would perceive that that skin was what the tower was built for. I reckon they would, I dunno.

(Mark Twain 1903)

9.1 Introduction

The fundamental elements that accelerated the rise of the Anthropocene were already in place by the second half of the seventeenth century. Although humans had burnt fuels, including fossil fuels, and changed land use prior to this time, this is the period where we first have evidence of increased greenhouse-gas concentrations attributable to human activity. It also coincides with the generally accepted date range given to the onset of the Industrial Revolution – the most likely source of those gases. Like most revolutions, the Industrial Revolution depended on a wide range of component processes to make it possible. We can only briefly mention a few of these, with the primary focus on the changing relationship between the economy and the environment.

At the start of the fourteenth century the population of England is estimated to have reached about four and a quarter million people, probably close to the maximum carrying capacity of a basic agrarian economy (Broadberry *et al.* 2011). Various famines around this time suggest that it was unlikely that much greater numbers could have been reliably supported under the prevailing systems of production. However, the plagues of the fourteenth century killed around 40 per cent of the population of England, relieving the stresses on the productive capacity of the environment. Depopulation led to large-scale abandonment of villages and settlements across the country. London's population halved and, presumably, its demand for resources by an equivalent amount. The clearing of woodland ceased, and some regenerated (Rackham 2000). For the next 150 years, England's population numbers remained largely unchanged. The population crept back above 3 million by 1550 and had returned to fourteenth century levels by the early 1600s. From here on, the total population was to grow slowly but the agricultural population remained largely unchanged. By 1800 the total population was above 8 million, while the agricultural population was essentially the same as it had been in 1300 (Apostolides *et al.* 2008). Using figures compiled by Wrigley (2006), we can see that agricultural productivity, as measured by output per agricultural worker and output per hectare of agricultural land, had increased significantly. In 1300, some 80 per cent of adult males were directly engaged in agricultural production (note that this does not imply females did not work on the land – just that the records do not readily indicate how many of them did with what percentage of their time). By 1800, this figure had fallen to 40 per cent. During this time agricultural output had doubled, or in some cases tripled, producing significant food and non-food surplus organic resources. This meant that many workers were able to work in sectors of the economy other than primary production, because adequate surpluses were available to sustain them. Most of these workers migrated to towns and cities, creating an urban population that was to grow as total population grew. In addition, the increased production of grains, specifically oats, could support a large population of draught animals whose power was crucial on-farm, but also off-farm in transport, communication, and for work in pre-steam engine industries and manufacturing. With a significantly larger urbanized workforce employed in secondary sectors of the economy, trade and commerce, including imports and exports, was dramatically increasing. Economic activity, the profits from which flowed disproportionately to the mercantile capitalists who owned the systems of production, drew in resources from overseas. Chief among these were cotton, sugar, and wood, representing the products of significant external land areas and the labours of large numbers of individuals not resident in the country.

In the late seventeenth century, England was an 'advanced organic economy' (Wrigley 2006). There was a strong reinforcing feedback process between increased agricultural productivity, driving increases in the manufacturing workforce, leading to increasing urban population levels, and increasing trade and commerce – all requiring more food and non-food organic outputs, and thus (to close the loop) demanding increased agricultural productivity. Yet the system was probably approaching the limits to further increases in the efficiency possible under an economy fundamentally limited by the rate of photosynthesis. Gains had accrued from changing societal arrangements (for example, the enclosure of common land and the eviction of peasant and small-scale farmers; changes to environmental-management practices (such as reducing fallow periods) made possible by the increased rates of manuring from more farm animals). However, as Wrigley says:

> [N]o organic economy, however successful, could escape from the constraints common to all. Asymptotic growth was possible and could lead to major change; exponential growth was beyond reach. A ceiling was set by the productivity of the land. The ceiling itself might be raised by technical or institutional change, but a slowing of growth was inevitable as the ceiling was approached ... As long as the land remained the principal source not only of food but also of almost all the raw materials used in manufacture, it was inevitable that the productivity of the land should set limits to possible growth.
>
> (Wrigley 2006: 475–476)

Here we see just a few of the key processes that would give rise to the Industrial Revolution (Davies 1999: 999 lists some 48 interrelated variables). However, what is missing is the power needed to make the Industrial Revolution possible. Fossil fuels, together with the technology needed to harness their energy, would provide the answer. Slowly growing across the nineteenth century, this power would eventually give rise to the fully established Anthropocene in the twentieth century, where human culture was unleashed as a force in nature, capable of affecting the Earth system on a global scale. A new paradigm would arise to explain, legitimize, and normalize this novel social–environmental system – the idea of Limitless Growth.

9.2 The Paradigm of Limitless Growth

The belief that growth in the human economy is *not* limited by the productivity of the land is the central driving belief of the Anthropocene. Consequently, we label this belief the 'Paradigm of Limitless Growth'. The central innovation that gave rise to this paradigm was the large-scale use of fossil fuels, notably coal. Coal had long been used as a direct source of heat in home heating, and in a number of industrial processes, brick-making or the firing of ceramics. By the early eighteenth century about 3 million tonnes of coal per year was being mined (Smil 2008). However, with the invention of relatively efficient steam engines, in the late eighteenth century, the thermal energy of coal could be harnessed as a source of kinetic energy. For the first time, the amount of work that could be done by a group of people and their available technology was no longer shackled by their access to environmental stocks of biomatter or flows of wind or water. Now economies could be powered with energy reserves that had been captured by ecosystems millions of years ago. The reserves were so large as to seem inexhaustible – hence the belief that the growth they could fuel would be limitless. Today there is recognition, grudging in some quarters, that on a finite planet such resources must, in fact, be limited. However, the Paradigm of Limitless Growth endures – most notably in the belief that, with the right settings, *economic* growth is limitless. Human ingenuity will take on the challenge of innovating to circumvent any environmental limit economic growth encounters. Like the once-revolutionary steam engines, the technologies of today will, it is held, be consigned to history as they are supplanted by as-yet unimagined new technologies. Similarly, it is imagined that alternative sources of energy will be discovered and harnessed long before existing stocks of coal and other fossil fuels are exhausted. In this way, the human economy will climb to ever greater levels of prosperity and progress.

The Paradigm of Limitless Growth is unlikely to deliver a just, worthwhile, and sustainable future. Not only is indefinite growth not possible on a finite planet, it is ultimately in no one's interest that we continue to pursue it – not even the wealthy few who are reaping the short-term benefits. A major problem is that technology provides no ethical standards. As Marx (2010: 577) has observed: 'The popular belief in technology as a – if not *the* – primary force shaping the future is matched by our increasing reliance on instrumental standards of judgement, and a corresponding neglect of moral and political standards.'

Describing the current trajectory of the Anthropocene as a runaway 'suicide machine', Wright (2004: 131) notes that wealth will provide scant protection in the chaos of global social–environmental collapse. Although we do not want to present a 'doomsday' narrative, we do argue that if we are all to 'live well' in the Anthropocene, then the growth paradigm that has dominated since the Industrial Revolution must give way to a new one. We need to develop a belief system that is compatible with both our collective needs and the ecological realities of the world. Only within a paradigm that supports such a belief system can the Anthropocene become an era that we can celebrate rather than fear. The challenge of living well in the Anthropocene is not an environmental one – it is a human–ecological one.

9.3 Anthropocene communities

The energy and technology available to communities in the Anthropocene has driven increases in just about every material dimension imaginable. This includes total population numbers. The estimated global population of 3 million when Cheddar Man was hunting and gathering has risen to over 7 billion today, and is estimated to reach 9 billion by 2050. Urban populations have risen from around 2.5 per cent at the start of the Anthropocene to now account for more than 50 per cent of the global population. We have entered an 'urban age' where the most typical habitat for humans is the city (Sukhdev 2013). The land area that had a carrying capacity for a single group of 20 humans 500 generations ago is now home to over 8 million Londoners (Figure 9.1). The land area required to provide the resources that the population of London demands, and to assimilate its wastes, is estimated to be 340,000 square kilometres – more than two and a half times the land area of England (Best Foot Forward Ltd 2002). In terms of the variables of the extended Ehrlich–Holdren relation I = PCT (Section 6.5), global population levels (P) have exploded in the Anthropocene.

So too has average consumption (C). We can use energy as an indicator of total consumption (PC). Global energy use rose from 217 million kilojoules in 1970 to 400 million kilojoules in 1997 (Steffen *et al.* 2004: 84) . Global averages are of course

Figure 9.1 London in the Anthropocene. The land area once home to 20 hunter-gatherers.
Source: © High Level Photography.

skewed by the disproportionate amount of affluence-driven consumption in first world countries. For example, in 2000, when the population of London was 7.4 million, the city consumed the energy equivalent of over 13 million tonnes of oil, producing 41 tonnes of carbon dioxide, consumed 49 million tonnes of materials, generated 26 million tonnes of waste, and imported 6.9 million tonnes of food. Londoners travelled 64 billion passenger kilometres (the number of passengers multiplied by the number of kilometres within London (2002). Holiday travel by Londoners, including flights overseas, was not estimated.

Against this background the contribution of the technology impact factor (T) has to be placed in context. Technology is constantly being adapted and refined, and can vastly improve the efficiency with which energy and material resources are converted into a useful form. Twentieth-century charcoal furnaces produced iron at about 30 megajoules per kilogram of hot metal – a small fraction of the energy required in the Iron Age (Box 8.2). Today's computers are smaller, and less energy and material intensive, than their clunking forebears. Today's combustion engines are far more efficient than those of one hundred years ago. The downside is that there is far greater demand for all these things, driven by far larger populations, consuming much more per capita. What technology cannot do is overcome an open-ended process, whereby whatever gains innovation makes in efficiency per unit of service are swamped by the generation of insatiable demand.

9.4 Ecosystem health in the Anthropocene

Access to fossil fuels in the Anthropocene helps to maintain the average person's material lifestyle at levels far above the 'elite' of any period in the photosynthetic-limited era. Use of these fossil fuels is not sustainable. Fossil fuels are a non-renewable resource and the rate at which they are being used far exceeds the rate at which they are being substituted by sustainably used renewable resources (Section 6.2). However, it is not just that the energy that powers the process of material consumption is being used unsustainably – so too are the materials themselves.

The planetary boundaries of nine essential environmental variables have been estimated (Rockström *et al.* 2009). For many of these resources, the rate of consumption far exceeds the rate of replenishment, and the resource collapse threshold is dangerously close. In terms of the impact scale shown in Figure 6.9, we would say that impact is now close to, or in, the buffer zone where social–ecological processes are at risk. In some cases it is estimated that impacts are above the threshold limit, and so current social–ecological processes are unsustainable. Again, we emphasize that the amount that different communities contribute to these impacts are not equal. Each of the planetary boundaries are discussed below in relation to the capacity to produce food for human consumption. Here we can see the degree of vulnerability to which global populations are now increasingly exposed (from Deutsch *et al.* 2013).

Land use change

The greatest driver of land use change, food production, is driving the conversion of natural ecosystems to croplands and pastures. Around 40 per cent of Earth's ice-free land surface has now been converted to agriculture. That figure is much higher if considered as a percentage of land that is, or could be made, suitable for agriculture.

Further expansion would push agriculture into marginal landscapes that would require intensive inputs and modification to achieve substantial yields, and risk triggering soil degradation. Alternatively, or additionally, expansion of agriculture by area would come at the expense of the production of some other resource, such as woodland for the production of timber.

Phosphorus and nitrogen cycle

The production of fertilizers for agriculture is the main driver of human interference in phosphorus and nitrogen cycles. Agricultural production is impossible where these elements are deficient. All agricultural production removes stocks of these elements from the environment and unless the natural rate of their replenishment is respected, they have to be replaced by human activity. The problem is particularly acute in farming systems that do not have animals in rotation with cropping, as the manure from grazing livestock is one way to replenish elements absorbed by plants. The phosphorus cycle is particularly problematic as it has no atmospheric pathway. The main natural path for phosphorus to return to the land is through the droppings (guano) of seabirds. Natural reserves of guano have been largely depleted, and current demand far exceeds their rate of replenishment. Much phosphorus in artificial fertilizers is mined from rock deposits – the volume of these reserves is unknown. Some estimates are that global reserves could be as low as 50 years' supply.

Unlike phosphorus, nitrogen does have an atmospheric path – about 78 per cent of the atmosphere is nitrogen. Nitrogen is fixed by soil microorganisms and leguminous plants, and so can be naturally returned by fallowing and by legume rotation, including green manuring and animal feed. However, most conventional farming methods depend upon artificial nitrogen, which is synthesized from ammonia at an energy cost of 50–100 megajoules per kilogram and applied at rates with an embodied energy cost of 40 gigajoules per hectare (Smil 2008). As much as one-third of global food production today is subsidized by artificial nitrogen fertilizers. In excessive concentrations, both nitrogen and phosphorus can cause significant environmental harm, such as algal blooms in waterways.

Freshwater use

About 70 per cent of all freshwater diverted to human use is for irrigated agriculture. Dams, impoundments, and excessive diversion from rivers directly harms river ecology (Chapter 2). This activity also reduces the amount of fish protein available to other users of river resources. Where water is drawn from groundwater it is crucial to not surpass the long-term rate of replenishment. In many places the rate of extraction for irrigation greatly exceeds the rate of replenishment, and groundwater reserves are diminishing. A notable example is in the Punjab of India where 75 per cent of irrigation draws on groundwater, with significant declines in reserves. Access to water is likely to be the source of increased future conflict between upstream and downstream users, including between nations.

Rate of biodiversity loss

Converting natural ecosystems to agriculture results in major loss of habitat and is one of the primary causes of biodiversity loss. Excessive use of insecticides and herbicides also contributes to erosion of biodiversity. Significant on-farm biodiversity conservation is possible, where farmers are encouraged and rewarded to retain native vegetation or wildlife corridors on their properties. In such cases, the higher levels of on-farm biodiversity can directly benefit the farmer through, for example, retaining natural predators of pest species. However, industrialized intensive agriculture is a major contributor to biodiversity loss, as its heavily mechanized high-input, high-output regime favours monocrops. For example, in Australia the sowing of rice seeds across vast tracts of land using small aircraft requires extensive clearing of remnant trees as they present a collision hazard.

Climate change

Fossil fuels are used extensively at every stage in the food system, from production, processing, packaging, distribution, and consumption (Ingram *et al.* 2010). Agricultural systems also emit methane from sources such as livestock and rice paddies, and nitrous oxide from fertilizer use. The initial conversion of land to cropland and pasture releases large volumes of carbon into the atmosphere, including significant losses from soil carbon stocks. Dominant industrial agricultural production methods make agriculture a significant contributor to climate change, including emissions from fertilizer manufacture, refrigeration, long-distance transportation, warehousing, and distribution. Agribusiness also promotes more highly refined and manufactured products for their higher retail value. When the entire food chain is looked at, it accounts for as much as one-third of all greenhouse gas emissions (Gilbert 2012). Food systems will in turn be significantly impacted by climate change. This includes affecting the point of production, as changes occur in rainfall patterns, minimum and maximum temperatures, and frequency and duration of drought. However, climate change will affect other stages of food systems, such as the impact of extreme weather events on food distribution and storage. Populations with low levels of food reserves, and this includes most cities, are potentially vulnerable to even relatively short disruptions in supply (Porter *et al.* 2014).

Ocean acidification

Carbon dioxide emissions contribute to ocean acidification. Increasing acidification will negatively affect marine ecosystems, including their capacity to provide food. This is both directly as a source of food, for example as shellfish lose the capacity to form calcium carbonite, and through loss of important fish nurseries, such as coral reefs. Ocean acidification will then significantly drive further changes to terrestrial food production, as it will reduce the oceans' capacity to remove carbon from the atmosphere, potentially stimulating a runaway feedback effect.

Ozone depletion

The chlorofluorocarbons that were the major cause of stratospheric ozone depletion were primarily used in refrigeration. Refrigeration is a significant element of industrial food systems in particular, as it makes possible their extensive transport, storage, and distribution networks. Refrigeration is also ubiquitous in home food storage, at least in developed nations. This includes the cold storage of many food products, such as jam, that don't require cooling because they are already preserved. In the post-war years the commercial production of frozen goods, including pre-prepared convenience food, has made home ownership of a freezer a necessity for many. The chlorofluorocarbons that these appliances used have now been largely replaced by less damaging compounds, and the ozone layer has consequently begun to recover. This is the only one of the planetary boundary variables that is showing some improvement.

Atmospheric aerosol loading

In many parts the world, food production makes a significant contribution to aerosol loading from the use of wood for cooking fires. Food production also contributes to fine particles, dust, and smoke in the atmosphere. The use of fire to clear land and remove stubble, windblown soils from eroded agricultural landscapes, and trucking for food distribution all contribute to air pollution. The health consequences of breathing particulate matter are significant, but it is not currently possible to estimate the actual contribution food systems make to air quality. To date, no value has been estimated for this planetary boundary.

Chemical pollution

Fertilizers, herbicides, and pesticides are used in large volumes throughout industrial food systems. They are some of the most toxic and pervasive chemical pollutants that humans release into the environment. Bio-accumulators, that is chemicals that become more concentrated as they move up the food chain, are especially pernicious – DDT is a classic example. Although theoretically regulated to low, safe, exposure thresholds, key individuals – such as the person doing the spraying – may be exposed to very high levels. In certain contexts, regulations, including application rates and handling safety, might be routinely ignored, particularly, for example, by low-skilled labour in a developing country. It is also not easy to predict how chemicals that are nominally safe by themselves will behave when they encounter other chemicals in the environment. Life in the Anthropocene sees most individuals routinely exposed to thousands of novel chemical compounds every day. What health implications this has, if any, is extremely hard to estimate. As with atmospheric aerosol loading, this planetary boundary currently has no estimated value.

A significant source of pressure on these essential planetary boundaries arises from a commoditized food system whose production, processing, and distribution networks primarily reflect the economic imperative of food system efficiency, and not of ecological functioning. Such commoditized systems do not have operational standards that deal with social justice issues or environmental consequences.

9.5 Human health and wellbeing in the Anthropocene

This discussion of social–environmental systems in the Anthropocene has focused on affluent communities in developed nations, because their activities are the primary drivers of change in the system. However, no discussion of the environmental impacts of food production can ignore the massive disparities in consumption levels around the world. In developing nations, 20 per cent of children under five years of age –

nearly 100 million children – are underweight (FAO 2012); 850 million people are estimated to be chronically undernourished, again mostly in the developing world (FAO 2012). In many cases, these malnourished populations are economically marginalized and very poorly served by a food system that treats food as a market commodity. Often, they are sold unhealthy products, such as soft drinks and infant formula. In a global free-market system, locally produced food is not necessarily devoted first to satisfying local consumption needs, because an affluent remote community can pay more for the resource than is possible for the local community. Even if they are held responsible for their local environmental conditions, poor communities typically have the least capacity to change their behaviour. For example, a family facing starvation is likely to eat its own seed stock, even knowing that means it will face famine the following year. Such communities face conditions that are driven by circumstances outside their sphere of control. At the largest time and spatial scales these drivers can include international relations and historical legacies of a colonial past. In terms of the extended Holden–Ehrlich equation (Section 6.5), the consumption levels of these communities are below the base consumption levels necessary for a minimum dignified existence. At the same time, poor communities are especially vulnerable to the changes resulting from exceeding planetary boundary thresholds – changes that are largely driven by activities in affluent communities. By any measure, this situation is grossly unjust.

It is difficult to establish cause-and-effect relationships between what consumers in affluent communities choose to consume and what markets produce. Nevertheless, it would be naive to ignore the massive advertising and political lobbying power of the food industries. Increasingly, global markets see 'Western' dietary profiles dominating in affluent communities across the planet. These diets consist of highly refined, convenience-oriented and processed products that dominate over the less 'value added' basic foods. Fats, oils, sugars, and meat are eaten in increasing amounts at the expense of basic carbohydrates, fresh fruit, and vegetables. A consequence is that undernourishment is rare in these societies, although pockets of it do exist. But, massive health disorders are arising from poor dietary choices and excesses in consumption of certain categories of foods. Diet-related disorders, including obesity, have seen increases of 400 per cent in the past 25 years and are emerging as 'diseases of affluence' – diseases that arise in the Anthropocene for the first time as major causes of death and disability.

The effect of consuming energy-dense commoditized foods is amplified by processes that tend to reduce the level of an individual's somatic-energy expenditure. Growth-based economies develop marketable commodities that reduce the energy expended by individuals. Consequently, many people (again, mostly in affluent societies), are surrounded everyday by devices that serve to save time, energy, and effort in the delivery of comfort and convenience. From private motorized transport, to electric kitchen appliances, to armchair entertainment, much of our daily activity involves manufactured surrogates for what our forebears had to do for themselves using their own body's energy. In such a world it becomes increasingly difficult for individuals to burn the energy that the same system encourages them to consume. For many the solution is offered by other commoditized sectors of the system – gymnasiums, weight-loss dietary programmes, and medication.

Although the Paradigm of Limitless Growth has delivered a wide range of benefits to humanity, collectively we have now reached the limits of the planet's capacity to sustain us at current population and consumption levels. Yet even a cursory application of the extended Holden–Ehrlich relation clearly demonstrates that the impacts arising from consumption are unethically skewed between affluent and poor communities. However, well-intentioned programmes to bring the poor up to the levels of profligacy enjoyed by the rich cannot work – the world does not have the resources to support the required levels of consumption. What is required is global convergence where the rich consume less, and the poor consume more (Figure 6.10). The burden of keeping the impact of the global human economy within planetary boundaries has to fall disproportionately on those who consume the most, not the least. Affluent communities in the developed world have the greatest capacity to act, have the greater per capita responsibility for the problem, and they set the benchmark levels of consumption to which the developing world aspires.

9.6 System dynamics of 'Limitless Growth'

In terms of our dynamic hypothesis, developed through Part II, a hypothesis concerning consumer cultures in affluent nations is depicted in Figure 9.2.

The state of a community depends on the extent to which the Paradigm of Limitless Growth dominates community activities (link L1 in Figure 9.2). The strength of this paradigm can change, via L2, if the community learns and adapts when the state of the community is seen to be unsatisfactory. But, when the belief in limitless growth is strong, such adaptation is unlikely. When economic growth is seen as the cure-all for a community's ills, the most likely response to a problem is not less growth but more. Thus, the paradigm is insulated from any concerns about the state of the community, and learning in response to other signals is unlikely.

The policies and practices (L1) reflecting the Paradigm of Limitless Growth drive levels of consumption. This consumption supports the provision of goods and services that, by and large, people enjoy – after all, this is the consumer culture's primary *raison d'être*. Growth in the system is driven by unsatisfied market demand, as well as by fragmenting markets into more and more niches. Average levels of consumption are excessive and few people are chronically underprivileged. With the exception of those (such as the homeless) who have essentially dropped out, lower socio-economic

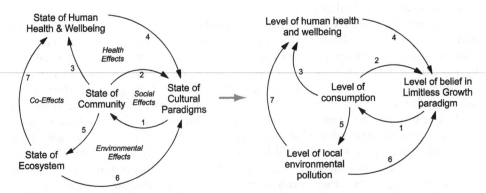

Figure 9.2 A consumption problem space. The diagram on the left is the cultural adaptation template (Figure 7.5). On the right is the problem space of consumption within the Paradigm of Limitless Growth.

groups become simply another target market for differentiated product lines. Here, social inequities arise mostly from disproportionate consumption of certain products, such as junk food, rather than from inadequate consumption itself. This system is perfectly content to further diversify, as delivering new products to new niches – the marketing of 'green' products, for instance – is what it does best.

The 'environment' that the community is aware of is a small fraction of the actual environment impacted by human consumption. For example, immediate and point-source pollution in the local environment are typically perceived as major issues of concern. Consequently, the building of urban parklands or removal of nearby smoke-stacks (L5 in Figure 9.2) is considered as evidence of environmental improvement (L6). People may enjoy the perceived improvements, thereby creating a reinforcing feedback loop that drives additional improvements in the local environment. There is a strong cap on this process, however, as environmental improvements are often seen as luxuries to be had only if the economy can afford them. Within the logic of the Paradigm of Limitless Growth, arguments to improve the environment become arguments to first improve the economy.

In the modern world the 'actual environment' that community consumption affects is globally extended. With the exception of some media reports, however, few feedback signals from these environments are received by the consumers. Further-more, as many environmentally damaging practices manifest as cheaper products, the economic signal to the paradigm is actually positive. As a result, for example, the observation that 'this Asian river is badly polluted' is not made. In other words, since signals about the health of the river are not received (L6), concern for the remote environment is weak or absent. Instead, the observation is made that 'this Asian product (the making of which pollutes the river) is cheap'. Even if a consumer knew that the production that satisfied their needs was damaging a distant river, they might well feel that to curtail their activity of buying that product (L5) would not clean up the river, or that going without the product or buying its more expensive non-polluting alternative was too great a personal inconvenience. Furthermore, they might comfort themselves with the thought that, by buying products produced in distant lands, they were contributing to the growth of the distant economy. After all, if the distant economy were to grow, as required under the Paradigm of Limitless Growth, then it would be possible for the distant communities to repair their damaged rivers.

The health and wellbeing of an affluent community is generally good, certainly in comparison to a chronically poor one. Many of the products and services that consumers choose enhance their personal physiological and psychological wellbeing (L3). However, some of the products that they choose (such as junk food, alcohol, and cigarettes) have unwanted health consequences. The affluence of the community may buffer the effects of these choices to a certain extent through, for example, the provision of medical treatment. Less obvious, more insidious harm may well be occurring at the levels of social functioning. Evidence for this is in the often-expressed observation (L4) that excessive consumerism and individualism in modern societies harms the community by eroding social capital, resulting in loneliness, stress, or depression. However, if addressing negative outcomes of consumerism requires consumption levels to be reduced, this tends to oppose the core values enshrined in the Paradigm of Limitless Growth – consume more in order to grow. In addition, complex systems often push back on efforts to change their state. Such 'policy resistance' occurs when calls for action to remediate the negative health impacts of over-consumption by banning sales of junk food are resisted by market pressures. Sales of junk food generate economic activity, which is what the growth system prioritizes. In this context, the problem of over-consumption is characterized as arising from an individual's choice, for which they are personally responsible. The solution is then seen as the individual choosing to 'eat less and exercise more', rather than by addressing the social and environment context within which the individual behaviour occurs – that is, the presence of tasty, cheap, readily available and highly promoted junk food.

To the extent that the immediate environment is relatively healthy in an affluent community, there are co-benefits for human health and wellbeing (L7). For example, communities that can afford to build and maintain adequate water-treatment facilities can essentially eliminate exposure to waterborne diseases. However, there are also co-costs. Other factors, such as levels of vehicle emissions, might be high, with associated negative health consequences. Where the built environment has been designed badly (for example, where inadequate footpaths make walking difficult), sedentary behaviour is promoted, contributing to obesity and other poor health outcomes. One problem is that negative health impacts arising from, for example, excessive exposure to plastics, heavy metals, or novel chemical compounds, can occur in ways that are very hard to detect and isolate.

As well as affecting distant ecosystems, the consuming community's behaviour has major negative health and wellbeing impacts on other groups outside its sphere of concern; for example, the workers and communities in distant locations who make the products that the community consumes. These individuals are not seen as 'part of' the community but as external providers to it – if thought of at all. So, for example, the buyer of a mobile phone may well feel happier as a result of acquiring it (L3). The harm is felt by the underpaid sweatshop worker who assembled the phone. In the logic of the system the consumer rewards the worker economically. This is seen as sufficient to discharge their moral obligation for any harm done to them. Also, it might be assumed that the worker made the item as willingly as the consumer acquired it, since the worker has been remunerated. Yet, the two parties have not entered into the exchange on fair and equal terms.

Finally, the environmental harm that a community's activity causes in the remote environment (via a link equivalent to L5) has a co-effect felt by the worker and community that live in the remote environment (via a link equivalent to L7). For example, by not paying to clean up heavy metal pollution caused by cotton dyeing, the resulting T-shirt is cheaper than it otherwise would have been. The benefits flow to the consumer's community and the costs flow to the worker's community.

9.7 Conclusion

Application of the cultural adaptation template to this account of life in the Anthropocene has drawn attention to a number of important elements that might not otherwise have been considered, or seen as connected. We can see there is a danger of promoting local 'sustainability' agendas that simply displace the point of impact and come at the cost of social justice elsewhere. Often, the community into which the impact is displaced has less social and environmental capacity to absorb that impact, in which case the net result is to make the problem both socially and environmentally worse. Part of the problem that allows this displacement to happen is an inability to see those more-distant environments and communities as being 'part of the system'. Economic signals alone are incapable of stabilizing the wider social–ecological system, as they simply do not provide the necessary information. This missing feedback prevents the necessary learning and adaption in the group whose behaviour is causing the problem. While there are strong moral arguments as to why the group that is causing problems for remote social–ecological systems ought to do something to change their behaviour, we contend that altruism is not the only motivation. The pragmatic reality is that the group causing the problem are ultimately dependent on all of the systems that they are damaging. Eventually, they too will feel the consequences, and their ignorance or lack of concern for the harm they are causing makes them vulnerable. For all of the planetary boundary issues, the sooner serious and concerted intervention begins, the less cost, effort, and suffering it will take to rectify the situation. The affluent communities of the world currently have the economic and social capacity to address the problems of sustainability. As communities delay, however, the cost of remediation is rising exponentially and they will eventually lose that capacity. If global tipping points are reached, and collapse ensues, no one will be able to buy back what has been lost.

Current levels of production and consumption are seen as normal due to the power of the Paradigm of Limitless Growth. Within this paradigm, socially and environmentally destructive outcomes are seen as perhaps regrettable but, ultimately, unavoidable. Trying to reduce the destructive consequences of one's behaviour by purchasing alternative products can be helpful, and the development of fair-trade and environmentally sound products can see real benefits flow to the producer. However, by itself the consumption of 'green' products is unlikely to transform the system. The system thrives on creating, and then satisfying, an ever greater plethora of product lines. That is how it continues to grow, even though the greater proportion of its consumers have had their basic needs satisfied. A more strategic, ultimately political, form of engagement with the system by the consumer is needed in order to achieve more widespread and structural transformation. This essentially requires pressure to redesign the system so that socially and environmentally destructive outcomes do not occur. In the short term at least, this will entail the involvement of those businesses and corporations whose current systems of production are currently causing harm.

Finally, we can now recognize that agents in the system act according to the logic of the Paradigm of Limitless Growth, which encourages communities to consume more in order to enhance their perceived levels of comfort and convenience at the lowest possible cost to themselves. By and large, they enjoy the things that they consume, and it is unlikely that someone would willingly consume less of what they enjoy without a compelling reason. For many, being told that they are 'destroying the Earth' is not a reason that they respond to positively. As discussed, they see their activities as perfectly normal and believe that their behaviour is well within their rights, and clearly encouraged by the system. Consequently, we need an alternative paradigm that embeds other values. Within this alternative paradigm, consuming less would not seem so onerous if in so doing something of greater value was achieved. Within the framework of an alternative paradigm, the consumer would perceive it to be in their own interest to consume less, with less social and environmentally destructive consequences. We can further note that an individual cannot possibly know or care about *all* the consequences of every action he or she takes. However, as discussed, the present sum of all human action is unsustainable. Consequently, it is in the immediate self-interest of every individual (but especially those in the affluent developed nations) to support systems of production and consumption that deliver just and sustainable outcomes at all levels. Living well in the Anthropocene requires individual behaviour to be globally just and sustainable, *despite the individual not knowing the full consequences of his or her actions*. This outcome will occur only if the dominant paradigm changes, and this will require political engagement from an active, concerned citizenry.

In summary, a paradigm that promotes the goal of 'sufficiency' must come to dominate the human economy now that it is global (Section 6.3). The question is how over-consumers in affluent communities might be motivated to reduce their current levels of consumption. The arguments for ethical change presented in this book indicate that, ideally, this must be done as a matter of willing choice, rather than some forced reallocation. Apart from anything else, those who have the most are typically the most powerful, so it is not clear who could do this reallocation other than the powerful themselves. It is certainly unlikely that the oppressed could force them to do it. The possibility that affluent consumers might willingly consume less is discussed in the next chapter.

References

Apostolides, A., Broadberry, S., Campbell, B., Overton, M., and van Leeuwen, B. (2008). 'English Agricultural Output and Labour Productivity, 1250–1850: Some preliminary estimates'. *Reconstructing the National Income of Britain and Holland, c.1270/1500 to 1850*, The Leverhulme Trust.

Best Foot Forward Ltd (2002). *City Limits: A resource flow and ecological footprint analysis of Greater London*. London, Chartered Institution of Wastes Management – Environmental Body.

Broadberry, S., Campbell, B., and van Leeuwen, B. (2011). 'English Medieval Population: Reconciling Time Series and Cross Sectional Evidence'. *Reconstructing the National Income of Britain and Holland, c.1279/1500 to 1850*, Leverhulme Trust. Reference number F/00215AR.

Davies, N. (1999). *The Isles: A history*. London, MacMillan.

Deutsch, L., Dyball, R., and Steffen, W. (2013). 'Feeding cities: Food security and ecosystem support in an urbanizing world'. *Urbanization, Biodiversity and Ecosystem Services: Challenges and Opportunities*, Springer: 505–537.

Food and Agriculture Organization (2012). *The State of Food Insecurity in the World*. Rome, Food and Agriculture Organization.

Gilbert, N. (2012). 'One-third of our greenhouse gas emissions come from agriculture'. *Nature* doi:10.1038/nature.2012.11708.

Ingram, J., Ericksen, P., Liverman, D., and Ebook Library. (2010). *Food Security and Global Environmental Change*. London, Earthscan: 1 online resource (385 pp.).

Marx, L. (2010). 'Technology: The emergence of a hazardous concept'. *Technology and Culture* 51(3): 561–577.

Porter, J. R., Dyball, R., Dumaresq, D., Deutsch, L., and Matsuda, H. (2014). 'Feeding capitals: Urban food security and self-provisioning in Canberra, Copenhagen and Tokyo'. *Global Food Security* 3(1): 1–7.

Rackham, O. (2000). *The History of the Countryside*. London, Phoenix Press.

Rockström, J., Steffen, W., Noone, K., Persson, A., Chapin, F. S., Lambin, E., Lenton, M. Scheffer, T. M., Folke, C., Schellnhuber, H. J., Nykvist, B., de Wit, C. A., Hughes, T., van der Leeuw, S., Rodhe, H., Sorlin, S., Snyder, P. K., Costanza, R., Svedin, U., Falkenmark, M., Karlberg, L., Corell, R. W., Fabry, V. J., Hansen, J., Walker, B., Liverman, D., Richardson, K., Crutzen, P., and Foley, J. A. (2009). 'Planetary boundaries: Exploring the safe operating space for humanity'. *Ecology and Society* 14(2).

Smil, V. (2008). *Energy in Nature and Society: General energetics of complex systems*, Cambridge, MA, MIT Press.

Steffen, W., Sanderson, A., Tyson, P., Jäger, J., Matson, P. A., Moore III, B., Oldfield, F., Richardson, K., Schellnhuber, H. J. , Turner II, B. L., and Wasson, R. J. (2004). *Global Change and the Earth System: A planet under pressure*, Berlin, Springer Verlag.

Sukhdev, P. (2013). 'Foreword'. *Urbanization, Biodiversity and Ecosystem Services: Challenges and opportunities*. New York, Springer.

Wright, R. (2004). *A Short History of Progress*, Melbourne, Text Publishing.

Wrigley, E. A. (2006). 'The transition to an advanced organic economy: Half a millennium of English agriculture'. *Economic History Review* LIX(3): 435–480.

10 Consumers and global food systems

There are two spiritual dangers in not owning a farm. One is the danger of supposing breakfast comes from a grocery, and the other that heat comes from a furnace. To avoid the first danger, one should plant a garden, preferably where there is no grocer to confuse the issue.

(*Good Oak*, Aldo Leopold 1966)

10.1 Introduction

In this chapter we focus on the production and consumption of food – our conclusions can be generalized to other products. Food production has direct environmental impacts and food is something that everyone must consume. What food is consumed, and in what amounts, affects the health and wellbeing of the consumer. These effects can be positive – for example, when people eat a balanced diet of fresh, nutritious, and flavoursome food. Or they can be negative, when there is over-consumption of fats, sugars, and salts, as might be obtained from a diet based primarily on junk food. The two extremes also have social implications. Home-cooked food can be a source of pride for the chef, convivial exchange between family and friends, and a cause for celebration. Consumption of junk food and pre-prepared TV dinners requires no skill, is not socially enriching, and may suppress social exchange – the cultural process of 'eating a meal' is treated as merely fuelling the human body. That said, consumers of junk and highly pre-prepared processed foods nevertheless do find them enjoyable.

There are also significant ethical dimensions relating to how food is sourced, distributed, and made available. Again, these can be positive, such as under local food movements and fair trade networks, where producers are valued and receive adequate compensation for their efforts, or negative, where producers work in poor conditions for little return, including not having adequate access to the food they themselves produce.

This chapter is centrally concerned with how a consumer might generate the necessary concern for how the food they consume is produced, such that currently unjust and unsustainable food systems are transformed into just and sustainable ones. Following the argument of the previous chapter, it focuses on affluent urban communities who currently enjoy high levels of food security. These communities have the prerequisite freedom of choice to change what and how they consume, and to bring political pressure to bear to transform current systems of production and distribution nationally and internationally.

10.2 Food system paradigms

In their book *Food Wars*, Lang and Heasman have characterized the dominant approach to food systems in the affluent west as operating within a Productionist Paradigm (Lang and Heasman 2004). Food production within this paradigm is driven by a commitment to raise volumes of output through intensive high-energy inputs. Commodities mass-produced in ever greater amounts are cheaper, with lower prices paid per unit of product, driving farmers to produce more to achieve an equivalent income. In this paradigm, the environments that provide food resources are global, with price being the prime criterion for selection. Aside from minimum standards indicating the quality of the commodity, produce from any one source is taken to be like-for-like substitutable for produce from anywhere else. The assumption that all products can be substituted results in them being treated as if they are inexhaustible. Global networks for transporting and processing bulk commodities are underpinned by cheap and readily available energy. Environmental harm or negative impacts on the health and wellbeing of producers and consumers are seen as tangential. Economists refer to such negative impacts as 'externalities' whose costs should theoretically be factored into the price of the goods and services that generate them. In practice, this requires regulatory intervention that is difficult to achieve. As a result the approach to food production is primarily concerned with making food physically available in large, cheap volumes and is typically not concerned with outcomes such as obesity or rural decline. Food processors value-add by converting these basic commodities into highly refined and diversified product lines. This delivers a plethora of choices to the consumer, including a range of exotic cuisines that would otherwise require considerable skill to prepare. Crucially, consumers' only engagement with the food system under this paradigm is as economic agents, selecting on the basis of the cost of the product weighted against the benefits they believe it will deliver.

The Productionist Paradigm is clearly a version of the Paradigm of Limitless Growth, and the reasons society needs to shift away from these consumptive paradigms were outlined in the previous chapter. It is not in the interests of consumers or producers that food is produced in this way. It is not simply that Productionist food systems tend to promote unhealthy food choices, such as highly processed pre-prepared meals. The system can and does produce healthy food choices. Indeed, the system offers product lines across the spectrum – it loses nothing if a consumer oscillates between eating junk food and putting on weight and eating a low-calorie weight-loss programme. Typically, however, the internal driver of economic efficiency in the Productionist Paradigm results in food commodities that deliver different health outcomes to different market demographics. For example, the wealthy members of a community might be able to afford to eat lean meat, such as an expensive cut of steak, with relatively low negative health impacts. The Productionist Paradigm then ensures that the balance of the animal is eaten by, for example, packaging the fatty offcuts into cheap sausages. These are consumed in disproportionate amounts by members of the community in lower socio-economic groups, resulting in excessive intake of fats with high negative health impacts. From the system's perspective an efficient outcome has been obtained, with the entire animal converted to marketable 'product' and sold to consumers based on their ability and willingness to pay. If all members of the community ate equal shares of 'good' and 'poor' cuts (in moderation), intakes of 'lean' and 'fat' would not be concentrated in any one social demographic group, and the negative health outcomes would largely be avoided.

The capacity of the wealthy to secure sufficient amounts of nutritious food is a major health advantage. Beyond this, the capacity of wealth to guard an individual against the negative impacts of the Paradigm of Limitless Growth is limited. Industrial food production across globalized networks has resulted in a range of disease pathways that wealth cannot necessarily protect against, such as bird flu, mad cow disease, and salmonella poisoning. At a larger scale, as the impacts of current production systems reach and exceed planetary thresholds (Section 9.4), it is likely to become increasingly difficult for wealth to provide access to good, nutritious, and healthy food. Obviously, wealthy individuals and wealthy nations will be able to outbid their poorer counterparts for dwindling supplies of healthy food, but ultimately all will be affected. Even if wealthy communities consider that it is in their interest to continue to depend upon Productionist food systems, this does not alter the fact that these systems, in addition to being unsustainable, are unethical. As discussed in Chapter 1, human ecology holds that the prudent and ethical dimensions of sustainability are inseparable, and so this unethical dimension is also a driver of paradigm change. However, as illustrated below, it is likely that with a broader sense of self-interest, consumers can see that it is both prudent and ethical for them to promote more just and sustainable food systems.

The discussion now turns to food consumption in three affluent nations, Australia, Denmark, and Japan, to show that it is *at least* prudent that wealthy consumers support alternative, just, and sustainable approaches to food production, processing, and distribution.

10.3 Urban food system vulnerability

All urban populations are vulnerable to processes that could disrupt the food-supply systems on which they depend. Factors such as the productivity of food-producing landscapes, issues of ownership and access to the products of those landscapes, attitudes to interstate and international trade, distance from markets, and supply-chain complexity all play a role in determining how and from where a city derives its food. Because different cities have structured their food systems differently, each has unique elements. Consequently, it is necessary to understand a city's socio-environmental history, and its current sociopolitical context, in order to accurately assess the resilience of its food system and make policy decisions that will improve that resilience. There is no 'one size fits all' solution and we should take care when we learn from what worked in one context and attempt to apply it to another. However, through the application of the cultural adaptation template (Section 7.5), we can identify common aspects of the food-system problem space.

In some places, including in affluent nations, significant quantities of food can be produced within the city itself. However, in practice this is most likely to happen in areas where there are large numbers of urban poor, already exposed to chronic food insecurity. This occurs in Africa, for example, where 43 per cent of the urban population live below the poverty line, and slums account for 65 per cent of urban populations (Anderson *et al.* 2013: 455). The amounts produced vary, but figures of around 10 per cent of urban households practising horticulture have been reported, with a high of nearly half in the Cameroon (FAO 2012). Population growth and immigration often drive the physical growth of a city over what remains of its prime agricultural land. When a community has very little economic capacity to import food from outside the region, widespread urban malnutrition results. In such situations, urban agriculture can make significant increases to human health and wellbeing through the provision of nutritionally important fresh vegetables and some animal protein for consumption by individual families. Such local production is unlikely to disrupt the economic and social viability of the region's farming communities, since the individuals concerned are typically unable to afford regional farm produce anyway. Indeed, in many cases significant exports from the city region occur, despite the local population's consumption demands not having been met. For example, the city of Kumasi in Ghana is estimated to export 50 per cent of its local produce, even during lean seasons when local supplies are inadequate to meet local demand (Pearson and Dyball 2014: 116). Exports like these are typically shipped to more affluent communities, who have been able to outbid local communities to secure access to the produce in question. For local urban production to provision local urban consumption, access to land needs to be secured so that the people working the plots can be confident they will receive the benefits of their labour.

In affluent urban communities the primary food security issue is not one of inadequate supplies leading to general malnutrition and starvation. Consequently, there is less motivation for the community to spend time and effort producing its own food. Total volumes of food produced by affluent urban communities, as a percentage of total volumes consumed, are typically very small and seasonal, but nevertheless significant. For example, Luxemburg's *Office International du Coin de Terre et des Jardins Familiaux* represents 3 million garden allotments in Europe, and there is a growing movement of community gardens in North America. Although pockets of urban dwellers, including some of the poor, may obtain important nutrition from urban gardens, overall the value of urban food production in affluent cities is likely to lie more in its educative, active lifestyle, and community-building role, than in its ability to contribute significant percentages of total amount of food consumed.

In affluent cities, the main issue is who eats what meals in what proportions. Poor health outcomes typically arise not from under-consumption per se, but rather from over-consumption, or the consumption of a nutritionally poor diet – behaviour that results in such conditions as obesity, Type II diabetes, hypertension, and cardiovascular diseases (Section 9.5). Food producers are influenced by how the food they produce is valued by consumers, and whether this value is transmitted back to them through the food production, processing, and distribution chains. The long-term health and wellbeing of consumers is inextricably linked with the sustainable production of adequate and nutritious food by farmers whose own social–environmental systems are healthy.

More generally, the way that the Productionist food system secures food for affluent communities produces global, social, and environmental distortions that result in inadequate levels of consumption in poor communities. These distortions need to be addressed if the global resource impacts of affluent consumption are to be reduced, while at the same time allowing the consumption levels of the poor to increase. As discussed in Section 6.5, there must be a convergence of the total resource consumption of the affluent and the total resource consumption of the poor, raising the latter to at least minimally dignified levels. The resulting impacts of globally averaged food consumption have to be in the safe and equitable operating zone (Figures 6.9 and 6.10), and below the planetary thresholds discussed in Section 9.4.

10.4 Australia: net food exporter

Australian farms are not particularly productive per hectare by world standards (Box 10.1). However, the very large areas under production, coupled with low population densities, result in Australian farmers producing large surpluses above domestic requirements. It is claimed that the 120,000 farmers in Australia each feed 600 people on average. Of these people, 150 reside in Australia and 450 overseas

---

Box 10.1 The Australian Capital Region

Canberra, the national capital of Australia, is a city with a population of about 380,000, located 150 kilometres inland in the south-east of the continent. Together with its hinterlands it forms the quasi-official Australian Capital Region (ACR). The ACR comprises about 5.86 million hectares, with a total population of 550,000 (including Canberra). The hinterlands of the ACR are mostly under agricultural production, with farms operated as large landholdings of several thousand hectares by a few individuals, typically as family businesses. The farming community is ageing as a result of a general inability to attract young people to careers as farmers. Because of their size and low labour levels, the farms are highly mechanized, with relatively nutrient-poor soils, and often severe water constraints.

Agriculture in the ACR is dominated by grazing (sheep and cattle), and broadacre wheat and canola production (Porter *et al.* 2014). There is some horticulture (fruit and wine grapes), dairy (in the wetter areas), and fairly extensive forest cover (much of which is managed commercially). Generally speaking, it is unlikely that the output of the ACR could be increased by additional land-use change, as land use is constrained by soil fertility and water availability. Lands devoted to commodity production are producing at close to maximum yields. For example, the land devoted to grazing would simply not sustain cropping. Increased output may be achieved through additional fertilizers, although the benefits are limited. There is also a growing trend to de-commodification, through the production of specialist crop varieties to meet niche markets and on-farm value-adding on smaller properties. In the event of drought, for example, there is potentially zero financial return on the very high level of inputs. In the longer term, these highly geared, artificial, input-dependent farming systems are likely to encounter one or more social or environmental limits.

A small but growing number of farmers are developing alternative approaches to high-input industrial farming systems, by focusing on basic principles of agroecology. These strategies support on-farm ecosystem structure and function, by building and restoring soil health and harnessing the capacity of life processes to power greater rates of nutrient cycling and carbon capture. Such approaches ultimately enhance productivity. Because they have lower dependence on artificial inputs, these alternative farming strategies have lower exposure to risk, and so are more resilient. The farmers' intimate knowledge of the land is restored to its key role in determining his or her skill and ability to work with natural processes, reverse landscape degradation, and produce healthy food – delivering both psychological and environmental benefits (Soils for Life 2012).

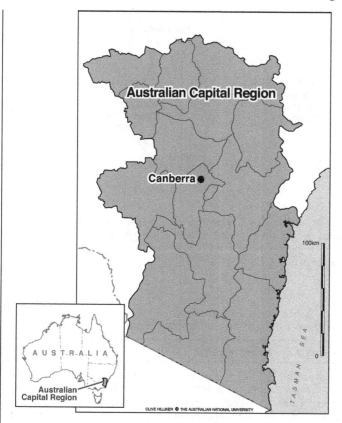

CLIVE HILLIKER ℗ THE AUSTRALIAN NATIONAL UNIVERSITY

The Australian Capital Region

The population of Canberra could sustain itself on the food produced in the ACR (Porter *et al.* 2014). The resulting diet would be nutritionally adequate but less varied year-round than currently enjoyed – although there would be no shortages of meat pies and hamburgers. Highly seasonal produce, such as tomatoes, would have to be either preserved or eaten only at certain times of the year. Foods such as rice and tropical fruits that the region is incapable of producing would have to be foregone. Processing facilities would need to be located in the region. Large infrastructure items, such as abattoirs, grain mills, and warehouses, would require major investment. However, one benefit would be that consumers would be more closely connected to food producers, and so would have a direct concern for farmers' social and economic wellbeing and the environmental sustainability of their production methods.

Shorter distribution networks, the greater possibility of nutrient recycling, fresher seasonal produce, a larger number of smaller producers, and greater economic support to the local region, are among a host of reasons why greater use of local food resources is highly desirable. Regional initiatives, such as farmer's markets, local food cooperatives, and local food labels, can all help maximize consumption of local production. However, while an increase in the consumption of local produce is possible, it is likely that ACR consumers will continue to demand food that is brought in from more remote landscapes.

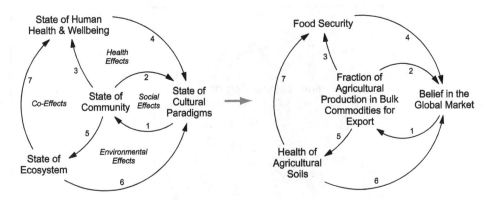

Figure 10.1 Food security in Australia. The diagram on the left is the cultural adaptation template (Figure 7.5). On the right is a system-of-interest diagram that focuses attention on some implications of a belief in global markets. The links are described in Table 10.1.

Table 10.1 Influence links in the Australia system-of-interest (Figure 10.1)

Link	Actions/processes/mechanisms represented
1	Belief in the efficacy of the global market leads Australian decision makers to establish policies that set Australia up as 'the granary of the world'. Australia's need for guaranteed access to overseas markets means that free-trade negotiations are entered into with enthusiasm. Economic arrangements support export-oriented farmers, who favour bulk commodity production over other forms of production.
2	In general, the downsides of a dominant export focus are not seen. Little concern for the way that overseas consumers drive decisions about the future development of Australian agriculture. No pressure to reduce dependence on export markets.
3	Economic processes driven by the need to meet overseas demand, rather than Australian food security. Australian farmers driven to compete in global commodity markets, which drives down terms of trade (Sawin *et al.* 2003). Corresponding dependence on importation of food (even vegetables) decreases profitability of Australian farms.
4	In general, little concern for food security. No pressure to reduce involvement in global markets.
5	Soil nutrients exported along with agricultural products. Nutrient loss compensated for by application of artificial fertilizers.
6	Health of soils is considered, but as a technical problem that can be solved, for example, by application of fertilizers, using no-till methods of crop production. No pressure to reduce dependence on global markets.
7	Poor soils reduce resilience of food-production system. Low soil-nutrient levels reduce nutritional value of foods.

(National Farmers Federation 2012). There is a limit on the fraction of total Australian production that Australians can consume. Domestic production meets about 93 per cent of Australian consumption, but that consumption accounts for only about 25 per cent of total production (National Farmers Federation 2012). This means that some 75 per cent of consumers are overseas. It is their preferences, and the prices that they are prepared to pay, that have the greatest influence on the nature and viability of Australian agriculture. Under current arrangements, food commodity prices trend down, forcing farmers to produce more each year for the same return, which in turn drives the unit price of the commodity down further. This reinforcing feedback effect drives intensification of agriculture, which eats into the environment's productive capacity by exporting nutrients faster than they can be replenished. Whether they know it or not, international consumers are vulnerable to the social and environmental dynamics affecting Australian rural communities, since it is these landscapes that are feeding them.

Embedded in the Productionist Paradigm is a belief in global markets and their capacity to secure food supplies. In Australia local consumption is 100 per cent satisfied by national production, leaving the remainder surplus for export. The ratio of food consumed domestically to food exported is about 1:3, at least for bulk commodities such as wheat and beef.

Australia focuses on the production of bulk commodities for export, and imports niche and high-value products. The affluent Australian community is highly food-secure and, in principle, can secure that food from domestic Australian sources. In practice, however, only basic food commodities are actually secured from domestic producers. A range of other products, for example, frozen vegetables, are imported. Nevertheless, for most categories, the community can or could secure supplies from national and local produce.

With very large surpluses, Australia is not perceived as being vulnerable to food system shortages. In terms of raw numbers, this is true. However, Australia is one of the most urbanized countries in the world and only around a week's worth of food stocks are held in urban centres (Pearson and Dyball 2014: 118). Factors such as very long, road-based transport networks place certain aspects of the Australian food system at greater risk than might be expected. For example, fuel prices have a fairly direct flow-on effect to the cost of food, and weather events such as flooding can isolate quite large cities. Nevertheless, the assessment that security is high reinforces the belief in global markets.

Around 60 million people overseas are dependent on Australian food exports, and it could be argued that Australia is morally obliged to continue to support them. The consumption demands of this international community is a major driver of impacts on Australian agricultural soils. This impact is felt via a link equivalent to L5 flowing from this international, rather than local, community. For as long as overseas demand is for high volumes of undifferentiated bulk commodities bought at the lowest price possible, the impacts of this equivalent link will be negative. As bulk commodity prices decline, Australian producers will try to get ever greater yields from their land to maintain their income. This typically will lead to high-input fertilizer regimes, which cannot fully replace all the nutrients exported, leading to a net loss of soil nutrients and a decreasing mineral density of the food produced. The consequent reduction in Australian soil-nutrient stocks is unsustainable and, as these stocks were low to start with, likely to lead to collapse of agricultural output.

The negative impact of food exports on soil nutrient levels might be expected to erode belief in global markets as the solution to global food security. This is one of the arguments used by some advocates of local consumption of local produce – nutrients can be recycled when producer and consumers are geographically close to each other. However, this argument ignores the fact that local consumers cannot consume all local produce. Conventional economics would suggest that the price of the exported food could be exchanged for imported replacement fertilizers, but that is not currently happening. Nutrient loss is recognized as an issue by some, but the level of concern is not great enough to challenge (via L6) the widespread belief in global markets. Consequently, more innovative ideas about closing international nutrient loops – for example, by back-loading to Australia nutrients reclaimed from Japan – are not on the agenda of the Productionist Paradigm.

Ultimately the health of Australian agricultural soils directly affects Australia's ability to provide food security for local and international communities. There are alternative regeneration farming methods that work to build soil health. These approaches can lead to greater production, while avoiding the negative consequences of conventional high-input regimes. Such farming systems could underpin more sustainable food production in the future. However, only a small number of farmers are currently using these methods. For this number to increase, the support of consumers is required. Crucially, for Australia, this includes the majority of consumers who are located offshore. Such a multinational response will require a change in the belief that global markets solve food problems, and demands a move away from the Productionist Paradigm.

10.5 Denmark: food transformer

In contrast to Australia, Denmark has deep, fertile soils with ample rain providing reliable groundwater – conditions that are well suited to naturally high-yielding agriculture. Past land-use practice, designed to maximize agricultural output, led to almost total clearing of natural woodlands. The resulting high levels of production supported the exportation of wheat and other grains in the mid-nineteenth century, bringing significant revenue into the country. However, Denmark's capacity to act as a major food exporter was hampered by the nation's small size. New transportation networks enabled very large volumes of grain, grown in inland United States and central Europe, to be transported and sold into international markets at a scale with which Denmark could not compete (Jesperson 2004: 148). Consequently, Danish food exports moved away from bulk carbohydrates and into higher value products. Today, pig products dominate Danish agricultural exports (including to Australia) and are the main commodities for which Denmark is self-sufficient. The bulk of food that Danes consume is drawn from across Europe and elsewhere, the system primarily driven by considerations of economic efficiency.

A significant percentage of Danish pig production relies on the primary productivity of landscapes outside Denmark, as the country imports a significant (and growing) proportion of its pig feed. A major component of this feed is soybeans grown in South America. Partly because it no longer has to set land aside for growing feed for pigs, Denmark is able to allow land previously used for this purpose to revert to forest cover. The national goal for reafforestation is about 20–25 per cent of land cover by the end of the twenty-first century (FAO 2010). These restored forests provide

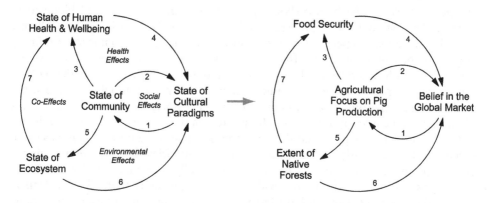

Figure 10.2 Food security in Denmark. The diagram on the left is the cultural adaptation template (Figure 7.5). On the right is a system-of-interest diagram that focuses attention on some implications of a belief in global markets. The links are described in Table 10.2.

Table 10.2 Influence links in the Denmark system-of-interest (Figure 10.2)

Link	Actions/processes/mechanisms represented
1	Belief in the efficacy of the global market leads Danish decision makers to establish a focus on the production of niche products to the global market. These actions lead to promotion of pig farming, supported by importation of pig feed.
2	The success of niche production leads to an increase in belief in the effectiveness of global markets.
3	A focus on niche production affects food security because a large proportion of essential foods (such as grains) must be imported. Thus Danish food security depends on the sustainability of imports from other countries, especially within the European Union.
4	In general, no serious problems with food security are seen. Thus, there is little pressure to change the basic paradigms. There is some concern over food standards, particularly the ability of other countries to produce organic foods that meet Danish standards.
5	Focus on pig production and importation of grain (for pig feed and human consumption) releases farmland for reafforestation. Action is also taken to improve the extent and health of wetlands. This action results in increases in ecosystem health.
6	Observation of increases in the extent of native forests and wetlands, increases belief in the global markets. This is an effective learning link.
7	Increased extent of native forest contributes to food security via increased health of agricultural ecosystems. But, the reduction in area of farmland acts to reduce the already small capacity for local production of foods other than pigs.

a range of functions, such as carbon regulation, cultural amenity, and biodiversity (Hansen and Vesterdal 2004, Zandersen and Termansen 2013). Although this is highly desirable from a Danish perspective, it does mean that the ecological impact of primary production has been displaced from Denmark to South America and elsewhere. Essentially, South American landscapes are cleared to produce pig-feed so that Danish landscapes can recover. The economic exchange of one commodity for the other usually ignores environmental consequences. Furthermore, the financial exchange is unequal, as value-adding always is. The money paid to the grain producers is not enough to purchase the pork that their grain was transformed into when it was eaten by the pig. Consequently, the landscapes and communities that provide the photosynthesized energy that supports life are economically marginalized. The economic rationalist's solution to the grain producers' predicament is that, like the Danish farmers, they should get out of basic carbohydrate production and into higher value products (such as wine). They can then sell the wine and use the profits to buy their staples from elsewhere. However, it is impossible that this displacement of primary production can be practised by everyone. Somewhere, someone on the planet needs to stay in the business of producing the basic carbohydrates that support global food systems.

Food production in Denmark reflects the Productionist Paradigm, with its belief in the efficiency of global markets. A particular regional manifestation of this is the free trade of commodities across the European Union. If 'local food' is interpreted as Danish food, most of what the Danes consume is 'imported', and much of that from elsewhere in Europe. However, as the European Union itself is less than 60 per cent the land area of Australia, it could be argued that this product is more 'local' than much Australian product consumed in Australia. While local production is valued as part of the aesthetic of Danish landscapes, greater emphasis is placed on the importation of food, especially basic grain commodities, over local production of those commodities. The rationale is that it is more economically efficient to import cheap grain and add value to it by transforming it into pork for local consumption and export. This reinforces the belief in the efficiency of global markets.

The affluent Danish community is highly food secure, as it can readily access the food it needs from the European Union and other international imports. Denmark has maintained a fairly constant self-provisioning capacity (of about 40 per cent of those food products that it is capable of producing) for the past 50 years. The sustainability of this production is based in part on approximately constant population levels. It could secure more food from landscapes over which it has sovereign jurisdiction, but sees no need to expand domestic production. The fact that Denmark's food security stems from its capacity to source foods from outside its sovereign jurisdiction is not seen as a risk. But, in the case of one commodity – pork – production relies on imported pig feed. This does not equate to self-sufficiency. If, for whatever reason, that flow of feed ceased, Denmark would have to reduce its pig population, or increase the land area devoted to growing feed at the expense of native forests. However, their inherent vulnerability to disruption of these flows is largely ignored.

The importation of significant percentages of the food consumed in Denmark, including that fed to livestock, relieves Danish soils from the impacts of the associated production processes. Consequently, large areas of land are able to revert to 'natural' wooded conditions, with generally positive consequences for the health of the environment. The observation of increasing afforested areas in Denmark is greeted positively. Both for environmental reasons, such as reduced impacts from farming and increased carbon sequestration, and for social reasons, such as the important place forests have in the Danish national psyche, increased forest cover is welcomed. This reinforces the belief that relying on global markets for food imports is a good idea.

However, the benefits of reafforestation are not necessarily as great as they appear to be – human-created grazing meadows can have greater biodiversity than the dense 'natural' woodlands. As it is not economically viable to graze these areas, some land managers now mechanically clear them. Furthermore, as discussed above, the local consumption of imported food has negative impacts on the overseas landscapes that produce the food. Given that Danish landscapes are highly productive, displacing the point of production to sites overseas can see total environmental impacts increase. For example, retiring Danish agricultural land (with an average wheat yield of 7.2 tonnes per hectare) and substituting wheat imports from Australia (with a national average yield of around 2 tonnes per hectare) results in over three and a half times more land area being devoted to wheat cultivation (Australian Bureau of Statistics 2006).

Danish consumers have, and can afford, a high level of concern for healthy produce from healthy soils. For example, the demand for organic produce has grown strongly in the past decades and now over 6 per cent of all Danish farms are organic (Landbrugsinfo 2014). However, given the amount of food imported, Danish concern for organic produce will need to expand to include concern for healthy food produced from healthy landscapes, wherever on the planet they are located. Ultimately, this extension will require an adaptation of the belief in global markets to provide this, through new signals sent through L4. The Productionist Paradigm will have to give way to a new paradigm that insists that food systems must sustainably provision *all* consumers and support *all* producers.

10.6 Japan: food importer

Japanese landscapes are incredibly productive and, together with extensive fisheries, sustain a traditional diet based on fish, rice, and vegetables. However, Japanese farming output has been unable to meet the demands of the Japanese population. Part of the problem is the extremely limited amount of land that is suitable for farming due to the mountainous landscape. The other problem is social, and relates to the size and management of Japanese farms. As a matter of national security, Japan has sought to maintain self-sufficiency in its traditional primary carbohydrate staple, rice, which many Japanese farmers produce. Although yields are high per hectare, Japanese rice production is not particularly efficient. With a typical area of less than two hectares, most farms are extremely small, independently operated, and unable to achieve the efficiencies of scale that larger operations achieve. Many are run by part-time farmers, whose major income is not from farming. The price of rice is high but imports are restricted, so over 95 per cent of the rice consumed in Japan is domestically produced.

Traditional Japanese farming involves '*satoyama*' landscapes, with a mosaic of villages, paddy fields, sustainably harvested woodland, and other small-scale activities that function to conserve nutrients and build ecosystem health. Biodiversity in *satoyama* landscapes is high. Where *satoyama* landscapes have been abandoned, the regeneration that follows is seen by the Japanese as an undesirable deterioration into 'wasteland'. However, they are not very economically efficient, and despite the financial support provided to maintaining them, like much small-scale agricultural practice, these traditional farming systems are falling out of service. One problem is that farmers are ageing and Japanese youth show little inclination to take up farming – far more attractive lifestyles can be found in cities. A further problem is that Japanese dietary preferences are changing. Since the Second World War the Japanese economy has grown significantly and with it preferences for a more 'Western' diet. This has resulted in growing demand for products that Japan cannot easily produce itself, and that are consequently imported in growing volumes. In 1960, Japan had a population of 92.5 million who consumed 126 kilograms of rice per capita. By 2010, the population had climbed to 127.5 million but per capita consumption had fallen by half, to 67.4 kilograms. So, despite maintaining self-sufficiency in rice production, the proportion of rice in the Japanese diet has fallen and Japanese total food self-sufficiency has fallen to less than 40 per cent (Deutsch *et al.* 2013).

One strategy to address this has been to reduce subsidies for rice production, and instead subsidize the production of foods that form the basis of the new Japanese diet. This would entail switching to the production of wheat and grain products for animal feed – notably beef. However, the Japanese environment is not suited to these products. For example, rice yields are over six and a half tonnes per hectare (FAO 2013) while wheat yields are closer to four tonnes per hectare. Furthermore, the knowledge and skills of Japanese farmers would have to change, and they would have to layout and equip large-scale wheat growing enterprises. This would further drive the demise of traditional land management and its associated ecosystem services.

If you believe in the capacity of global markets to secure food, none of this is a problem. From a Productionist perspective, Japan would be better off abandoning farming altogether, and rely on its non-agricultural sectors' earning capacity to allow it to purchase all the food it needs from world markets. Instead of harnessing the ecological services of its own landscapes, it could use its economic power to appropriate the ecological services of landscapes in other countries, such as Australia. However, exchanging Japanese production for Australian equivalent is not a like-for-like substitution. Because the land productivities are so different, a much larger area of Australian land needs to be put into production to substitute for each hectare of Japanese land taken out of production. Assuming the additional land area was available, Japanese food security would then be dependent on Australian sovereign decisions about how it manages its lands, who it chooses to export to, how large it wants its own population levels to be, and so on. For example, in Chapter 2 we described how concern for the environmental health of Australian rivers is producing political pressure to have water currently allocated to irrigation returned to the rivers. Japan can do little to influence the outcome of this conflict, but in a global market it directly affects Japan's food security. As it is, food exports from Australia are exhausting Australian nutrient stocks and accumulating nutrients to problematic levels in net importing nations such as Japan. If Japan is to continue to consume food grown in Australia then some way to close this loop must be found, so that exported nutrients are returned to the landscapes of origin.

Finally, while Japan finds it hard to keep Japanese youth interested in farming, it has no capacity whatsoever to keep Australian youth interested in farming. Like their

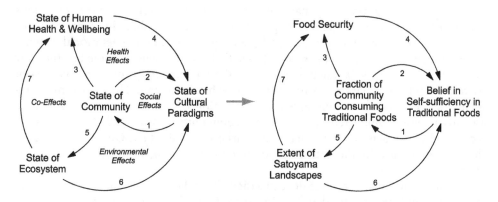

Figure 10.3 Food security in Japan. The diagram on the left is the cultural adaptation template (Figure 7.5). On the right is a system-of-interest diagram that focuses attention on some implications of a belief in the need to maintain self-sufficiency in traditional foods. The links are described in Table 10.3.

Table 10.3 Influence links in the Japan system-of-interest (Figure 10.3)

Link	Actions/processes/mechanisms represented
1	Belief in the importance of being self-sufficient in traditional foods prompts actions to protect domestic rice production. This belief in self-sufficiency also drives determination to remain aloof from the global market.
2	The paradigm is under pressure from those who want increased availability of commodities, such as wheat and beef, that must be imported.
3	Maintenance of traditional rice growing maintains food security by holding down dependence on imported foods.
4	Food security not seen as a problem by those who want to increase imports of commodities (such as wheat and beef). Those who believe that dependence on imports reduces food security will take actions to defend the self-sufficiency paradigm.
5	Adherence to traditional diets leads to determination to maintain traditional *satoyama* landscapes. Positive policy action is being taken to prevent abandonment of the traditional farming landscapes, and their reversion to natural forests.
6	The presence of policies to prevent the abandonment of *satoyama* landscapes supports the self-sufficiency paradigm.
7	Farming is dwindling in Japan as *satoyama* landscapes are lost. The resulting reduction in number of farms and skilled labour put food security at risk.

Japanese counterparts, few young Australians are keen to pursue a career in agriculture, and Australian rural communities are slowly declining. Again, Japanese food security is vulnerable to this demographic change, which it cannot influence. For all these reasons, it would seem that Japan is right to be concerned about its very low levels of food self-sufficiency, and its vulnerability to processes that could affect its food security, but which are outside its control.

Changing demographics in Japan are changing food preferences. There are various drivers of this change, including exposure to Western media, the penetration of Japanese markets by international fast-food corporations, and generational changes that see traditional cuisine as 'old fashioned'. Beef and wheat dominate the new demands. Programmes designed to encourage the Japanese to eat more rice have been tried. So too have programmes to grow more wheat in Japan. These have met with limited success. Japan has increased its production of beef, but the feed for these animals is mostly imported. The Japanese community has the affluence to readily secure these products from international markets, and does so. One consequence is the rise of obesity in the Japanese population. Declining food self-sufficiency is another.

Japanese consumers are generally concerned about the relationship between healthy landscapes and healthy foodstuffs. One reason for the fairly widespread political support for costly subsidies to local rice farmers is the belief that Japanese products are safe to eat. This stands in contrast to food imported from regional neighbours, which is seen as having a high risk of contamination through poorly conducted and monitored production processes. However, as has been discussed, healthy food produced from healthy Japanese soils currently cannot meet Japanese food requirements. If, as seems inevitable for at least the medium-term future, Japan will have to rely on imports for the difference, then it might be expected that its concern for food safety will extend to support, and preferentially purchase from, overseas farmers who are producing wholesome food that is safe to eat. A Japanese consumer may have no particular ethical concern for the wellbeing of, for example, an Australian farmer. However, for as long as they are depending on the food that that farmer produces, it is in their self-interest that a link equivalent to L7 exists, linking healthy Australian soils to the imported component of their food. This concern for food safety requires a new paradigm that encompasses a different set of values that go beyond the Productionist Paradigm's focus on quantity.

10.7 Shifting paradigms

The establishment of just and sustainable food systems is in the long-term self-interest of affluent consumers – it would be prudent for them to politically resist the industrial Productionist Paradigm. Failure to do so will inevitably lead to the collapse of the systems they depend upon for their health and wellbeing. Arguments from the preceding chapters demonstrate that the political pressure for this paradigm shift should be applied now. The longer that current systems of production and distribution continue the greater the damage to key planetary boundaries, and the greater the cost and more problematic recovery becomes. Key variables that are already significantly overloaded may well be approaching tipping point, beyond which recovery will become impossible. For these variables, every day that remediation is delayed is essentially a gamble that the planet can continue to tolerate the activity in question. Given the catastrophic consequences of triggering one of these tipping points, set against the relatively minor benefits of further delaying the cost of intervention, this would seem a highly imprudent gamble indeed.

However, the motivation for affluent consumers to change their behaviour cannot rely solely on their perception of self-interest. A common feature of a wide range of sustainability issues is the failure of people to privilege the long-term consequences of their behaviour over short-term benefits. If affluent consumers wait until they have direct experience of personal harm before they act, it will be too late. By the time the citizens of Australia, Denmark, and Japan start to run out of food, the poor of many African countries will have long since starved to death. As discussed in Chapter 1, acting now is both prudent and ethical. Affluent citizens of the world must move to avoid conditions that are *already* being experienced by the poor. Based on the argument advanced by Christensen (2014), ethics demands the extension of our self-interested concern to these morally significant others, whom we can be certain feel the same way we do about the desirability of living above minimal social and environmental thresholds.

The external costs of food production, such as social and environmental harms caused at the site of production, and the health impacts of highly processed foods, are currently not factored into Productionist industrial food systems. While this situation exists, ethically and sustainably produced food is unlikely to be cheaper or more convenient to buy than the high-impact produce of the Productionist industrial food systems. Nor is the same variety likely to be available. Broadly speaking, food consumption with lower total impacts is likely to favour food produced with lower on-farm inputs for which the farmer receives better economic return. Although low-input agricultural systems do not necessarily yield less or cost more than their high-input counterparts, it is difficult to imagine they could actually be cheaper. The Productionist approach to farming places overwhelming emphasis on performance as measured by economic efficiency, and it is unlikely that an approach to farming that embraced a broader range of values would perform better on this measure. Lower impact food consumption also requires fewer convenience products, with fewer pre-prepared, processed, and packaged options, because the energy and resource costs of their manufacture are extensive. The range of choice is likely to be narrower, as greater reliance would need to be placed on foods that are locally available in season. Meat consumption would need to regain a luxury status, being consumed far less often and priced to reflect sustainably and ethically reared animals. This would not mean that exotic items were never consumed, but rather that they were not habitually consumed. Similarly, consumers could not expect that a local supermarket would always hold stocks of any culinary delight that happened to come to mind. The social and environmental costs of constantly maintaining such a range of choices are simply too great, with much going to waste and very little capacity to return nutrients to the landscapes of origin.

It is utopian to suppose that consumers will willingly choose sustainable food products, with greater cost, less convenience, and narrower choice, without some compelling reason. Without such a reason, people are likely to choose just and sustainable alternatives only if they perceive the personal impact to be small. This is not to suggest that people choose only options they perceive as having no negative impact upon their self-interest. People hold a range of values that express the sort of person they like to think they are – values that are strongly influenced by the dominant paradigm of the culture in which they live. By and large, these values constitute what it means to be a 'good person', and most people for most of the time try to act in accordance with these values. Clearly, people recognize that doing this will inevitably entail a degree of altruism and self-sacrifice from time to time. However, the clash between the requirements of ethics and people's perception of their self-interest cannot be unbearably or unliveably great.

The threshold at which people believe that concessions to the ethical become too great is not fixed. People can discover that the sacrifices required of them to act ethically are not as great as they initially expected. For example, an ethical commitment to buy less meat overall, but a smaller amount of better quality organic produce for specific dishes, could lead to a greater appreciation of both meat and vegetarian food choices. Instead of seeing 'giving up meat' as a sacrifice, the consumer might instead find it opened their eyes to a range of cheap, flavoursome, and healthy options they had not considered when they insisted on meat being central to every meal. This is not just a process in which the consumer comes to see that what they thought intolerable can in fact be tolerated. It is also a process in which people reconceive and reconfigure their understandings of their self-interest. In this example, a commitment to eating less meat could stimulate learning to prepare low or no meat dishes, exploring interesting cuisines that traditionally rely more centrally on vegetables; improve dietary intake and consequently health; reduce food costs; and provide the satisfaction of mastering a new range of dishes that impress family and friends. In this way, acting ethically with a moderate degree of sacrifice to their self-interest can lead to a paradigm shift in which people's beliefs about what constitutes their self-interest is changed, leading to further ethical concessions. This is a crucial component in people coming to willingly embrace just and sustainable systems, including food systems.

Switching the narrative of sustainability from one in which consumers are rather implausibly expected to willingly embrace going with less of what they enjoy, to one that focuses on the reinforcing relationship between the ethical and the prudent, opens a range of options. Alternative, more sustainable food systems can be designed that allow urban consumers to re-engage with the process of accessing food. This can include fishing; participation in urban gardening; directly interacting with local and regional food producers, for example, through farmers' markets; and reinvigorating the social dimensions of preparing and sharing meals, including backyard barbeques and other gatherings. There is no reason to believe that cafés and restaurants cannot deliver sustainable foods – indeed they may offer efficiencies of production over home cooking. Urban consumers can value these aspects of engagement, conviviality, and solidarity, which they will themselves appreciate over a moderate decline in convenience and variety. This can play a crucial role in the process of shifting the threshold beyond which concessions to the ethical become intolerable. In this way, the very understanding consumers have of what it is to live well can be shifted to the point where they recognize they can contest industrial commodification of food systems as active ecological citizens without having to somehow become enthusiastic about campaigning against their own self-interest. Only if consumers' understandings of their own self-interest – in effect, their expectations of cost, convenience, and choice – can be shifted can one expect consumers to move beyond a private concern for their own desire or satisfaction to a genuinely public and political concern for rights and responsibilities implicated in food systems.

However, as the case studies in this chapter demonstrate, consumers cannot be expected to draw upon only the produce of local producers in local environments. Limiting urban consumers to the seasonal food output of local environments is either impossible (because there simply is not enough local production to meet local demand) or so excessively inconvenient or restrictive as to undermine efforts to shift consumer understandings of their self-interest. And for some products the local option may be the less sustainable option – it may, for example, be more energy and resource intense than its imported counterpart. Consequently, as the case studies indicate, a percentage of urban food will likely come from rural communities working on remote landscapes, including through international imports. It is highly unlikely that urban consumers can have detailed knowledge of, and care for, how such landscapes are managed or how justly those producing food from them are treated and rewarded. Even so, through consumer awareness of their relationship with and concern for local food systems, political support for minimum social and environmental standards can be extended to all the food-producing landscapes and producers, wherever these land-scapes and producers are. The argument is that engaged biosensitive citizens, who are prepared to demand local sustainable food systems, even at greater cost, inconvenience, and less choice, would extend their ethical principles and standards to all environments and remote land managers.

10.8 Conclusion

What has been demonstrated for food choices can be generalized to other consumer choices. Wherever we are concerned about the impact of peoples' behaviour, we see that people have to willingly ascribe to an alternative belief system that lowers their environmental impact. They have also to be able to operate reasonably easily within that belief system. This would allow people to more closely align their actual behaviour with the ethical standard to which they aspire. Under the Productionist Paradigm, this alignment is either not possible, or so difficult that only a minority consider the attempt, as it appears to demand too great a self-sacrifice. Under the guidance of a more biosensitive paradigm people can see that what they previously took to be in their self-interest was narrowly framed around a range of material values that the old paradigm promoted, and that obscured a broader range of values. In such cases there is every possibility that people will be as content with low-impact modes of consumption as they were with modes of consumption that had high levels of environmental impact. What is needed are ways of seeing the world that lead affluent consumers to willingly reduce the impacts of their consumption and to support the necessary increases in consumption for the less affluent and the poor. That is, to achieve the impact convergence required for a just and sustainable society (Section 6.5).

No one can possibly know all the environmental consequences of their every choice and action. However, individuals can extend a generalized concern from the small sphere of relationships they do rationally engage with to the broader systems that they sit within. Politically engaged biosensitive citizens can expect that the systems of production that supply them are configured to be just and sustainable. In this way the adage 'think globally: act locally' is turned on its head. We must 'think locally' because it is the only sphere of concern that is small enough for us to engage with rationally. But, when we act our actions almost certainly have global consequences. Hence, 'think locally: act globally'.

References

Anderson, P. M., Okereke, C., Rudd, A. and Parnell, S. (2013). 'Regional assessment of Africa'. *Urbanization, Biodiversity and Ecosystem Services: Challenges and opportunities.* Dordrecht, Springer, 453–459.

Australian Bureau of Statistics (2006). *Yearbook Australia 2006*. Canberra, ABS.

Christensen, C. (2014). 'Human ecology as philosophy'. *Human Ecology Review* 20(1): 31–49.

Deutsch, L., Dyball, R., and Steffen, W. (2013). 'Feeding cities: Food security and ecosystem support in an urbanizing world'. *Urbanization, Biodiversity and Ecosystem Services: Challenges and opportunities*. Dordrecht, Springer, 505–537.

FAO (2010). *Global Forest Resources Assessment 2010: Country Report Denmark*. Rome, Food and Agricultural Organization of the United Nations.

FAO (2012). *Growing Greener Cities in Africa: First status report on urban and peri-urban horticulture in Africa*. Rome, Food and Agriculture Organization of the United Nations.

FAO (2013). *Rice Market Monitor*. Rome, Food and Agriculture Organization of the United Nations.

Hansen, K. and Vesterdal, L. (2004). 'Guidelines for planning afforestation on previously managed arable land'. *Water, Air and Soil Pollution* 73(1–4): 61–82.

Jesperson, K. (2004). *A History of Denmark*, trans. Ivan Hill, Basingstoke: Palgrave Macmillan.

Landbrugsinfo. (2014). 'Organic farming in Denmark'. Available online at www.landbrugsinfo. dk/oekologi/sider/engoeko.aspx

Lang, T. and Heasman, M. (2004). *Food Wars : The global battle for mouths, minds and markets*. London, Earthscan.

Leopold, A. (1966). *Good Oak: A Sand County almanac*. New York, Oxford University Press.

National Farmers Federation (2012). *Farm Facts*. Canberra, National Farmers Federation.

Pearson, C. and Dyball, R. (2014). 'City Food Security'. *Resilient Sustainable Cities*. L. P. P. N. P. I. Roberts. New York, Routledge, 113–122.

Porter, J. R., Dyball, R., Dumaresq, D., Deutsch, L. and Matsuda, H. (2014). 'Feeding capitals: Urban food security and self-provisioning in Canberra, Copenhagen and Tokyo'. *Global Food Security* 3(1): 1–7.

Sawin, B., Hamilton, H., Jone, A., Rice, P., Seville, D., Sweitzer, S. and Wright, D. (2003). *Commodity Systems Challenges: Moving sustainability into the mainstream of natural resource economies*. Hartland, VT: Sustainability Institute.

Soils for Life. (2012). 'Innovations for Regenerative Landscape Management: Case studies of regenerative land management in practice'. Available online at www.soilsforlife.org (accessed 20 January 2014).

Zandersen, M. and Termansen, M. (2013). 'Assessing recreational values of Danish forests to guide national plans for afforestation'. *Socio-economic Importance of Ecosystem Services in the Nordic Countries: Scoping assessment in the context of The Economics of Ecosystems and Biodiversity (TEEB)*. M. Kettunen, *et al.* Copenhagen, TemaNord, Nordiska Ministerrådet Denmark. Available online at www.teebweb.org/wp-content/uploads/2013/01/TEEB-case_TEEBNordic_Assessing-recreational-values-of-Danish-forests-to-guide-national-plans-for-afforestation.pdf.

11 Stewards of a full Earth

(T)here is nothing more difficult to plan, more doubtful of success, nor more dangerous to manage than a new system. For the initiator has the enmity of all who would profit by the preservation of the old institution and merely lukewarm defenders in those who gain by the new ones.

(*The Prince*, Machiavelli *c.*1532)

11.1 Introduction

In the Anthropocene, humans have emerged as a new Earth-system force, exerting strong evolutionary selection pressure on the biosphere and significantly affecting energy and material flows at a global scale. Having developed such capacity, humans must assume moral responsibility for the consequence of their actions. To the extent that humans can understand the relationship between their behaviour and its social and environmental impacts, they must be held accountable for their actions in ways that, for example, a hurricane cannot (Palsson *et al.* 2013). For better or worse, humans are now 'Earth stewards' (Power and Chapin 2009), or literally housekeepers. The meaning of 'steward' holds connotations of managing an estate in trust on behalf of others – stewards do not own the estate, nor can they do with it as they will. If, in the Anthropocene, the 'estate' is planet Earth itself, then for humans to assume the role of steward is to assume the duties of care and maintenance for others into the future. Furthermore, Earth is now 'full', to use Daly's expression (Daly 1996). In the past, environmental systems had the capacity to absorb the impacts of human activity (Chapter 8), but the global economy has now grown to the point where no such surplus exists. The Paradigm of Limitless Growth (Chapter 9) that allowed humans to 'fill the Earth' is unable to regulate behaviour so that all people can live equitably and sustainably. Accordingly, humans need a paradigm shift to a new way of understanding their relationship with each other and the environment – one that will allow them to conduct themselves well as stewards of a full Earth. Human ecology, as originally seen by Ellen Swallow Richards in 1892 as working towards 'knowledge of right living' (Clarke 1973: 120), can help establish the goals of this new paradigm. As Richards said, our 'normal lives' should be 'healthy' and 'happy' – to which we would add, in the language of today, 'and sustainable'.

11.2 From 'Limitless Growth' to sufficiency: the need for a paradigm shift

In Chapter 1 we defined 'paradigm' as the collection of worldviews, beliefs, assumptions, and priorities that dominate in a particular community. The Paradigm of Limitless Growth was discussed in Chapters 9 and 10. It entails the belief that growth, most specifically economic growth, provides the means to solve environmental and social problems. This paradigm has been instrumental in driving human colonization and transformation of the vast majority of the planet's ecosystems (Ellis and Ramankutty 2008). Its specifically modern industrial 'productionist' incarnation originated in north-west Europe and has been spreading across the cultures of the planet for the past 200 years or so. Irrespective of the morality of this paradigm, to the extent it promotes limitless growth and expansion on a finite planet, it cannot continue to drive human behaviour. There must be a shift to a new paradigm, one that recognizes and works sustainably with natural processes, in socially just and equitable ways.

Figure 11.1 illustrates this paradigm shift. The portion of society that genuinely believes that either we do not face significant social and environmental problems today or, if we do, that current activities will solve these problems in a timely manner, is described as committed to 'business as usual'. The portion of society that believes a new paradigm is necessary is described as being committed to 'biosensitivity'.

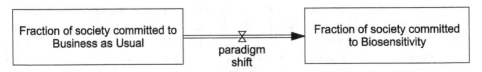

Figure 11.1 Stewards of a full Earth. The cultural change needed, if humanity is to establish and maintain a dignified existence, requires a shift from a 'business as usual' society to a biosensitive one. This diagram is a version of Figure 7.7 with the direction of the required paradigm shift made explicit.

The 'business as usual' worldview assumes that humanity need have no particular dependence on 'nature'. This belief holds that environments provide certain services that are in principle capable of economic valuation. If need be, technological means can be used to develop perfect substitutes (see, for example, Simon 1981). This is a very high-risk strategy. If it works then all is well. If it fails – for example, if some novel technology fails to adequately replace a lost ecosystem function – the consequences are potentially catastrophic. A commitment instead to working with the life processes that have been generated by 4.5 billion years of evolution would seem to offer a much lower risk strategy. The 'natural technology' is known to work as long as humanity has sufficient humility to work with and respect its limits, rather than attempting to overpower, control or replace it. The main challenge is having to place limits on the endless material consumption (which is often equated with happiness) promised by the future trajectory of the Paradigm of Limitless Growth (Costanza *et al.* 2000).

In contrast to this worldview, a biosensitive society holds that the principle of continual growth is not sustainable in a finite world and that human health needs can be regularly and reliably met only if the ecosystems upon which they depend are themselves healthy (Section 7.4). A major role for technology and human ingenuity remains, but not as a mechanism for subverting natural processes. The dominant paradigm of a biosensitive society would foster the belief that maintaining the physical (clean air and water, a healthy diet, appropriate physical activity) and psychosocial health needs (including creativity, conviviality, and access to emotional support networks) of all humans was the ultimate goal of society.

Indeed, the never-ending pursuit of ever higher levels of pleasure and happiness, especially if based predominantly on material consumption, would seem to be a dubious psychological goal (Burkeman 2012). Rather, a biosensitive society would hold that a more appropriate goal lies in the 'just right' levels of consumption – the 'Goldilocks Principle' (Section 6.5) – where equitably distributed 'sufficiency' replaces limitless growth as a material goal, with 'contentment' rather than hedonism as its psychological counterpart (Princen 2005; Wilkinson and Pickett 2010; Christensen 2014).

11.3 Social learning for biosensitivity

Proposals for ways to reach just and sustainable futures often encounter the blanket objection that 'it will never happen'. For example, observations that private car-based transport systems inevitably lead to congestion and air pollution can lead to proposals for public transport-based alternatives. But then it is objected that 'citizens will never give up their cars'. In one sense, this is obviously false. Citizens will certainly give up their cars if there is no longer fuel to run them. So what the objector really means is something like, 'I cannot imagine the circumstances in which people would *willingly* give up their cars'. People who frame the world according to a fixed paradigm, and so see a limited range of possible futures, find it difficult to conceive of other possibilities. This difficulty is compounded by the fact that the social and physical infrastructure created by a dominant paradigm means that it is often inconvenient and sometimes impossible to avoid the kind of behaviour that the paradigm promotes as 'normal'. Human ecology is interested in understanding how people and communities might change the way they see the world around them and imagine its future, so that what currently seems impossible is perceived as plausible and, indeed, desirable. This is essentially about social learning, but not merely in the sense of coming to know what one did not know before. It is *transformative* learning that changes what one thinks is the right and sensible thing to do (Mezirow 1997; Keen *et al.* 2005; Dyball *et al.* 2007; Taylor 2007). Transformative learning involves changes to the dominant paradigm.

As discussed in Chapter 7, the state of a community has a wide range of social and environmental impacts. If these impacts are to drive a desire to modify behaviour towards a Paradigm of Biosensitivity, we must understand the relationship between our behaviour and its impacts. That is, as shown in Figure 11.2, we must have some idea about the cause-and-effect relationship between processes represented by the links L1, L3, L5, or L7. If we do not know that a heavy metal, such as mercury, can bio-accumulate in food chains, thereby causing severe health impacts (L7), then we might think that discharging such substances into local waterways (L5) is not a risk. But for most sustainability issues, and their associated dimensions of justice, we are not ignorant of what is causing the harm. Often we understand the consequences of damaging activities, yet we do them anyway (Fischer *et al.* 2012). Knowing that mercury is a poison does not necessarily prevent a chemical factory from continuing to discharge it into local waterways as a waste product of its operations. If the dominant paradigm places overriding importance on the economic activity that the factory generates, and has policies in place to protect and encourage its operations, pressures to modify the paradigm will be resisted. In this example, the L1–L2 feedback loop would be maladaptive, acting to encourage the factory to continue to produce in a 'business as usual' fashion. It would override adaptive health and environmental learning that would otherwise generate a desire to modify the dominant paradigm, but which remains too weak to actually do so until or unless the harm done becomes so catastrophic that it is acted upon.

Observations and knowledge about activities, including scientific knowledge, can make a major contribution in a society shifting to a Paradigm of Biosensitivity. However, any such knowledge is always embedded in a broader social context. It is this social context that determines whether scientific findings and recommendations will be incorporated into decision making and subsequent behaviour change. By itself, knowledge will not produce desirable change. Political influence arising from vested interest of those with social power is, of course, a major source of this resistance to change.

An awareness of negative social, health, or environmental effects does not necessarily result in a desire to modify the processes that are causing them. For a host of reasons – social, pragmatic, economic, physical, and political – individuals, groups, and institutions can and do resist change, including change that is ultimately beneficial to them. People often tolerate conditions that they are used to and readily perceive risks in proposals for new ways of doing things. For example, the risk that a passenger travelling at night on new public transport might get mugged could be promoted as a major disincentive to building the system (Latour 1996). The far greater risk of harm that passengers currently experience in their daily commute by car is discounted. Furthermore, individuals and groups disadvantaged by the current

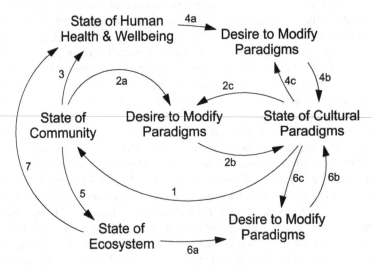

Figure 11.2 Willingness to learn. This is a reproduction of Figure 7.6.

arrangements might be concerned that proposed changes to improve their lot will mean the loss of the little they already have. This phenomenon was famously recognized by Machiavelli, as reproduced in the epigraph to this chapter. The underlying message is that change cannot be imposed upon people just because by some measure it is 'good for them'. Individuals and groups must desire the change for themselves, and this requires extensive community engagement, dialogue, and other means of envisioning alternate futures. We can note that in exploring new ways of living a special role falls to the young, who are less likely than older age groups to be captured by the dominant paradigm, having not yet developed a vested interest in perpetuating it.

In the face of this understandable reluctance to pursue the unfamiliar, small-scale alternative systems have an important role. For example, urban communities producing food in their backyards, although small in volume, may act as prototypes for more sustainable systems. Rather than being valued in terms of the actual volumes produced, the significance of the contribution of what is often viewed as an 'alternative' activity may demonstrate other ways of living in the future. These activities can function as 'rehearsals for change' (Altman 1980). Instead of modifying the dominant paradigm from within, we can think of these alternative communities as operating outside the dominant paradigm. These activities can show the 'business as usual' community that it is indeed possible to live well within a different paradigm. This model requires the 'business as usual' community to overcome prejudice about 'alternative' behaviour and to be inspired to adopt the new activities.

A less radical approach might be to work within the dominant paradigm, but push the boundaries of what is seen as conventionally 'possible'. From small beginnings, with initially low levels of commitment, an ever greater number of people can over time be drawn into different systems of production and consumption. As participants build confidence and trust from the feedback of experiencing success, much greater, widespread, and radical transformations can emerge and develop, ultimately resulting in pressure to change the status quo. An example is a small farmer's market, which starts out as simply another place to buy foodstuffs, in a model not unlike 'business as usual'. From insignificant beginnings the market might grow to transform the regional rural economy, reintegrating local consumers with local producers for mutual benefit. This could be an important step in a broader societal shift towards a paradigm of biodiversity, which in turn could influence mainstream supermarkets to change how they source their supplies. This more gradual approach may be more successful in generating the desire to modify paradigms by working from within rather than challenging from outside.

The modern world is incredibly complex. The systems of production and distribution that make the vast array of consumer goods available are spread across the planet. No one can see all the consequences of all that they do, and then rationally choose between options based on some exhaustive comparison. Although people make daily choices about how to access things to which they feel entitled in a morally defendable fashion, this kind of deliberation is possible only in relation to very few everyday behaviours (Christensen 2007). For most goods and services consumed, people have to trust that adequate legislative and policy checks and balances are in place to regulate how those things are produced and made available. Within the Paradigm of Limitless Growth, people cannot and should not trust that constraints are in place to ensure that the things they consume are produced in a manner that is just and sustainable – often they are not. Nonetheless, everyday action and life would grind to a halt if everyone was forced to critically examine their every action.

A paradigm shift at the global community level is ultimately required. Within the Paradigm of Limitless Growth, an impossible level of detailed knowledge is required for individuals and communities to make ethical choices. With a shift to the Paradigm of Biosensitivity, just and sustainable goals would be the 'new normal' throughout the entire social–ecological system. Within such a society there would be grounds to trust that the everyday practices of citizens would have positive social and environmental impacts.

11.4 Self-interested motivations for modifying paradigms

There are two main reasons why communities should be motivated to become biosensitive. The first is practical – within the Paradigm of Biosensitivity people can satisfy their reasonable desires without causing unacceptable social and environmental harm. The second reason is ethical – that the right to satisfy reasonable desires should be extended to all. Christensen (2014) argues that it is only when individuals can satisfy their reasonable desires in an ethical manner that they can be said to be 'living well'.

Even for individuals who are self-interested and content with 'business as usual' there are practical grounds for shifting to a biosensitive paradigm. Within the Paradigm of Limitless Growth, fixing problems equates typically to short-term interventions aimed at treating symptoms rather than addressing causes. Usually the underlying problem stems from the commitment to Limitless Growth, which cannot be reconciled with social or environmental reality. Continuing in this paradigm will allow social and environmental problems to multiply, which ultimately affects all members of society. The social–ecological system seen by a self-absorbed individual is illustrated in Figure 11.3.

To live is to consume. Human life is possible only if and when humans obtain sufficient basic resources from the environment. It follows that individuals are entitled to seek the resources they need to satisfy their reasonable desires. In other words, referring to Figure 11.3, they are entitled to maintain the values included in 'State of My Universe' at reasonable levels. The variables involved are those that affect the biophysical and psychosocial aspects of Boyden's universal human health needs (Section 7.4). Activities that allow someone to more fully satisfy those needs would improve the state of their 'universe', and can be said to be good for them. Activities that made the state of their universe worse would be harmful. Such activities would oppose the individual's dominant commitment to look after themselves, and would be relayed to them by one or more of the feedback links L2, L4, or L6. A 'Commitment to Looking after Myself' helps ensure that the required balance is maintained, through corrective action taken via link L1. It is unreasonable to expect the individual to ignore situations where they perceive that their living conditions have worsened.

If an individual's personal paradigm entailed a commitment to extreme altruism, then perhaps they would be prepared to sacrifice their own welfare for some other cause. This is not unheard of, as, for example, when parents sacrifice themselves to save the life of their child. But there is a purely practical reason for a self-interested

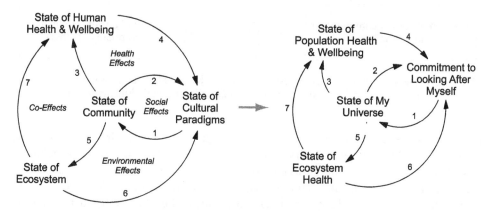

Figure 11.3 Individualism. The diagram on the left is the cultural adaptation template (Figure 7.5). The problem-space diagram on the right illustrates the limited worldview of a self-absorbed individual. Links L3 and L5 are dashed to indicate that this individual pays little attention to their impact on ecosystem health and overall population health and wellbeing.

individual to be concerned about the health of the environment and the welfare of others. The impact that their actions have on others will eventually impact upon themselves. Consequently, it is in the self-absorbed individual's interest to understand their impacts on the environment, and on those aspects of society that support their own health and wellbeing. Links L3 and L5 in Figure 11.3 are dashed to indicate processes that this individual is largely unaware of, but that will affect them eventually. An individual who understands the effects of these processes would see that a commitment to look after oneself entailed a commitment to live within a biosensitive paradigm. Individuals who see this reality could choose to modify their behaviour and reduce consumption that, for example, led to the erosion of environmental health or community health and wellbeing. They might still desire a reasonable sufficiency of goods, but would be content with more moderate levels of consumption (the Goldilocks Principle; Section 6.5). They would do this not through some implausible drive to forgo the things that they genuinely desire, but because they believe that consuming materially less, and putting higher value on intangible things such as relationships and experiences, constitutes what it means to 'live well'.

In reality, an individual's 'State of My Universe' is inevitably affected by the actions of others. For as long as the Paradigm of Limitless Growth continues, self-interested individuals will find that their capacity to look after themselves alone is eventually eroded, irrespective of what they themselves might do. It would be impossible for someone to find a refuge that could indefinitely support their physical and psychosocial health needs, while the world around them underwent social and environmental collapse.

11.5 Ethical motivations for modifying paradigms

The motivation for shifting to a Paradigm of Biosensitivity does not arise only because it is in one's self-interest; there are also ethical motivations. This moral extension is twofold. First, in pursuing one's own reasonable desires, one must consider the

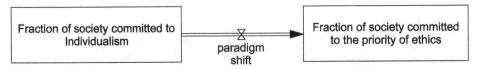

Figure 11.4 The priority of ethics: an essential shift of belief. This diagram is a version of Figure 7.7 with the direction of the required paradigm shift made explicit.

impact on others. Second, if a person has a right to pursue their own reasonable desires, the right of others to pursue what they reasonably desire must be acknowledged. Human ecology thus proceeds from the conviction that most human beings are both able and, under normal circumstances, prepared to consider whether their purposeful activities result, or are likely to result, in benefits or harm to 'morally significant others' (Christensen 2014: 3). We argue that the Paradigm of Limitless Growth *necessarily* prevents people giving adequate consideration to morally significant others. This in turn means that in a 'business as usual' society people are prevented from living well. Recognition that society needs to give priority to ethics is essential to achieving the worthwhile, just, and sustainable futures that are the goals of a biosensitive society. This shift is illustrated in Figure 11.4.

What it means to 'live well' is the condition where one can satisfy what one believes to be one's own entitlements while at the same time respecting the entitlements of others. As Christensen (2014) argues, people are usually prepared to do the right thing provided the cost is not too high. Furthermore, the point at which people feel that the cost of 'doing the right thing' is too high is not fixed.

All humans are predisposed towards living well, but can do so only in circumstances in which they can mediate reliably between the pursuit of their desires and the ethical ramifications of satisfying them. Mediation between desire and ethics will not happen if it demands large sacrifice, where individuals have to forgo things that they regard as necessary. But the character and extent of an individual's needs has a strong cultural and historical component, stemming largely from the dominant cultural paradigm (see the discussion of three paradigms in Chapter 8). While this can cause considerable inertia in the system, it is possible to modify what is regarded as being genuinely needed. As Christensen points out, people will tolerate certain levels of discomfort and inconvenience that they would otherwise not accept *if certain alternative rewards are in place*. In other words, it is possible, as described in Chapter 10, to discover that what was originally thought to be an intolerable sacrifice is not so. We can indeed bring desire, satisfaction, and ethical requirement into alignment with one another – when new, less resource-intensive behaviour delivers alternative non-material outcomes that we value (Christensen 2007). Examples of such outcomes would be time with family and friends, pride in mastering a new skill, or simply living at a slower pace.

This is not to imply that people always give moral consideration to the consequences of their action, or are always willing to behave in ways that reflect their considered moral judgement. At times they may regard the personal discomfort or inconvenience as too great. We suggest that most people most of the time are able and willing to do the right thing, provided that it is not discomfiting, injurious or inconvenient to them. Who and what they consider to be morally significant is subjective. But it at least includes 'other humans' affected by their activity. Many would extend that concern to 'future generations' – as yet unborn humans who will inherit the consequences of their forebears' activities. Others again would extend concern to other species or the intrinsic value of the biosphere in general. Whoever, or whatever, is included in the sphere of concern, it is enough simply to know or suspect that certain activities will harm these morally significant others. Under such circumstances, a person is obliged to take reasonable steps to ensure that obtaining what they desire does not come at too great a cost to others. Living well involves a healthy sense of one's own entitlements but is always constrained by consideration of and respect for the entitlements of others. Living well is almost impossible to achieve within the Paradigm of Limitless Growth, but would be habitual and normal within the Paradigm of Biosensitivity.

11.6 Conclusion: celebrating the Anthropocene

In the Introduction we quoted Borden (2014) as saying that human ecology concerned itself with two age-old questions of the human condition: 'what makes life possible', and 'what makes life worthwhile'. He then draws on a quotation from Lawrence 'Yogi' Berra, a famous American baseball player who was notorious for mangled, nonsensical sayings. A classic example is 'when you come to a fork in the road, take it'. However, as Borden explains, the instructions are not as uninformative as they would first seem. Yogi was giving directions to his house, which could be reached by taking either of two roads leading from an intersection. Extending this metaphor to the study of human ecology, Borden says that whichever of the two questions concerning the possibility or value of life you seek to address first, you will inevitably find yourself on a path leading to the other. Ultimately, human ecology addresses what it would take to live well in a humane, worthwhile, sustainable world. Whether approached via social pathways or environmental ones, eventually the same destination is reached. There does not need to be a trade-off between environmental and social goods.

Human ecology is a complex and challenging study, partly because of its concern for these interactions between the social and the environmental, but also because it is rarely satisfied with simple explanations of the cause of problems. It is, as philosophers say, drawn to ultimate rather than proximate explanations. Starting from concern for the health of a child, we can ask questions about why the child became sick. The immediate explanation might be that it came into contact with a pathogenic microbe that caused an infection. But human ecology wants to ask why that was; for example, by asking why was the water dirty and home to the pathogen, and why did the child drink from it and not from a more hygienic source. Why was the child's immune system unable to deal with the pathogen? These would invite explanations from the nature of the child's environment, and the state of the water treatment infrastructure, directed perhaps at engineers and urban planners. Human ecologists would also need to know about the microbe and the conditions in which it flourished and was transmitted to humans – questions directed at microbiologists and epidemiologists, and why the child's immune response was not functioning – questions directed to the medical profession. Questions about the socio-economic status of the child would elicit answers about why it habitually played in the gutter and lived in a shanty town with inadequate communal water and sewerage services. Exploring these threads could lead to interrogating the sociopolitical systems of governance of the city, region, or country. This questioning could eventually reveal that poverty, corruption, and institutional dysfunction were hindering the nation's sustainable development. These circumstances in turn might be explained with reference to the legacy of a colonial past that had created power imbalances, indebtedness, and social instability. Ultimately, the overarching paradigm of economic progress, in which the resources of the nation flowed out to wealthy and powerful international elites, could be seen as causing the child's ill health.

Human ecology seeks to draw these multiple threads of explanation together. Seeing the connections is crucial to seeing the issue of concern more comprehensively. The search for ultimate rather than proximate answers is a search for solutions that address the root causes of those problems rather than merely addressing their symptoms. Tracking down these ultimate causes, and devising enduring solutions to the problems of modern society, requires a systems approach such as that outlined in this book. From a systems point of view, it is essential to identify the goals of the system. According to Meadows and Wright (2009), a focus on the goals of a system always leads to a critical appraisal of the dominant paradigms that set, legitimize, and perpetuate those goals. Pursuing goals of justice and sustainability, without awareness of the goals set by the overarching paradigm, can lead to perverse outcomes. Examples include buying 'green' products from businesses whose only interest is to capture all consumer niches; proposals for public transport systems and corridors of urban infill that are primarily designed to increase property values and economic return to developers; or development initiatives designed to convert subsistence farmers to producers of bulk export commodities. Just and sustainable outcomes can be delivered, but great care needs to be taken to ensure that these outcomes are the focus of development activities, and not subsumed by the hidden agenda of the dominant paradigm.

Human ecology's contribution to the question of 'what makes life possible' is that ultimately humans cannot live at all if they cannot live sustainably. To the question of what makes life worthwhile, human ecology would suggest that a worthwhile life was one that was lived well, and this entails living ethically, content with sufficiency. In the Paradigm of Limitless Growth, humans are neither living well nor sustainably. However, human ecology is firmly committed to the possibility that this does not have to be the case. Human ecologists are motivated by the belief that all people can and do care about the future, both for themselves and for their fellows. Furthermore, it holds that, under the right conditions, humans can work collectively towards achieving that future. Within a Paradigm of Biosensitivity, living sustainably and living well would be concomitant aspects of everyday normal behaviour. Whichever direction you choose from the fork in the road, the common address that it will bring you to is the need for a shift in the dominant cultural paradigm of our time, to one that recognizes the priority of ethics and the ecological realities of the world. Under such a paradigm life in the Anthropocene would be something that all humanity could celebrate. Within this aspirational goal of moving towards a celebratory future, a significant role for human ecology is to help imagine what it might be to live and do well in a humane, sustainable, and worthwhile world, and to invite and enthuse others to work towards realizing that future.

References

Altman, D. (1980). *Rehearsals for Change*. Melbourne, Fontana.

Borden, R. (2014). *Ecology and Experience: Reflections from a human ecological perspective.* Berkeley, CA, North Atlantic Books.

Burkeman, O. (2012). *The Antidote: Happiness of people who can't stand positive thinking.* Melbourne, Text Publishing.

Christensen, C. (2007). 'The material basis of everyday rationality: Transformation by design or education?' *Design Philosophy Papers: Collection three.* A.-M. Willis. Ravensbourne, Australia, Team D/E/S Publications.

Christensen, C. (2014). 'Human ecology as philosophy'. *Human Ecology Review* 20(1): 31–49.

Clarke, R. (1973). *Ellen Swallow: The woman who founded ecology.* Chicago, IL, Follett Publishing .

Costanza, R., Daly, H., Folke, C., Hawken, P., Holling, C. S., McMichael, A. J., Pimentel, D., and Rapport, D. (2000). 'Managing our environmental portfolio'. *BioScience* 50: 149–155.

Daly, H. E. (1996). *Beyond Growth: The economics of sustainable development.* Boston MA., Beacon Press.

Dyball, R., Brown, V., and Keen, M. (2007). 'Towards sustainability: Five strands of social learning'. *Social Learning Towards a Sustainable World: Principles, perspectives, and praxis.* A. E. J. Wals. The Netherlands, Wageningen Academic Publishers: 181–195.

Ellis, E. C. and Ramankutty, N. (2008). 'Putting people in the map: Anthropogenic biomes of the world'. *Frontiers in Ecology and the Environment* 6(8): 439–447.

Fischer, J., Dyball, R., Fazey, I., Gross, C., Dovers, S., Ehrlich, P. R., Brulle, R. J., Christensen, C., and Borden, R. J. (2012). 'Human behavior and sustainability'. *Frontiers in Ecology and the Environment* 10(3): 153–160.

Keen, M., Brown, V. A., and Dyball, R., Eds. (2005). *Social Learning in Environmental Management: Towards a sustainable future.* London, Earthscan.

Latour, B. (1996). *Aramis, or, the Love of Technology.* Cambridge, MA, Harvard University Press.

Meadows, D. H. and Wright, D. (2009). *Thinking in Systems : A primer.* London, Earthscan.

Mezirow, J. (1997). 'Transformative learning: Theory to practice'. *New Directions for adult and continuing education* 74: 5–11.

Palsson, G., Szerszynski, B., Sörlin, S., Marks, J., Bernard A., Crumley, C., Hackmann, H., Holm, P., Ingram, J., Kirman, A., Buendía, M. P., and Weehuizen, R. (2013). 'Reconceptualizing the "Anthropos" in the Anthropocene: Integrating the social sciences and humanities in global environmental change research'. *Environmental Science and Policy* 28:3–13.

Power, M. E. and Chapin, F. S. (2009). 'Planetary stewardship'. *Frontiers in Ecology and the Environment* 7(8): 399–399.

Princen, T. (2005). *The Logic of Sufficiency.* Cambridge, MA, MIT Press.

Simon, J. (1981). *The Ultimate Resource.* Princton, NJ, Princton University.

Taylor, E. (2007). 'An update of transformative learning theory: A critical review of the empirical research (1999–2005)'. *International Journal of Lifelong Education* 26(2): 173–191.

Wilkinson, R. and Pickett, K. (2010). *The Spirit Level: Why equality is better for everyone.* London, Penguin.

Index

Note: 'b' following a page number means box; 'f' refers to a figure and 'n' to note.